AN ECONOMIC AND SOCIAL HISTORY OF LATER MEDIEVAL EUROPE, 1000–1500

This book examines the most important themes in European social and economic history from the beginning of growth around the year 1000 to the first wave of global exchange in the 1490s. These five hundred years witnessed the rise of economic systems, such as capitalism, and the social theories that would have a profound influence on the rest of the world over the next five centuries. The basic story, the human search for food, clothing, and shelter in a world of violence and scarcity, is a familiar one, and the work and daily routines of ordinary women and men are the focus of this volume.

Surveying the full extent of Europe, from east to west and north to south, Steven A. Epstein illuminates family life, economic and social thought, war, technologies, and other major themes while giving equal attention to developments in trade, crafts, and agriculture. The great waves of famine and then plague in the fourteenth century provide the centerpiece of a book that seeks to explain the causes of Europe's uneven prosperity and its response to catastrophic levels of death. Epstein also sets social and economic developments within the context of the Christian culture and values that were common across Europe and that were the cause of constant tension with Muslims, Jews, and dissidents within its boundaries and the great Islamic and Tartar states on its frontier.

Steven A. Epstein is Ahmanson-Murphy Distinguished Professor of Medieval History at the University of Kansas. He is the author of numerous articles and five books on aspects of medieval social and economic history, including *Genoa and the Genoese, 958–1528* and *Purity Lost: Transgressing Boundaries in the Eastern Mediterranean, 1000–1400*.

An Economic and Social History of Later Medieval Europe, 1000–1500

STEVEN A. EPSTEIN

University of Kansas

CAMBRIDGE
UNIVERSITY PRESS

CAMBRIDGE UNIVERSITY PRESS
Cambridge, New York, Melbourne, Madrid, Cape Town, Singapore,
São Paulo, Delhi, Dubai, Tokyo, Mexico City

Cambridge University Press
32 Avenue of the Americas, New York, NY 10013-2473, USA

www.cambridge.org
Information on this title: www.cambridge.org/9780521706537

© Cambridge University Press 2009

First published 2009

A catalog record for this publication is available from the British Library.

Library of Congress Cataloging in Publication Data

Epstein, Steven, 1952–
An economic and social history of later medieval Europe, 1000–1500 / Steven A. Epstein.
   p. cm.
Includes bibliographical references and index.
ISBN 978-0-521-88036-7 (hardback) – ISBN 978-0-521-70653-7 (pbk.)
1. Europe – History – 476–1492. 2. Europe – Social conditions – To 1492. 3. Europe –
Economic conditions – To 1492. 4. Economic history – Medieval, 500–1500. 5. Social
history – Medieval, 500–1500. 6. Middle Ages. I. Title.
D117.E67   2009
940.1'7–dc22   2009005515

ISBN 978-0-521-88036-7 Hardback
ISBN 978-0-521-70653-7 Paperback

CONTENTS

ILLUSTRATIONS

CHAPTER 9

ACKNOWLEDGMENTS

A book like this one depends on the accumulated research and insights of many scholars, some of whom are noted in the chapter bibliographies. I am deeply grateful to all these people whose work I have borrowed, and from whom I have learned so much over the last three decades. Beatrice Rehl suggested this project to me, and I thank her for setting me on this interesting path. William Caferro and Ann Carlos read the entire manuscript and made many excellent suggestions for improvements. Pam LeRow and Paula Courtney provided invaluable help with the tables and illustrations. Ellen Tirpak expertly copyedited the manuscript, and Ken Karpinski skillfully managed its production. I am also grateful to the many students whose good questions have made this a better book.

INTRODUCTION

YOU HAVE OPENED THIS BOOK ON THE ECONOMIC AND SOCIAL history of later medieval Europe, so you are entitled to know its limits and biases. This is a big Europe of open horizons, especially shaped by Mediterranean and Asian influences that draw our story to North Africa and the Middle East (see Figure I.1). The year 1000 is an arbitrary beginning so, in Chapter 1, we must take a step back to examine the social and economic history of early medieval Europe. The year 1500 is not, in some respects, a good ending, but we can worry about that later. By 1000, the Europeans were basically at home, although there would still be some migrations within Europe. These Europeans were far from being the most comfortable or prosperous people on the planet. Two other peoples, the Turks and Mongols, came into Europe during our five-hundred-year period. By 1500, the Europeans, equipped with good weapons, institutions, and reasonable numbers, were on the verge of bringing their distinctive society and economy to the rest of the world. The entire story of this remarkable change is not contained within these five centuries, and the causes of change are not limited to social and economic history. Nevertheless, these vital subjects – economic and social history – warrant opening this book.

Economic history is easier to define. Its subject is human choices about consumption and is generally limited to the material circumstances of life. "Human" means women and men, always. Yet, men and women make choices about how to choose, and some reject materialism while others thrive in the world of making, buying, and selling. Here, we must study those who are trying to survive by satisfying their own basic needs – food, clothing, and shelter – while also, in some way, satisfying the needs of others. In other words, we are examining rational maximizers of self-interest, operating under the constraints of the real

1

Figure I.1. Big Map of Europe, listing frequently mentioned places (map by Keith A. French and Darin Grauberger, University of Kansas Cartographic Services).

world, its rules, resources, climate, and all of the rest. As Gregory Clark has recently pointed out, wealth alone is the most important factor that enables lifestyles and therefore social history. This is the inevitable bias of economic historians – the privileging of the search for wealth as the activity motivating most people most of the time. Such an assumption does not make economic historians crude materialists. What they tend to hate is the absence of wealth – poverty. They see wealth and poverty as two sides of the same coin. Much of economic history is the search for an antidote to poverty and the ways that poverty hurts people.

Social history, a vast subject, considers how people live together in society as members of groups. How they survive is the story of the constraints – how climate or clean air, or personal traits, such as health and religious opinions, come together with personal capabilities to affect survival. The emphasis here will be on how people live in families and how they work together, or do not. Because social history takes in almost all of human experience, in practice we must limit our focus here to those aspects of society most connected to choices about work, comfort, and the economy. This social history has little to do with past politics and is no substitute for a textbook on medieval history. Material culture matters here, so, for example, tools are discussed. Cultural history is discussed occasionally when values or luxuries emerge as topics. The approach taken to social history excludes most of cultural history, a regrettable but necessary decision if the book is to be short.

One of the subjects that unifies social history and economic history is the standard of living, that is, the level of comfort a person enjoys. In our time period of study, many people had no choice about these matters, especially those who were born and died as slaves. In practice, comparatively few people had any sort of standard of living that we might envy. Only at the end of our period of study does any sort of consumer society emerge that shared its products with any substantial amount of people – still perhaps the top percent in terms of wealth. It is practically impossible to measure the standard of living in the Middle Ages, but sometimes, at least, we have a sense of what direction it was going. Precise numbers are lacking on topics, such as gross domestic product, wages, literacy, caloric intake, and other factors that shape how people live and die. Whether or not the average person was experiencing any real improvement depends on how we measure or estimate what they valued. The privilege of praying in a great cathedral like Chartres has to be weighed against a grumbling stomach or cold feet. Free lands in Iceland or in the Ukraine experienced a burst of productivity, but it would not last. Clark's perspective on this problem was so wide that he contended that the average person was really no better off in 1800 than he or she was in 100,000 BCE. What he means must be taken seriously, even if he is wrong.

We must resist the temptation in social and economic history to focus on elites, lords, and great merchants. The great mass of people, poor with very little or nothing, subsisted in a standard of living that their distant hunter-gatherer ancestors may very well not have envied. Our later Middle Ages were in the middle of the Malthusian world in which economic success equaled reproductive failure. In this environment, the stern message was that, for most people, the only ways to raise the standard of living were to decrease the birth rate and/or to increase the death rate. A pie of a stable size gave bigger slices to fewer people. The rich had more children because they could afford to, but if they had too many they would end up poorer. Yet, those factors we might assume improved the lives of people – peace, hygiene, freedom from epidemic disease – reduced the standard of living because they lowered the death rate! This way of looking at the world made economics, at first, seem to be truly the dismal science of death. Most medieval people viewed this world as a brief stop on the way to either a pleasant or hellish eternity. But they thought that what they did here mattered, not only to their salvation, but also to their choices about how to live. Their institutions, the sets of rules or norms by which they regulated social and economic life, are perhaps their most durable legacy to the modern world.

This textbook is a summary of vast scholarly literatures which are growing exponentially every year in a variety of languages. Even at this moment, it becomes slowly out-of-date. This is the normal fate of textbooks. This introduction and each chapter mention the most important works for the topics discussed. Some major studies influenced every chapter and are not listed again. The bibliographies of these works, in turn, become a guide for the huge literature that you may wish to consult on any special subject that seems neglected or omitted. Wherever possible, I have emphasized readings in English, but I have tried to keep a proper perspective on the social and economic history of later medieval England. This vast and intensively studied subject cannot be allowed to overwhelm a text that must illuminate Europe as a whole. This textbook is a filter standing between you and the known facts and opinions about medieval social and economic history. I have selected some themes and not others, and I have chosen one example over another. My biases and ignorance will become apparent as you read. For now, I want to make it clear that this is not the first textbook on this subject. I will briefly set out the major influences on the ways I have shaped this book, so that you can think about these limits in advance.

Let us consider a few old and great books for what they have contributed to the current wisdom on medieval social and economic history. Not all of this will make immediate sense to you, but down the road it will ring bells, and even now it explains the biases of this textbook.

Henri Pirenne's *Economic and Social History of Medieval Europe* (1937) rightly commanded the field for most of the twentieth century. This book stood the test of time because of its big ideas. Pirenne claimed to be guided by the facts rather than theories. In practice, this means that he was in the grip of theories that he did not understand or had suppressed. Yet, his judgment was excellent and where the book fails is in the lack of up-to-date information. In the last seventy years, more research has rendered obsolete most of what Pirenne wrote about credit, customs duties, employers, and entrepreneurial landlords, among other topics. He knew well northern Europe, commercial fairs, banking, manors as social institutions, trade, in general, and many other things. Pirenne saw Europe from the perspective of what he knew best – his native Flanders, its leading medieval city, Bruges, and another city he seemed to admire above all others, Venice.

Pirenne's book is filled with *bons mots*, really striking points revealing his biases, partly inherited by me. He thought that the merchant improvised at the will of his circumstances. This means he focused on entrepreneurs, opportunities, and accidents. The rise of a merchant class struck him as a fundamental issue in this period. Jewish merchants seemed to be accessories, and when they were largely excluded from commerce Pirenne thought society had lost nothing essential. He was the first, but by no means the last, historian to ponder the exact role Jews played in economic development, as their social fate became dominated by discrimination and even expulsion from parts of Europe. Feudal society hovered over the world Pirenne studied, and he thought that the few common people who preserved their liberties were of no consequence. Piracy struck him as the first stage or indeed the root of commerce (he had the Vikings in mind), validating Balzac's view that behind every fortune there is a crime. Commerce was contagious according to Pirenne, so being neighbors to more prosperous trading civilizations was a stroke of good luck. His characteristic open-mindedness inclined Pirenne to value the contributions of Islamic practices to medieval economic life. Yet, he saw the one important result of the Crusades (not a subject that much interested him) as the ways Italians, Provençals, and Catalans came to dominate the Mediterranean at the expense of the world of Islam. Usury laws on the interest rate on loans struck Pirenne as a hindrance rather than a barrier to economic development.

Above all, Pirenne was convinced that the later Middle Ages witnessed the rise of commercial capitalism and that anyone who failed to see this was blinded by theory or bias. He surely had in mind Max Weber, Karl Marx, and others who, for one theoretical reason or another, denied the existence of a medieval capitalism. Europeans did not have to wait for Protestantism or the end of the feudal mode of production to invent capitalism. Pirenne claimed that capitalism required an entrepreneurial class of rational maximizers who owned private property, who produced for a market, and who employed people to work for them. These basic hallmarks of a market economy, commercial capitalism, appeared together in Western Europe precociously in twelfth-century Flanders and northern Italy. Elements of a market economy had been long present in the Muslim and Greek East, legacies of the ancient world. Nevertheless, some people, be they peasants or nuns, continued to exploit some lands in common ways. One economic system does not automatically drive out others. The search for food, clothing, and shelter can be an individual, familial, or collective endeavor.

Most economic historians have joined with Pirenne in locating the rise of free markets in the Middle Ages. Disagreements still exist about the degree to which the market's rise, which was admittedly impressive, had become the dominant engine of the European economy by 1500. This textbook tries to avoid abstractions like "the market" or "capitalism." I put forward here a view of economic development entirely consistent with a clear market economy in some regions by the end of this book. This does not mean that markets prevailed everywhere or overcame more traditional means of organizing production – for example, durable forms of peasant servitude. Pirenne also understood this inevitable mixing of styles of production and degrees of personal and material freedom. Pirenne was not infallible. For some reason, he was convinced that no one had economic policies in the Middle Ages, but as we will see, there were many policies.

Marc Bloch's *Feudal Society* (1961) was conceived in the 1930s and reflects the French *Annales* school approach to medieval social history. This school aimed to fuse economic, social, and cultural history into a total synthesis, enriching the previous emphasis on past politics and the Church. Bloch rooted his understanding of society deep in the soil worked by generations of peasants or serfs – both farmers under duress. A lordly class of professional warriors and landlords subjected this peasantry and lived off of their labors. Whatever surpluses the feudal regime generated sustained early markets and noble consumption. Bloch understood that feudal society did not prevail everywhere and was not even present all parts of medieval Europe. Nevertheless, we owe to him an abiding interest in medieval agriculture – its farming and pastoral regions that sustained cities. The role of the warrior in medieval society, and the social value placed on contracts among people, became distinctive medieval social legacies to the subsequent development of Europe. Some later historians have turned a skeptical eye toward "feudalism" as an anachronistic and useless legalistic construct imposed on the rich variety of local medieval experiments in self-help and farming. Bloch's social insights suffuse this text and its assumptions.

John Hicks, *A Theory of Economic History* (1969) synthesized the lessons of nearly a century concerning how to write economic history, a subject hard to disentangle from all the other types of histories. Hicks wondered about how exactly history benefits from quantitative analysis, but he concluded that it did. Economic theory was relevant to general phenomena, but not the stories that remain the staple of the historical narrative. Hicks was interested mainly in markets, which he saw as rising from custom and command in a society. The rise of the market is not a good or dramatic story; it is a general phenomenon. Yet, most people eventually work for a market. Like Pirenne, Hicks loved city-states, such as Venice and Florence, because they revealed how merchants ruled and specialized. It is natural for economic historians to have a fondness for merchants. So the things that engage merchants tend to absorb economic historians, because these things leave behind records and numbers to ponder. Hicks drew attention to risk – the merchant was above all in the business of reducing risk and enduring uncertainty. Yet, we must be careful to ask exactly what risk entailed in specific contexts. Law and money were the great Roman legacies to the medieval economy. Medieval merchants had to reinvent credit. For Hicks, the real point to disputes about usury was the morality of interest on unsecured loans. He saw feudal society as primarily a military system, and economic historians cannot forget about the costs of war. Finally, according to Hicks, everyone understood that the theoretical benefits of free trade did not always work out, in practice, to enrich everyone. Economic historians tend to take free trade as an obvious good thing, as almost a religion. Social historians tend to worry about how the powerful rig trade to their private gain at public cost.

Carlo M. Cipolla published the first edition of his fundamental *Before the Industrial Revolution: European Society and Economy 1000–1700* in 1973, and its third edition appeared in 1994. The title and dates reveal his most important premise – the later medieval world was a prequel to what really mattered – the Industrial Revolution. Cipolla's interests and statistics thickened as he came to the end of this story. Yet, he accepted the basic connectivity of economic and social history. One of the common themes was scarcity – the basic constraint operating to shape and to distinguish needs from wants. Choice was always necessary, because there were always more wants, let alone needs, than resources. Basic choices concerned food, clothing, and shelter. Cipolla always had an eye out for those whose choices were most constrained: the many beggars in medieval society and the foundlings left on church porches. Charity was a prime example of a voluntary transfer of wealth. Cipolla saw the important distinction about savings: before 1000 – hoarding and dishoarding, and after 1000, the rise of investment. An important question to ask about any society is: who can save and invest? He too rightly observed that the public debt was unknown in the ancient world and was thus a great medieval invention. The very high percentage of the medieval work force in agriculture was proof of its low productivity. Some medieval work, such as weaving, saw considerable increases in productivity while others, such as domestic service or building, saw virtually none. Fixed capital was mainly in livestock, tools, and weapons. Cipolla had no doubts that warfare was negative economic production and a social waste. He also wondered if free trade was always a good thing and if protectionism was sometimes wise policy. Finally, Cipolla was a close student of the rise of the professional in later medieval Europe, and he gave pride of place not to the banker but to the physician. Cities were death traps but frequently hired doctors to serve the public. This was an amazingly astute and caring public health policy.

These thoughts on the current status of medieval economic and social history prepare us to enter this complex world. Medieval people had no reason to believe that what we know as their social and economic history affected their own values, or history in general. We are imposing these categories of analysis on the medieval world. Important themes take us to the calamity of the Big Death in the fourteenth century. This world did not end. Europe contained enough grounds for optimism so that its people chose to continue making choices to live. Without their endurance, many of us would not be here. From the perspective of the rest of the world, with its own stresses, the arrival of the prosperous and well-armed Europeans, with their new institutions and diseases, was far from a blessing.

Nevertheless, we may see these five hundred years as an interval between the great migrations of Europeans during the early Middle Ages, and their subsequent adventures after 1500 across the planet. During our period of study, some Europeans (and not others) began to triumph over poverty and backwardness. Of course, any competitive society produces losers as well as winners. The grim side to the expansion of Europe remains a persecuting culture rightly credited with the origins of modern racism and slavery. Yet, on the other side of the argument, a judicious mix of property rights, reliable ways to resolve disputes, and useful mediating institutions, such as guilds, and policies such as protectionism, among other causes, helped Europeans to astonish their near and distant neighbors.

SELECT BIBLIOGRAPHY

Janet L. Abu-Lughod, *Before European Hegemony: The World System A.D. 1250–1350*. Oxford, 1989.

Daron Acemoglu and J. A. Robinson, *Economic Origins of Dictatorship and Democracy*. Cambridge, MA, 2005.

Robert C. Allen, Tommy Bengtsson, and Martin Drake, editors. *Living Standards in the Past: New Perspectives on Well-Being in Asia and Europe*. Oxford, 2005. Nothing before the seventeenth century – the modernist stance on medieval economic history.

Marc Bloch, *Feudal Society*. Translated by L. A. Manyon. Chicago, 1961.

Carlo M. Cipolla, *Before the Industrial Revolution: European Society and Economy 1000–1700*. 3rd ed. New York, 1994.

Gregory Clark, *A Farewell to Alms: A Brief Economic History of the World*. Princeton, 2007.

Christopher Dyer, *An Age of Transition? Economy and Society in England in the Later Middle Ages*. Oxford, 2005. If only such a book existed for every place in Europe . . .

John Hicks, *A Theory of Economic History*. Oxford, 1969.

Henri Pirenne, *Economic and Social History of Medieval Europe*. Translated by I. E. Clegg. New York, 1937.

1

EUROPE AT THE MILLENNIUM

T O START OUR ECONOMIC AND SOCIAL HISTORY OF EUROPE with the Tenth-Century Crisis, we must take a step or two back in order to make a good beginning. First, the ancient economy ended in the early medieval West but continued on in some fashion in the Byzantine Empire in the East. Great movements of peoples occurred across early medieval Europe. Vast migrations brought Germanic- and Slavic-speaking people into new lands that they claimed as their own. Second, the rise of Islam affected the entire Mediterranean economy and society. Third, the Carolingian state experienced an economic revival whose strengths and problems define the Tenth-Century Crisis. Let us start with the legacies of the ancient economy as they are currently understood in light of the latest research.

In the Barbarian kingdoms of the early medieval West, the imperial economy, with its sophisticated tax structures, collapsed by 700. Nearly everywhere in Europe, kings were increasingly unable to draw on local resources for military purposes in the ways that the most effective late-Roman emperors were able to do. This fact suggests that the survival of the Byzantine state depended on some continuity in fiscal structures and public income in the eastern Mediterranean. Later, Muslim caliphates would be able to draw on these legacies. In the period from 400 to 800, aristocracies became weaker everywhere except in Francia and in the Greek East. In most places, the ruling elites were poorer and less comfortable in their material circumstances than they had been in the fourth century. Peasants, who were farmers working under some form of duress, became more autonomous, and those who had originated as rural slaves in many places found servile status to be less well defined and more onerous. Weaker aristocracies changed their cultures and identities as Christianity set

down deeper roots and ethnic and linguistic differences became more pronounced after the universal empire's fall in the West. The Roman state's policies had concealed the regional differences that became more obvious in early
medieval Europe as tribal kingdoms that were in a diverse patchwork replaced
the old imperial provinces. As regionalism began to matter more, the pace of
the important social and economic changes varied. In some places, such as
Britain, the collapse of the Roman Empire was so complete that it wiped out
many aspects of the old regime, while in Italy, and especially in the Byzantine
south, some of the fiscal and urban traditions endured. The end of the Roman
Empire in the West was the beginning of an early medieval Europe. Increasingly defined by its church as Christendom, it was a fragile spiritual home
surrounded by formidable pagans in northern Europe and Eastern Europe,
and sophisticated Muslim societies and economies to the south and to the
east.

The end of Roman imperial unity in the West and its partial survival in
the East had long-term consequences for population levels, styles of government, tax policies, coinage, and many other aspects of daily life. Although the
collapse of the empire was a catastrophe for its emperors, their armies, and
urban societies, for most people life continued largely unchanged. Christianity's triumph over classical paganism endured, and its rules on marriage would
gradually percolate through Barbarian society. Still, the Barbarians wrecked
much of the empire's infrastructure and manufacturing or allowed it to decay.
Lead, copper, and silver mining, which were common across Roman Europe,
collapsed to prehistoric levels and did not surpass these levels until the early
modern period. Comforts, such as good ceramics and roofing tiles, gradually
disappeared, as did international trade in staples, such as olive oil and wine.
Patterns of shipwrecks across time in the Mediterranean suggest that Roman
levels of trade have not been reached again until comparatively modern times.
Mass production and consumption, a feature of the Roman economy, did not
survive the barbarians. Their invasions were violent, and many people suffered
and died, as in the Vandal sack of Rome in 455. Justinian's efforts to reestablish Roman authority in the West in the 530s and 540s resulted in further
destruction and waste of resources, which included his subjects. A great plague
in 541–542 devastated large portions of the Greek East and Italy, compound-
ing the social and economic problems arising from the empire's difficulties. A
more-prosperous and better-nourished society might have withstood this new

epidemic more easily, but that argument was little comfort to the nearly half of the population that succumbed. Although the exact nature of this illness remains unknown, its effects were severe, not to be repeated in Europe until the Big Death of the fourteenth century. Evidence for a sudden global climatic change beginning in the 530s is mounting. This period of cooling for Europe, known as the Vandal Minimum, occurred from about 400 to 850, with the coldest temperatures around the year 700. Cold climates probably spelled harder times for agriculture across Europe and, in some places, may be responsible for the low crop yields that seem typical in this period.

The general picture of economy and society before the Carolingian period suggests that the material complexity and comfort levels for both ordinary people and aristocrats plummeted in the West. Nearly everywhere, both slavery and literacy rates declined, but these legacies of the ancient world continued to endure. New barbarian groups continued to arrive in Europe. The sixth century witnessed the arrival of the Lombards in Italy, and in 582 the Avars and the Slavs penetrated the Balkans and sacked Athens. In the Byzantine lands, economic decline also occurred, but a relatively strong government kept alive such necessities as manufactures for the army, a supply of small change for the market, and ships for trade. The best-documented early medieval society, Roman Egypt, seems to have experienced the fewest problems, and its economy survived intact the Arab conquest of 639–642. The first Arab siege of Constantinople in 674–678 shows how quickly Islam affected the geographer's Europe, but we, like the Byzantines, must not forget about the Roman, now Arabic, East and its continuing prosperity. At the other extreme end of the early medieval world, Ireland, never Romanized, came over to its faith and escaped the waves of invasions that Britain experienced. Ireland's prosperous kingdoms preserved classical and early Christian learning.

Historians have written for centuries about the fall of Rome, and more recent labels, such as "The End of Ancient Civilization," "The Transformation of the Roman World," "The Rise of Christendom," or even "The Birth of Europe," have become sound bites summarizing big arguments about this period. By 700, in a barbarized West, land and booty remained the principal forms of wealth for those emerging aristocracies and peasantries that the Carolingian kings forged into a temporarily cohesive state. What Georges Duby called "an economy of gift and pillage" partially explains a system of exchange where status and violence had at least as much to do with the ways goods circulated as did markets and local bartering.

CAROLINGIAN ECONOMY AND SOCIETY

A quick survey of European society and economy in 800 in the heyday of Charlemagne's reign helps establish a baseline from which to measure the crises his successors faced at the end of the ninth century and through the tenth century. This highly selective summary can only skim the surface of a big subject, but let us begin with Figure 1.1 and some large generalizations. The vast extent of forests nearly everywhere except the drier Mediterranean south, where tracts of scrub prevailed, suggests that as the amount of land under cultivation had contracted. In what was once Roman Europe, rural population levels were certainly lower. Cities had shrunk, and some had virtually disappeared. The largest city in Western Europe, Rome, was perhaps at 5 percent of its population at its ancient height, while the greatest city in Europe by far remained Constantinople, which was a bit smaller than the Roman city but was still a giant compared to the settlements to the west.

Surveying the regions from west to east, we first find the great exception to decay in the west, a prosperous, urbanized Muslim Spain still connected by North African trade routes to the heartlands of Islam in the eastern Mediterranean. A few small Christian kingdoms in northern Iberia looked north to the Carolingian Empire for support. The most important non-Carolingian sphere in the West was the British isles – Anglo-Saxon kingdoms connected by a still relatively peaceful and vibrant trading network in the northern Atlantic and in the North and Baltic Seas, where pagan Norwegians, Danes, and Swedes traded and occasionally raided their neighbors. Italy was fractured into a northern area incorporated into Charlemagne's empire while, in the south, independent Lombard and Byzantine areas existed. The central fact here is the absolute decline of Italy, which was now cut off from North African and above all Egyptian grain and other items of trade. Even so, Italy still was, apart from Muslim Spain, the most urbanized place in the west. Between those areas of Europe controlled by the Carolingians and the Byzantines, various largely pagan tribal groups of Germanic- and Slavic-speaking peoples, along with the Avars from Central Asia, controlled the trade routes through their territories along the Danube and points east. Whatever unity Rome had once imposed on parts of Europe had clearly disappeared. In those areas that were never Romanized, such as Denmark, there is no reason to assume that the population had declined or that such comforts that had existed were gone. The movement of peoples from northern to southern Europe instead suggests that depopulation and riches in

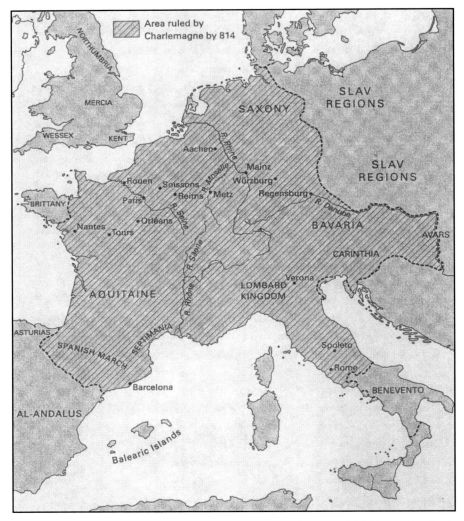

Figure 1.1. Charlemagne's empire in 814 (from Rosamond McKitterick, *Charlemagne: The Formation of a European Identity*. Cambridge 2008, p. 101).

the south had opened up niches for the wandering tribes and settlers to inhabit. A sophisticated market economy existed in Muslim Spain and in the Byzantine East, with some intrepid merchants, pilgrims, and travelers connecting these two systems. In Francia, as we will see, the land was the primary source of wealth. In less-organized areas of Europe, goods circulated in an economy of gift and pillage that was at least as important as the fragile worlds of buying and selling.

The monotheists (the Christians and Muslims) were clearly prevailing, and therefore, certain features of these faiths were becoming more pervasive. In the Christian lands, which were really a federation of regional faiths tied together by the Latin language and Mass, the Benedictine rule for monks and nuns, and the activities of missionaries, some basic social rules were emerging. The teachings of the faith were slowly establishing a nondivorcing, monogamous family life as the rule. Charlemagne reinforced this basic unit of society by requiring that everyone he controlled have godparents, which augmented the family when it proved unable, for whatever reason, to protect its children. He also tried to require paying a tithe to the church, and this custom as well as a constant stream of donations in exchange for prayers and the hope of salvation increasingly made the Church the greatest landowner across Europe. Christian teachings required that a proper burial should take place in consecrated ground, so cremation was disappearing and grave goods were an increasingly rare relic of pagan values.

In Muslim Europe, Arabic provided a linguistic commonality for what was still a federation as these Muslims stood apart from the caliphate in Baghdad. As much of Spain became increasingly Muslim in faith, burial practices shifted to simpler and speedier burials. Some wealthy men, who were able to support up to four wives, practiced polygamy. But the similarities in social practices among the monotheists, including the Jews, who were the most numerous in the south and above all in Muslim Spain (but still a tiny minority even there), are striking. In matters of diet, the Jews and Muslims denied themselves, for example, the pig herds that were such a common feature in Christian Europe, while the Christians needed fish on certain days and times of the year. Different specifics mask a common belief that rules about food help define a people. Monotheistic, literate societies have obvious common features, such as making wills, something that is not shared by the world evoked in the poem *Beowulf* or the by great ship tombs of northern Europe. Women remained socially subordinate among these monotheists because both of these faiths sanctioned such treatment, admittedly in slightly different styles. Christians had convents of religious women living outside secular society; Muslim women might initiate divorce. This is not to say that the polytheists in the north created paradises for women, but in a world like Sweden, with goddesses and a gender division of labor that left high-status tasks, such as brewing. in the hands of women, a rougher equality between the sexes may have prevailed.

Both polytheists and monotheists had strong ideas about honor, and much of their literature concerned admirable defenses of it in the face of monsters, infidels, and other threats in the world. No group had a monopoly on honor; for what society would claim not to value a reputation for valor and integrity? All of the societies in Europe cherished honor. The lords, or the aristocracy, were the warrior classes who controlled the land, usually claimed to have the most honor because their style of life was in itself the definition of honor – was not their sword mightier and more dignified than the hoe of the peasant? Men claimed the right to define female honor and defend or violate it at their whim. The vast majority of the population, who were the tillers of the soil and the herders, found their honor invested in family life, village traditions, and the minute gradations with which the Carolingians in particular defined personal liberty. Slaves were by definition both without honor and debased items of commerce, who were either captured or born into their lowest status. Slavery was the great common theme – a social and economic fact of life in all parts of Europe, and a major staple of the commerce that still existed among the regions. In most spoken languages, slave hunting in the southern Slavic lands gave an ethnic label to human chattel – the slave. Trafficking in people was one of the important links between Europe, North Africa, and the Middle East, and no society had any scruples or sense of guilt about dealing in captives and born slaves who were more valuable than wood or even fur.

One of the most distinctive features to emerge from the Carolingian documents is the manor. This form of agricultural estate stands at the end of a long tradition of organizing rural society to benefit the aristocratic or ecclesiastical landowners. What is new about the Carolingian manor, so far as we can tell, is that a few sources, the polyptychs, served individual lords, in the surviving sources usually abbots, as catalogs of their estates, broken for convenience into manors. An individual manor was a big farm that was usually divided into two parts. The lord, a monastery or Charlemagne himself, reserved part of the land, the demesne, and the local productive assets for his own benefit and use, to be run by a steward or estate manager. Records survive because absentee landlords, such as the king or a bishop or a religious community, needed produce – grains, meat, vegetables, cloth, wine, whatever the particular estate could provide – in order to move these supplies to where they were needed. Or, a peripatetic ruler might move from estate to estate and live off the surpluses generated by his part of the enterprise. The other part of the manor consisted of tenants – peasant laborers who held land and other assets on a bewildering array of terms ranging from true rents paid by people who were personally free to work the servile lands clearly assigned to people originating as slaves and who, in some cases, were still called slaves. Other tenants, the lidi, or half-free, occupied a nebulous status between the slaves and the free peasants and may have originated from mixed marriages between these groups.

The main source for this rural world was the polyptych – the most famous is the one prepared for Abbot Irminon between 825–829 for the estates of the great abbey of St. Germain des Près near Paris. Three other documents of this type survive from other church estates, and a few scraps of information from Italian lands are also available. In addition, we have a famous capitulary or royal edict, _De Villis_, which Charlemagne issued to his estate managers about 800. This document presents an ideal portrait of what a utopian manor might have supplied to its owner, from the horses and fishponds to fruits and nuts, in addition to the staples in grains and firewood that the tenants were obligated to cart to wherever the ruler or religious community needed them. Archaeology has also helped illuminate village buildings and the ways fields were laid out and cultivated. The study of place names has enabled scholars to determine types of rural settlements and even speculate about the ethnicities of their original inhabitants. On these slender sources, historians have been trying for more than a century to establish the basic features of the Carolingian rural economy, the engine upon which everything else, from war to trade, depended. The main debate has always centered on the manor – how pervasive was this institution, and how reliable are the statistics that can be extracted from the polyptychs? In brief, such numbers are worth scrutinizing for what they reveal and what they hide. Also, it would be an immense error to assume that all of Europe was an orderly patchwork of manors, even if Charlemagne and the great landowners may have dreamed of such a world and the steady stream of wealth it would have provided. In the real world of violence and oral testimony that depended on village memories and traditions, much farming land remained outside this system and, in some places, peasants were comparatively free and worked their lands mainly for their own benefit. In vast tracts of Europe outside

Charlemagne's realms, the forests and the coastlines offered livings to many people who probably thought the manors were traps. Without records like polyptychs, we can only guess about the rural scene in most places, but the biggest mistake would be to assume that manors were everywhere. Whatever surpluses the Carolingian economy was able to generate flowed to the powerful from the manors they possessed rather than to the taxes that were so hard to collect.

POPULATION

The bipartite structure of the classic Carolingian manor reveals a domain (demesne) reserved for the landowner to exploit and other lands held by family units. These tenants originally occupied an amount of land sufficient to support the family – a recognizable group of parents and children. Usually delineated sometime in the past, this tenancy or farm, referred to by the continental sources most often as a *mansus* or, when the reference is found in England, as a *hide*, originally sufficed to keep the family alive and busy but produced enough surplus to pay rents and other services owed to the landlords. Some of these landholding patterns date back to late antiquity. Even in the ninth century, memories of the ancient Roman *colonate* (a system of rural settlement) endured as the relatively free status of the *coloni* and their lands testify. When the polyptychs are scrutinized, they can yield some statistics about the families occupying lands on the big manors. Once again, the sources are not good and the results are not necessarily applicable across Europe, but again the numbers are worth considering for what they reveal about rural life.

The survey of the tenants on the manors of St. German des Près showed, after correcting for various problems, a sex ratio of 119 men for every 100 women, and the wealth of the household did not change this rough relationship. In fact, the numbers of men became more pronounced in the lower status households where women seemed to be in even shorter supply. This sex ratio for the dependant peasants has puzzled social historians, and several hypotheses have been suggested to explain it. Some technical problems about the sources, which do not always note the sex of children, may undercount women. The cloth workshops on the manor, especially those controlled by powerful lords interested in collecting women to put to work at this trade, may have absorbed many workers and removed these women from the pool of ordinary tenants. There is no evidence that infanticide of baby girls accounts for the sex ratio, or indeed any reason to believe that any such practice would have favored the males over the females anyway. In addition to speculating about the missing women, it is also useful to ask about the extra men, many of whom, the sources tell us, were slaves. This type of source captures the male slaves who outnumbered the women who may have been living and working elsewhere. At the top of society, the households of the great collected women as economic assets, workers, and objects of prestige, and this admittedly demeaning practice would also skew the sex ratios in the countryside.

The average household size was 5.76 persons, and the median was 6. As usual across time and distance in medieval Europe, the richer households, those that controlled more land, contained more people. These households were generally flat in generational terms because grandparents were rare, which indicated comparatively low life expectancies or a delayed age at first marriage. These competing explanations will require a closer look because they will result in two quite different views of the Carolingian economy's vibrancy. Households frequently contained a brother or sister of one of the spouses as well as other hard-to-classify members, so this view of the household argues that the number of children present would barely suffice to replace the parents. All scholars assume high levels of infant and childhood mortality, as a rude index, perhaps at a mortality level of 50 percent by about age ten. After that point, the survivors had better chances for longer lives. Households replenished their ranks by people transferring in as other families collapsed from death or illness. Hence, the Carolingian family appears relatively flat in age but is extended laterally to the nearest kin of the spouses.

Records from the estates of the monastery of St. Victor in Marseilles have been used to generate credible figures suggesting that families in Provence contained between 2.9 and 3.1 children. This snapshot of the population, already reflecting the course of childhood deaths, could provide a reasonable basis for long-term demographic growth of perhaps 1 percent a year, which led to the population doubling every century – but this was not an example of Malthusian steady-state population. Lands available for clearing would have been able to sustain this growth, and pollen evidence from this period shows changes in plant species that are typical of farming and forest clearing activities. No widespread epidemics or famines would have provided the kind of external, positive Malthusian check on this type of population growth. It certainly makes sense that in an economy driven by agriculture, more farmers and lands under cultivation could have fostered economic growth. The overall ambitious programs of early Carolingian rulers, as well as their successful wars of conquest, argue for the idea that their economic base was growing. The kind of productive manorial enterprise the capitulary *De Villis* describes also presumes patient increases in both the scale and scope of farming in new crops and more diverse products. The most plausible Malthusian preventative check on population growth was to delay the age of first marriage. Child bearing in this society reflected familial notions of honor, and Christian values frowned on illegitimacy except among slaves and ruling elites. The dowry system, which required that the parents of daughters to transfer wealth to their prospective sons-in-law, may have accounted for a drifting up of the age of first marriage for men who needed to compete and establish themselves before seeming worthy of a bride and a dowry. Often, this marriage pattern resulted in lower ages of first marriage for women who were married off as early and as cheaply as possible. In fact, the evidence from the polyptychs shows, from the relatively high and equal numbers of bachelor men and women (and widowers and widows), that spouses were roughly similar in ages and that they were marrying in the later rather than in their early twenties. This early medieval marriage pattern, which was characteristic of a peasant society and was caused by the dowry system or some other factors, would have acted as a break on rapid population growth. In turn, this preventive check worked to increase per capita wealth – a temptation to have more children and reverse the improvements!

Much of the good land across Europe, from Ireland to the forests where the Slavic peoples of the East lived, escaped the manorial regime. Older patterns of individual farmsteads prevailed in northwest Europe. Migratory patterns of slash-and-burn agriculture were typical in the thinly populated areas along the Danube and Dniester rivers. But in the largest empire in the Christian West, manors supported the emperor, many of his soldiers, and much of his reformed Church.

TECHNOLOGY

Connections among technologies and social forms and economic changes have been investigated for early medieval Europe. The task here is to summarize briefly the Carolingian technological platform from which subsequent advancements took off, if we accept this approach to innovation. Two issues deserve notice. First, European societies had open horizons from the beginning with respect to borrowing technologies from neighboring cultures or invaders and quickly adapting them for local uses. At first, drawing on classical technologies that admittedly were stagnant whether as a result of slavery, limited education, or some other factors, Europe became an adept second adapter of other peoples' inventions. Second, written sources alone are poor witnesses to technology, so we must keep before our eyes the evidence from art and archeology throughout the Middle Ages.

Whatever its origin, the stirrup, by the ninth century, had spread across Europe and had made possible the heavy cavalry so characteristic of medieval culture, what Lynn White succinctly called the "union of man and horse." Supporting these mounted warriors became essential for anyone wishing to exercise military power. Because land and its uses remained the basic form of wealth, we will not be surprised to see that the needs of the man on horseback profoundly shaped rural society. Again, in rough terms, the ninth century also witnessed the widespread adoption of the nailed horseshoe, vital for keeping the horse on its hooves. At the same time the horse collar, which probably came west with the Turks, enabled another union, this one more humble but even more significant, between horse and plough. The heavy plough, usually wheeled, made possible the cultivation of dense clay soil in northern Europe. Slavic tribes perhaps brought this innovation to the west, and they may have borrowed it from some peoples farther east. A scratch plough, ancient technology suited to the dry Mediterranean lands, still served well there. Vast tracts of arable from England to Russia required a better tool, that is, one capable of digging a deeper furrow and turning over the soil. This deeper plowing helped to bring nutrients back up to crop roots and also made draining fields easier in the rainy north. Teams of horses or oxen efficiently harnessed to heavy plows made agriculture possible in areas where the Mediterranean plough was ineffective. Plow teams and peasants were another combination that affected social forms. Peasants often needed to share animals to put together teams. Long strips of land, for example, as shown in the origin of the furlong at 220 yards in England, made more sense because it was as long as these animals could pull together in one direction, and such plough teams were not as easily turned around as the simpler scratch plough was. Of course, the slower but steady oxen were still an important way to apply animal power to the need to feed people from the land. Horses and oxen also needed to eat. The availability of pasture and oats affected which animal would predominate in farming. Feeding these animals through the winter was always a problem and in parts of northern Europe they could not endure the bitter cold so they needed to be stalled.

Making coins and dies, the métier of the minter, is another ancient technological legacy of the Middle Ages. The big changes before Charlemagne had affected money and its uses. In the West, indigenous gold coinage had virtually disappeared, and the money supply consisted of silver pennies or deniers that were minted in vast numbers at mining sites or trading emporia, such as Frisian Dorestad and Flemish Quentovic. Enough silver pennies, in the millions, existed to sustain exchanges and tended to collect where they were needed along the trade routes and where they were hoarded and buried, as in the Viking north. Frisian silver ended up in England, parts of Scandinavia, and Rus long before any local coins were made. Francia was the main source for silver in the West. A basic standard had developed by which 240 pennies were struck per pound of silver. This standard naturally moved around according to silver supplies and the desire of those making the coins to stretch those supplies and their profits by making baser coins. A multiple of the penny by a factor of twelve, the shilling, also called the "sou" or "solidus," was a useful money of account – not yet a coin – but a way to keep track of all these pennies, as was the pound, livre, and lira. Charlemagne's reforms resulted in identical penny coins throughout his empire. This made possible by having the dies cut at a central point and distributed to the many mints across his realms. The Carolingian penny became a standard of exchange. This penny was a broad and thin hammered flan, a fragile and, at the beginning, a high-value coin that did not solve the problem of small change unless it was cut into pieces, as it apparently was.

By 800 in the Byzantine East, the gold nomismata had replaced the late Roman gold solidus and the empire also had an abundant supply of copper coins to facilitate market purchases. The Arabs had basically maintained the monetary systems they found in place. They had adopted the Persian silver dirham (a broad, thin coin probably serving as a model for the western penny) in the extreme eastern and western reaches of their conquests, where silver supplies in Iran and Spain, for example, made this possible. In the Arab heartlands, Spain, and Egypt, close to African gold supplies, the gold dinar was standard, but silver dirhams and even copper small change also circulated. Hence, the monetary map of Europe and the Middle East has a golden core stretching from the southern Balkans and Anatolia south through Syria and Egypt, with silver coinages prevailing in the Persian East and the Anglo-Saxon and Frankish West. Even in these places the occasional gold coin was minted, perhaps as a prestige item that imitated the more common Byzantine and Arab money.

The social function of coins is a much more complex subject to be addressed shortly in our look at trade. Monetary sums measured compensation for crimes in the form of wergild. Whether actual coins changed hands remains unclear, because bartering and payments in kind often replaced cash. Even on the estates of St. Germain des Près, in the Carolingian heartland and one of the most moneterized areas of Europe, three-quarters of rents were paid in kind, we assume for the convenience of tenants and the monks. During the ninth century, as silver and gold coins moved about Europe in the hands of raiders, traders, refugees, and pilgrims, a rough ratio developed between gold and silver in the monetary regions. In the Carolingian and Anglo-Saxon West, where gold was not mined and hence was rare and most precious, the ratio between gold and silver was 12:1. Among the Byzantines, who still controlled some mines and preferred gold to silver, the ratio was 7:1. For the Arabs, the elite traders from Spain to the Indian Ocean, dinars and dirhams coined from readily available gold and silver were usually about 10:1 in value. Silver and gold came out of the ground where they were, but they flowed in the direction of trade balances and cultural preferences. Astute traders understood enough about arbitrage to send metals where they enjoyed the greatest purchasing power.

TRADE

Under an effective ruler like Charlemagne, the Carolingian state from the late eighth century experienced levels of economic prosperity not seen since late Rome. The agrarian regime, better technologies for farming and harnessing the power of animals and moving water, a sound coinage, and successful warfare all worked together, in a favorable climate to produce the modest food surpluses sustaining demographic increases. Charlemagne extended Frankish authority deep into Italy and east of the Rhine, connecting Francia via roads and the sea with its prosperous neighbors. For sea power, the Franks could now depend on Frisian ships in the north and Venetian and Pisan ships in the south to augment and sustain their communications, trade, and travel across the great sailing trunk routes to the north and south. The map Figure 1.1 shows how the Carolingians might use their rivers and roads to facilitate trade between these two great regions and profit by these exchanges. What we now need to explore is the difficult subject of trade from the late eighth to the early tenth century.

A brief word on economic theory is relevant here, because in the absence of reliable statistics, all we have to analyze are impressions and theory, which is often a misleading combination. The classic factors of production are capital and labor. In the Western world, the main capital asset was good agricultural lands, partly mobilized by the manorial regime. Peasants extracted from the soils of Europe the food and products necessary to sustain Carolingian economy and society. This enclosed system seems a physiocrat's paradise – a productive, growing agricultural society that benefits from bursts of productivity resulting from bringing fresh, fertile land under better plows. Lay and church landlords at the top of the system envisioned a maximum of self-sufficiency, where manors would produce what they were best at: producing in some regions wine or cloth, and elsewhere wheat or horses. A modest internal trade would smooth out these comparative advantages and lead to a better life for all. Charlemagne would not have expressed his goals in these terms, but reading his legislation certainly leaves the impression that self-sufficiency at all levels was the goal. Even his armies were to draw on the manorial surpluses to wage successful wars and bring more resources under his control, just as the monks and nuns would pray more efficiently as they specialized in the work of God and left farming to the tenants. Ideally this world could thrive on its internal resources, needing nothing from elsewhere.

As nearby as Constantinople or Muslim Spain, fine things like steel swords, silk, spices, and drugs hinted at a world of comfort far superior to what even the emperor enjoyed in Aachen. Hence, trade was possible and in theory would extend the system of comparative advantage across the wider horizons of the world beyond the Carolingian frontiers. Transaction costs mattered in a world where being a merchant was dangerous, and all travel was difficult and expensive. Traders needed something to sell, and people remained the most profitable and easiest to transport item of commerce in Europe. Economic theory argues for the rise of trade and the enjoyment of its inevitable benefits, but it does not explain why trade will begin to matter more in a particular place in a moment of time. Trade's enduring appeal as both a panacea and a topic for study have made it a kind of proxy for all of economic history, which at times becomes simply the story of trade and complex maps with a lot of arrows. Far from privileging trade, let us remember how well this society was doing without it, how social values predisposed people to believe that trade was perhaps sinful, and what other moral issues might arise from dealings with the Byzantines and Muslims.

In the Frankish world, trade appears to recover in the period 750–775 and remains good until the end of the ninth century, when, as we will see, the long Tenth-Century Crisis begins. Sometimes trade with the Muslim lands was more important while at other times the land and sea routes to Byzantium displayed the most activity. These assumptions about trade accord well with the evidence on agricultural productivity and favorable climate – the main point is that the beginning of the European economy's long-term boom is in the ninth century rather than in the eleventh or twelfth centuries. Michael McCormick has made this argument by compiling a great deal of information about travel and communications in this period by arguing that evidence for these activities is also a reasonable proxy for commercial relations. After all, pilgrims, ambassadors, and even relics could not cross vast distances unless regular trade routes enabled goods as well as people to move. One of the most famous travelers was the elephant Abu Abbas, who made the long journey from the realm of Haroun al-Rashid across North Africa, and then by sea to Pisa and then over the Alps to Charlemagne's court at Aachen. This much-traveled Indian marvel ended his days at Haithabu in Denmark in about 806 while campaigning against the pagan Danes. The ability to move this elephant by ship presumes the existence of ports, shipping facilities, experienced mariners, and ways of communicating that our meager sources do not always illuminate. In similar ways, lost coins along trading routes and the little tags documenting the origins of relics can help demonstrate that both old and new sea and land routes of communication were open in the ninth century.

A few areas seem particularly vital to this trading system – for the Franks the Frisian coast, elsewhere the Tyrrhenian Sea stretching down from Liguria and Pisa to Campania and Amalfi, and Venice with its commanding position at the head of the Adriatic and close ties to Byzantium. Byzantine trading networks centered on the Aegean and its route to the Black Sea and retained a good knowledge of the sea lanes and ship building. Muslim trading dominated the southern shores of the Mediterranean, and their slow conquest of Sicily (827–902) and Crete (823–828) strengthened their grip on these sea lanes. Traders remain the most elusive travelers, not leaving specific records like those of the pilgrims and ambassadors. Still, Syrians and Jews remained specialists whose knowledge of languages, routes, and products gave them an edge over more recent entrants into the trading networks. The narrative sources may well exaggerate their significance in the West, because as strangers they were more likely to be noticed, mentioned, and occasionally despoiled.

McCormick has argued that the slave trade drove Carolingian commerce, and that Christian Europe was unable to keep up with the demand for slaves in the Muslim and Byzantine lands (see Figure 1.2). Charlemagne's conquests in Saxony and down the upper Danube yielded fresh supplies of slaves.

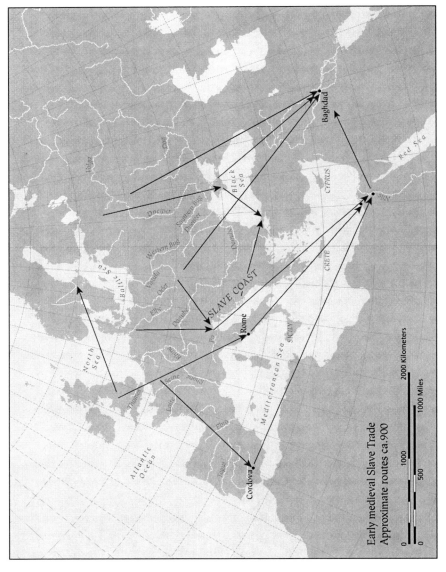

Early medieval Slave Trade
Approximate routes ca.900

Figure 1.2. Early medieval Slave Trade (map by Darin Grauberger, University of Kansas Cartographic Services).

Thousands of slaves traveled as captive goods south and east along the sea and the Dniester and Volga rivers, toward Muslim Spain and markets in distant Cairo and Baghdad. The eastern shore of the Adriatic was indeed becoming a "slave coast" where the capturing of people into slavery was a lucrative business for all concerned. Documents of practice, contracts, recording the activities of merchants do not exist. Archaeology for this period has not yielded the kinds of finds in ceramics than can sustain an argument about trade in commodities, such as oil or wine. The narrative sources tend to preserve notices of slaves, sometimes in the thousands, because the movements of slaves struck witnesses as memorable. Certainly no society – Carolingian, Byzantine, or Muslim – tried to stop the slave trade in the name of morality. The demand for slaves in the more prosperous Eastern economies does seem to have exceeded supply. What has not been demonstrated is that the income from this trade benefited the Carolingian economy or was put to any practical use. Much of the income disappeared into luxuries for a few, coin hoards, or the rapacious hands of raiders, such as the Vikings. Charlemagne's own income from booty seems to have been ploughed back into provisioning his war machine or his modest building program. The point here, as seems to be usually the case in societies that supply human capital to other economies, is that the income was not invested but rather consumed. Gathering of cash and valuable commodities like silks, spices, and steel for weapons (not plows) in nascent emporia and monasteries simply signaled to the pillagers where they might find the richest takings.

Carolingian and Anglo-Saxon societies did invest in the first round of stone parish churches scattered across the countryside in villages where people lived and where their numbers where increasing. Technologies for building in stone were not on a par with Roman accomplishments. None of the technological advances associated with this period affected in any discernible way craft man-ufacturing – which remained at low ebb. What cities as existed in the Christian West, apart from the interesting and poorly documented trading centers, such as Quentovic and Pisa, remained tiny and were not notable for artisan manufac-tures in easily tracked staples, such as pottery. Scriptoria were busy transferring what remained of the classical inheritance from paper to parchment, but we have no way of knowing what effect, if any, this accomplishment had on lit-eracy rates. Taking into account all the pluses and minuses to the Carolingian economy, most observers now conclude that Charlemagne and his successors presided over a period of growth that began in the late eighth century. A general crisis in the Tenth Century certainly challenged this economic and social progress. This problem is the beginning of our more intense study of the economic and social history of medieval Europe.

THE TENTH-CENTURY CRISIS

One key fact about this crisis is that it concerned Western Europe while its neighbors were either flourishing or preying on the West. Despite a Muslim sack of Thessalonike in 904 and problems with the Bulgars at the beginning and end of the tenth century, this was a good century for Byzantium. The empire was expanding in the Balkans and Asia Minor, Crete was retaken in 961, and missionaries converted the Bulgarians (864), Serbs (867–874), and the peoples of Rus (989) to Orthodox Christianity. These impressive accomplishments rested on the fiscal ability of the empire to raise taxes for armies and fleets, and these taxes largely came from hard-working peasants on the land. Even when under pressure, this remnant of the ancient world preserved enough of a state to marshal resources for defense.

Slavic peoples from the Baltic to the Black Seas, joined by Scandinavian raiders and traders, also established trading networks along the Volga and other river systems of Eastern Europe. Merchants from Rus brought furs and other goods south to Constantinople. Trading posts like Staraia Lagoda near modern St. Petersburg facilitated these exchanges, which initially relied for exchange on Muslim silver, and were replaced by German pennies during the later tenth century. By the end of the tenth century, the rulers of Bohemia were minting their own coins. Elsewhere in the Slavic East, pieces of iron, so valuable for tools and weapons, also served as a medium of exchange. Without cities or monasteries to be destroyed, and with much of Eastern Europe still cultivated by migrating peasants farming new lands until they were exhausted, the crisis was less severe here. Also, social fusion among Scandinavians and Russians and Ukrainians, and the Bulgars and southern Slavs, created some collaboration rather than simple mayhem.

For the Muslim world the crisis was not the result of external invasions and meant the political decay of the Abbasid caliphate in Baghdad and the subsequent fragmenting of the world of Islam. The emergence of a strong Fatimid dynasty in Tunis that conquered Egypt (969–1171) meant that all of the southern Mediterranean was united under a powerful Shi'te rule of a majority Sunni population. In turn, this aggressive state in the southern Mediterranean fostered, as we will see, a renewed wave of attacks above all on Italy. The other consequence of the conquest of Egypt is the famous Geniza records, a burst of information about the economy and society of the Muslim Mediterranean world in the tenth and eleventh centuries. These documents, that also illuminate trade with Europe and in the Indian Ocean, provide a wealth of details unavailable elsewhere. The activities of the Jewish Maghrebi traders from North Africa have become an important touchstone for understanding the different paths to economic development in the region. For the moment, all of this is in the future, but for Egypt the Tenth-Century Crisis was an unusual conquest from the West that incorporated the most populous and probably wealthiest part of the Mediterranean into the Fatimid Empire challenging for control of the sea.

For the Carolingian state, the crisis had internal and external causes. Charlemagne was lucky to be survived by one legitimate son, Louis, who became emperor in 814. The Frankish custom of partible inheritance meant that his three sons expected shares of the empire, and the political story of the ninth and tenth centuries is the gradual decay of the dynasty's power. Even though occasionally an able ruler, such as Charles the Bald, reassembled nearly all of the inheritance, the empire eventually fractured into an eastern German kingdom and a western Frankish/French one, with other kingdoms in Italy and Provence also surfacing. The relics of the famous Middle Kingdom stretching from Frisia on the North Sea down the Rhine into the Alps and beyond to the East and South became places where a state or empire ceased to have any real meaning. The complicated political story here can be reduced to a few important economic consequences. Once again the right to coin money slipped away from a central authority and numerous mints, producing debased silver pennies, appeared wherever anyone, lord or bishop, took the initiative. The public authority the effective Carolingian rulers had exercised through the counts was frequently usurped by these people or other strong men on the local scene. The great manors that had taken the place of direct taxes as a way for kings and emperors to fund war slipped out of royal control and were an increasing anachronism in an era of localism and violence. All these problems were more serious on the continent than in Anglo-Saxon England, where stronger monarchs were still able to raise revenues and men for defense, but there the external problems were, if anything, even more severe.

The renewed wave of attacks from all directions defines the crisis of the long tenth century (see Figure 1.3). The raiders must have found something

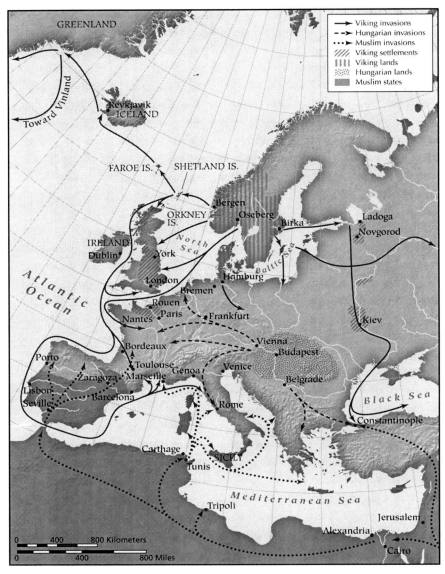

Figure 1.3. Tenth-Century Invasions (map by Keith A. French and Darin Grauberger, University of Kansas Cartographic Services).

attractive about this world and its goods – the external threats are evidence of an increasing level of prosperity from at least the ninth century. Apart from a few tiny cities and wealthy monasteries and churches, the wealth that these lands contained consisted of what the peasants had assembled through decades of hard work. Raiders passing through could sweep up livestock and captives and seize food supplies and whatever modest possessions came their way. Literate monks, of course, saw the threat to their institutions as paramount and so they might have decided to flee into the interior with their treasures in search of safety. Peasants stayed where they were, suffered, and endured. Raiders could not take their lands with them and only posed a permanent problem, when as in the case of the Danes in England, Scandinavians in Rus, and the Vikings in Normandy, they decided to stay and occupy land for themselves. Even this settlement substituted one warrior/farmer for another. The story the map tells looks terrible but this wave of invasions only challenged an agrarian society rather than destroying a sophisticated urban-fiscal network like the Roman Empire. These movements and migrations of peoples were the penultimate touches to making a Europe of recognizable peoples. After 1000, only a few new arrivals, the Tartars and Turks, changed the basic medieval ethnography of Europe.

To be in the path of the Magyars, Vikings, or Muslim raiders cannot have been a pleasant experience, and occasional chaos on the local level was bad for farming and hence the economy as a whole. These disturbances doubtless drove up the death rates for peasants living on the margins of subsistence. Western Europe, with its long sea coasts, many navigable rivers, and expansive plains open to the East, was difficult to defend and ideal to raid. The Magyars (later called Hungarians) were originally an Asiatic steppe people, the latest arrivals from Central Asia drifting west in search of pasture and opportunities. After helping the Byzantines defeat the Bulgarians, the Magyars found themselves to be unwelcome and pushed to the west, so they found a base in their permanent home, the Hungarian plain. Arriving there around 899, they quickly launched raiding expeditions of amazing distances, deep into Italy and the Carolingian heartland – as far south as Otranto, capturing Pavia and repeatedly threatening Rome, and by 917 they were across the Rhine. The Magyars killed many people, sold the survivors into slavery, and sacked monasteries. Otto the Great king of Germany defeated them at the Lech in 955 and by 1000 they were confined to their own kingdom and converted to Christianity. In this case, as awful as the raids were, we will be looking to how a king in Germany was able to mobilize resources to defeat and contain them. These Hungarians must have caused terrible problems for the Slavic peoples in the East, but the contemporary sources are not clear on the effects on these poorer societies. The new people now effectively occupied the great fertile plain of the Middle Danube, which separated the Poles and other Slavs in the north from their linguistic cousins, the southern Slavs.

Muslims from their bases on Sicily and in Iberia renewed attacks on Christian states. In Italy, the challenge was on the mainland, the Byzantines lost Bari in 840, Rome was sacked in 846, and the great Benedictine abbey at Monte Cassino was destroyed in 881. The surviving monks fled with their books to Rome. Raiders from Muslim Spain established a permanent base at Freinet (near modern Cannes) around 890 where they would remain until 973. Among their spectacular feats was the capture of the abbot of Cluny in 972, whom they held for ransom. Perched on the coast, generations of these robbers interrupted the cabotage trade (for a short distance) along the Riviera and controlled the main road south to Rome and the Alpine passes to their rear. Supplied by sea, these Muslims prospered because there was no credible Christian navy in the region and this area of the Mediterranean was too far from Byzantine areas for the Greeks to make a difference here. Muslim raiders from North Africa so thoroughly sacked Genoa in 934/935 that this little port took decades to recover. They repeatedly devastated other parts of the Mediterranean coast from the Pyrenees to Naples, as well as Sardinia and Corsica. In Iberia where a frontier of sorts existed between the Christian lands, such as Catalonia and the Muslim kingdoms to the south, a more regular form of warfare protected Europe north of the mountains from raids by land. But the sea routes remained open, and into the eleventh century Muslim sea power from Balearic Islands and Tortosa held the upper hand.

Above all, the threat from the Northmen began in the early ninth century and continued on past the pacification of the Magyars and the eventual taking of the offensive against the Muslims in the eleventh century. The story of the northern raids is a vast one as the Norwegians, Swedes, and Danes swept south in every direction, pillaging Ireland, England, the coast of Francia, and down the river systems of Rus into the Black Sea to trouble the Byzantines. Vikings, expert sea travelers, entered the Mediterranean from both ends during the ninth century. In some places, such as Normandy in Francia and the Danelaw in England, the raiders settled down and occupied lands. Elsewhere, the raiders remained a seasonal menace, appearing along the coasts or up rivers deep into Muslim, Christian, and Byzantine territories. Surely the ability of Scandinavia to sustain such raids and export so many people, even to distant Iceland, testifies to demographic growth, shipbuilding skills, and an ethos for adventure that brought them as far as Greenland, Seville, and Constantinople. Their settlements changed the destinies of peoples in Francia and Rus. We must take all these troubles from the Magyars, Muslims, and Vikings as a given, and also leave aside the motives internal to these peoples that put them on the move. What we must focus on is their victims and their responses to these challenges, for in these challenges many social and economic historians have found the origins of a feudal and commercial revolution and indeed the birth of Europe.

The crisis had some lasting effects on the old and durable geographic regions of the Roman Empire. North Africa, Cyrenaica, and Egypt were under a Fatimid rule that contested the control of Syria and Palestine. The Byzantine heartland remained in control of Asia Minor and the southern Balkans, with toeholds still in Italy. Increasingly over the early tenth century the old Lombard and the Frankish kingdom of Italy meant nothing and local strongmen prevailed. Venice's unique geography and fleet spared it the waves of raiders, and this undoubtedly helped secure its trading center an even more important role in the aftermath of the crisis. Iberia remained divided with most of it under Muslim control and economic cooperation across the confessional frontier was minimal. Here too the ancient economy had thoroughly collapsed in the northern Christian kingdoms. Only in the Muslim and Byzantine lands did the late ancient fiscal motors still run bureaucracies and standing military forces. These accomplishments were far beyond the petty rulers in Francia where these things had collapsed now twice – in the different Roman and Carolingian models. Ireland, Denmark, and Iceland were places that had never fit into ancient economic regionalism centered on the Mediterranean and Roman provincial boundaries, so their paths were new. England was drifting into a Scandinavian region unknown to the Romans. The repeated demands for tribute, the *Danegeld*, and the eventually Danish subjection of much of Britain may have provided the kind of fiscal demands that produced a more orderly exploitation and marshalling of rural resources. English agriculture, which was organized by the hundreds of farms and in a village structure that retained a sizeable numbers of slaves, fueled the ambitions of the Danish kings, such as Canute. East of the Rhine, the German kingdom faced the Hungarians as did their Slavic neighbors to the Byzantine frontier. This macropolitical picture of a big Europe now requires that we look beneath the surface to find the prosperity of the regions. Outside of the Byzantine and Muslim lands this will be peasant agriculture.

FARMING

The Europe in this chapter had a very wide range of climates and environments sustaining a broad number of farming, fishing, and pastoral systems. It would be a big mistake to impose an artificial and deceptive uniformity over these many forms suited to the microregions in which they existed, or to take one common type as symptomatic of all the rest. Once again, the nature of the surviving records causes distortions, because we are primarily informed about those peasant lands that fell into the control of the church through sale, exchange, or donation. These lands were already likely to be neighbors of whatever institution was eager to possess them, so they are already, in some sense, not typical. Let us search for some common types. The peasant freeholder who had enough land to sustain his or her family was the backbone of the economy. After the big Carolingian manorial regimes collapsed, this type of farmer was the most common through the villages of tenth-century Europe. How much land a family needed, and what such a unit was called (e.g., hide, mansus, curtilage) varied according to soil types and regions. These farming families often contained other relatives, and the more prosperous among them might have still had a few slaves. Above the free peasant farmers were families controlling more land than they could directly farm themselves, and these people, the big men on the local scene, leased farming units to the landless and also put slaves to work where slaves were available – as a result, rural slavery persisted in wide area of England, Francia, and Catalonia. In fact wherever the documents survive we see more than vestiges of a rural slavery. Below the self-sufficient were a mass of ostensibly free but landless people, who lived by doing seasonal agricultural work for others. Such people were always necessary in an agricultural regime with bouts of heavy labor demands at harvests and other activities.

The villages near tiny cities or on top of older ancient villas often had field structures like old Roman models – a mosaic of small, usually square holdings scattered around a village center. In the rural areas far from cities or wooden castles, the fields were larger. In some cases, by the tenth century individual plots were in long strips to facilitate plowing and perhaps to even out the risks of the microsoil qualities. Villages needed some sort of commons and wooded areas where peasants could gather firewood and pasture animals. These commons by old traditions remained a public right that free people used and needed. In Eastern European areas where peasants practiced slash-and-burn agriculture, the villages were very temporary settlements.

By the tenth century, in many regions, the surviving charters supply evidence of assarting – land clearing that usually takes the form of cutting down trees or draining wetlands to increase the amount of arable land. This movement made it possible to sustain population growth by bringing more land into cultivation, especially outside of the densely settled, regions. This was the beginning of a major wave of internal colonization across Europe. Sometimes assarts nibbled away at the commons, and in other places it was not clear who controlled the wastes, as land not used was often called. Big proprietors, secular or religious, funded assarting by offering landless peasants a share of the new land, usually half, in exchange for the hard labor of clearing trees and rocks or draining water-logged areas. Masters could put their slaves to work on these projects and then settle them on the farms that were created. These low-profile patient activities would escape the worst of the raiding and continued on during the troubles, especially in those places farthest from the rivers, coasts, and roads the raiders might take. In mountainous regions, fields were always tiny and bringing new lands under cultivation often required back-breaking digging to construct terraces. In a fishing village, rarely producing documents of any kind, we presume that increasing the scale of activities meant building more boats, extending a protective jetty by a few meters, or acquiring more salt to sell or to preserve more fish to trade. In a sense, these assarts went out into the sea, or mobilized the trees and salt pans. Soon the Dutch would begin the long-term process of literally assarting the sea. Several impulses guided assarting in general. New resources meant different things to different people – a free peasant with a few more acres had more to eat; a landless one might have a farm for the first time. A slave family on a new enterprise might hope for some event to turn them into tenants. Monks and nuns increased their income and supplies. Even where lords were still cultivating demesne lands with hired, traditional, or coerced labor, assarting improved their incomes as well. The bottom line here is that assarting only makes sense if an increasing population has some better tools, like horse collars, to do the work. Other labor-saving technologies, such as the water- and wind-driven mills becoming widespread in this century, freed considerable labor from grinding flour that could be put to more profitable ventures.

Despite the breakdown of Carolingian order and the fresh wave of invasions, parts of Europe show signs of a durable prosperity and continued growth in population over the tenth century. The most important factor driving this trend, given a favoring climate for farming, was peasant labor. A chronology of labor services, which brings the story down to about the year 1000, reveals that in some places, such as England, slavery remained an important rural fact, while in other areas like Catalonia and the Mâconnais slaves were becoming tenants and joining the ranks of an increasingly subjected peasantry. Over the tenth century, a new discourse about society described a tripartite world in which some people farmed while others fought or prayed. First articulated by the bishops Gerard of Cambrai and Adelbero of Laon, this social theory, for that is what it was, inevitably privileged those who prayed, but sought in the warriors a group who could be motivated to defend the spiritual hierarchy in an increasingly dangerous world. The overwhelming majority of the population had the duty to work to sustain the clergy and a lordly class. When strong kings like Charlemagne had maintained order the world seemed divided into two orders, secular and clerical. But as kings multiplied and became ineffective in dealing with the external threats, a new vision of society made more sense. Public authority no longer prevailed.

Private help on the local scene was required. Local lords eventually defeated the Muslims at Freinet, not some heroic king like Beowulf. In a prosperous but threatened rural Latium, these warriors built rural strongholds, primitive castles, from which to fight raiders and wage private wars. In the Midi (southern France), local violence among these warriors became so pronounced that movements known as the Truce and Peace of God began around 990 and continued on into the turbulent 1020s. Local clergy and small landowners initiated these desperate attempts to impose some rules on violence and those who claimed a monopoly over it. All of these trends constitute the beginnings of a feudal revolution and have three precursors that Marc Bloch noted sixty years ago – a subjected peasantry, a hereditary warrior class, and the collapse of public authority in the guise of effective kingship. As we will see in the next chapter, in some places none of this occurred, and free peasants or tribal systems or civic authority still counted for something.

Signs of trade, travel, and communications in the late tenth century present a perplexing picture. In some places, raiding and trading went hand-in-hand and the Vikings dealt in slaves and booty wherever they went. Important but small cities continued to be sacked, as was Barcelona on July 6, 985. Some riches there attracted pillagers but documents that might have illuminated the activities producing this wealth were also destroyed. What contributions cities and trade made to a profoundly ruralized society and economy in the West remain very obscure. Cities were headquarters for bishops, drew on local

Table 1.1. *Church property on the Continent Data (from David Herlihy, "Church Property on the European Continent, 701–1200,"* Speculum *36 (1961): 81–105 data, table 3, pp. 103–105).*

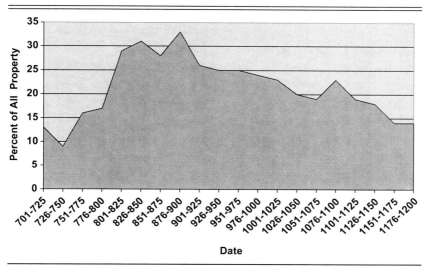

hinterlands for resources, and were frequently wrecked. Trading networks existed, and merchants from Amalfi and elsewhere, as pirates and adventurers, were already making their way to Egypt and the East by 1000. This thin and elusive commerce is not self-explanatory – trade does not somehow mysteriously rise by itself and the supply of luxuries will not create a demand for them unless someone has accumulated the resources necessary to buy them. These processes only emerged slowly from the years of crisis, but we should be alert to the signs of rural prosperity and, above all, in whose pockets the surpluses were accumulating.

The later tenth century emerges from the shadows in particular regions or places where large numbers of written charters survive – Anglo-Saxon England, Catalonia, and the region around Cluny, Bavaria, and Lucca, for example. The great mass of these documents concern property transfers and, in a classic article from 1961, David Herlihy used a vast sample of them to discover the probably percentage of all lands that belonged to the Church (see Table 1.1). Because even those transfers between secular owners only survive because the property ended up belonging to a bishop or monastery, the sample may be slightly biased in favor of ecclesiastical landowners. Herlihy was well aware of this problem and corrected for it by noting a special feature of nearly all charters, which scrupulously note property boundaries by naming, in the case of a square field, for example, the four neighbors. Counting all of these neighbors multiplies the number of property holders in the sample and captures many landowners who do not appear in any other records. Still, the great collections of charters, and monastic Cluny is the best example of this, show that church landowners pursued strategies of consolidating their holdings. Hence, the naming of the neighbors may be somewhat biased in favor of the very institutions collecting the records and lands. With all of these warnings in mind, we can still trust the general findings which have been ratified in many subsequent studies – that church property amounted to more than 30 percent of all of the lands in the Carolingian period, a time of enormous growth, and remained generally at more than 25 percent even during the troubled tenth century. (We will consider the post-1000 results in later chapters). Tithes and pious donations accounted for this great wealth. Waste, fraud, pillaging, and abuse kept the Church from owning everything.

Studying these charters has provided a treasure trove of new insights that range from particular villages to the land-owning strategies of great monasteries and bishoprics. Most of the findings in this chapter rest on careful work on some collection of charters – from the work of Guy Bois on the village of Lournand near Cluny in the Mâconnais to Michel Zimmerman's vast study of nearly 10,000 charters from Catalonia before 1200. Except for the charters in England, where local traditions created a charter tradition with documents in the vernacular Anglo-Saxon, nearly all charters are in a Latin increasingly special to the region where it was written. Outsiders at first find these tenth-century charters to be in a bizarre Latin that is annoying to anyone who learned his or her Latin from Caesar or Virgil. After setting aside prejudices about obtuse grammar and handwriting, students of charters ask: why there are so many of them? People required more and more charters over the course of the century. In a large number of cases, the parchment carries the marks or even the autograph signatures of the witnesses whose presence, along with the oaths of the parties, conferred validity on the business at hand.

This evidence prompts even more good questions – why were so many people donating land to the Church? How many could read or sign their names? Why did they need writing to validate an oral oath? What was the connection between memory and writing? We know from the charters that a fear of Hell and a desire for intercessory prayers prompted many donations to the Church. The subscriptions to charters reveal that a number of people who made their marks by a cross on a document could also sign their name. Whether that meant that they could read or not is a separate issue, but even if they could not speak Latin, it was the language of record. Finally, the greater reliance on the written word to keep track of land reveals menaced societies in crisis that needed to appeal to some authority outside of the parties literally to seal a deal. Recording speech was a new way of maximizing self-interest. Peasant memories in the countryside were one way to keep track of fields and rights and the folk memory remained a powerful repository. Anyone who could write or understand writing had access to a type of authority that could withstand the challenges of weak kingship, vague law, and even the raiders whose destructive ways meant that many charters were lost. But even more charters were kept, especially by the powerful landowners who now had a new legal tool in addition to their long memories.

This brief look at the forces shaping Europe at the millennium suggests that it would be best to begin looking at the next period by examining what most people did – farming.

SELECT BIBLIOGRAPHY

P. M. Barford, *The Early Slavs*. Ithaca, 2001.

Guy Bois, *The Transformation of the Year One Thousand*. Manchester, 1992.

Georges Duby, *The Early Growth of the European Economy*. Ithaca, NY, 1974.

David Herlihy, *Medieval Households*. Cambridge, MA, 1985.

Peregrine Horden and Nicholas Purcell, *The Corrupting Sea*. Oxford, 2000.

Michael McCormick, *The Origins of the European Economy*. Cambridge, 2001.

Joel Mokyr, *The Lever of Riches: Technological Creativity and Economic Progress*. Oxford, 1990.

Julia M. H. Smith, *Europe after Rome: A New Cultural History 500–1000*. Oxford, 2005.

Adriaan Verhulst, *The Carolingian Economy*. Cambridge, 2002.

Bryan Ward-Perkins, *The Fall of Rome and the End of Civilization*. Oxford, 2006.

Lynn White, Jr., *Medieval Technology and Social Change*. Oxford, 1964.

Chris Wickham, *Framing the Early Middle Ages*. Oxford, 2005.

Michel Zimmermann, *Ecrire et lire*. Barcelona, 2003.

2

AGRICULTURE AND RURAL LIFE

HE MATERIAL CIRCUMSTANCES OF EUROPE AROUND 1000 WERE defined by the fact that the vast majority (at least 90 percent) of the population lived off of the land in the countryside. Over the next three centuries, the story of the land and its people was the fundamental model of the European society and economy and the basis on which every other accomplishment rested. As Gary Holthaus writes, the issues that farmers faced included: "learning how to maintain the soil and water, animals, and crops; how to take care of the family, keep everyone healthy, and contribute to the community so that one can gain respect and create a meaningful life." Some peasants skinned that sheep or calf whose skin provided the surface on which the most erudite scholastic treatise might be read.

It seems obvious but essential to note that the tiny number of people at the millennium who prayed, fought, or did something else for a living needed farmers to produce the food their own hands no longer supplied. We need not romanticize these people into some sort of organic, unadulterated Volk from whom everything honest and worthwhile about Europe is derived. Nor should we be content to have these largely inarticulate peoples' stories be told by the literate classes who taxed, judged, and ordered the peasants to work. Most economic and social history has been written from the perspective of those who lived off of the peasants and who left behind the records and accomplishments that seem more important than the dull seasonal rhythms and proverbial idiocies of rural life. A crude environmental determinism is also an obstacle to understanding the people who pulled a living from the land or the seas. People and their needs were as much a part of nature as anything else. Climate and soil types are not destiny, any more than skin color, creed, or ethnic stereotypes.

Even with these warnings in mind, we must pick up the story somewhere, moving from the general to the particular across three centuries or ten generations. Needless to say, a survey must be selective and still provide a sense of the rich diversity of the microregions and microclimates of Europe. In a sense, every field and family would have a good story to tell, and historians have been trying to tell the story of an individual peasant or a particular village for a long time. Much of the warrior class also came from the countryside, and their hands rested heavily, in most places, on the backs of peasants. Summarizing all of this work into the blender of a survey risks a bland and even nauseating mixture; too many details will bore and bewilder. Let us then first look at climate, land, crops, and animals, and most importantly at the human settlements and the lives of peasants.

CLIMATE

Weather is what happens in the expansive present. Climate is the long-term situation, usually changing so slowly, if at all, as to escape notice by people living through climatic change. Hence, it is not surprising that medieval people did not notice the Little Climatic Optimum, a slow warming whose beginnings are vague. Usually defined as the period from 1000 to 1300, this optimum in northern Europe meant a slight warming (probably less than 1°C) bringing hotter summers, milder winters, and normal amounts of rainfall. The end of this period is sharper. Cooling began in the first decade of the fourteenth century. More severe winters did begin to strike contemporaries as well. Too much rain in 1313/1314 and from 1317 to 1321 resulted in harvest failures and famines across much of northern Europe. For now, let us concentrate on favorable climate. Certainly occasional bad weather, droughts, and storms caused famines and starvation in parts of Europe – the contemporary sources note widespread hunger in 1005–1006, 1032–1035, and 1195–1197. Scarcity of food could drive up prices and encourage speculators. True harvest failures or diseases in livestock could cause absolute shortages at any price. But, in general, the circumstances were favorable to agriculture, and nearly all problems in feeding people can be attributed to transport breakdowns, market failures, and greed. In other words, across Europe there was always enough food, even as some people starved or went hungry because there was no food to buy where they were or because they were too poor to pay the higher prices.

People did not cause these climatic changes and could not control them. In northern Europe, across the line extending from the Pyrenees, the Alps, and the Carpathian mountains into the plains of Poland and Hungary, the warming meant a longer growing season. Also, more land could be farmed, especially up the mountainsides, and farther to the north in places, such as Russia in the east and even distant Greenland in the west, where imported cattle ate hay crops now possible where formerly ice prevailed. In southern Europe, in the Mediterranean lands, the slight warming did not have a big effect on the already hot and dry summers, which became just a bit warmer. Between these extremes, in the great bands of deciduous forests still stretching across the central parts of Europe in about 1000, the good weather favored the continuing patterns of clearances and assarting that began back in the Carolingian era. All things (technology, farming techniques, seed types, etc.) being equal (which they never are) a favoring climate by itself would have allowed for an accelerating population increase that resulted from better yields from more lands – in theory. What the evidence on demography actually reveals is more complicated.

LAND

People had considerable power over the economics of land – how they valued, exchanged, and arranged it for their purposes. In Holland after 1000, the Dutch were adding to the stock of lands by raising it from the sea, but, in general, we should think of Europe's land as fixed in extent if not in use and unlike population levels. Hence the basic factors of production were – land (capital) and people. They could also improve land, patiently, by burning the heath, marling with lime, draining the wetlands, or fertilizing with seaweed for example in Ireland where it was possible, or pasturing animals on it for manure, and in other ways. What varied enormously across Europe was the natural quality of the soils, about which people could do little. Across wide stretches of northern Europe, glaciated in the last Ice Age, good top soils were thin to nonexistent and grazing was a better idea than farming. South of these areas the glaciers had pushed before them big deposits of stony clays. In theory, these soils were fertile and ideal for planting, but in practice, they were difficult to plow, even with a heavy wheeled plow with iron plowshares pulled by teams of oxen (see Figure 2.1). In river bottoms, the lower reaches of the Thames, Seine, Rhine, Danube, and

Figure 2.1. Types of Plows (from Robert Friedel, *A Culture of Improvement*. Cambridge, MA, 2007, p. 15).

Vistula, for example, where occasional flooding had piled up fertile deposits, the lands were generally ideal. Across much of Europe stretching from pockets in northern France and the Low Countries and becoming more widespread in the great steppes of Ukraine and southern Russia were lighter soils called *loess*. This windblown clay rested on top of heavier soils and was rich in nutrients and easy to plow. Loess also produced extensive grasslands ideal for migratory peoples, such as the Huns, Avars, Magyars, and Mongols, who periodically came west following these grass "highways." Mediterranean soils were thin and often alkaline because they rested on vast tracts of limestone just beneath the surface. The lighter scratch plow was well-suited to these lands, especially where keeping moisture in the soil was a priority. Many rivers entered the inland sea, and these delta and alluvial plains were important to prosperous agriculture in Catalonia (the Ebro), Provence (the Rhone), Lombardy (the Po), Tuscany (the Arno), and Latium (the Tiber). Many smaller rivers in parts of the Balkans, for example, the Achelous River coming out of the Pindus mountains and entering the sea at the western end of the Gulf of Corinth, created similar microregions of good alluvial soils surrounded by poorer ones. Floods could be even more of a problem in the south as good soils were continuously washed away into the sea. Natural processes created and destroyed soils. As yet, humans had only marginal ways to affect these changes, probably less than goats and sheep!

Forests were important natural resources since much construction depended on timber. Heating and cooking required firewood and charcoal. The north seemed to have limitless reserves of coniferous forests even in the face of the

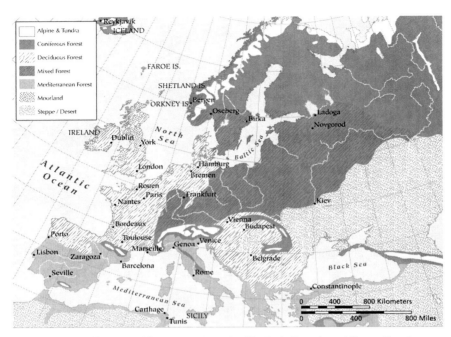

Figure 2.2. European Vegetation (map by Keith A. French and Darin Grauberger, University of Kansas Cartographic Services).

great clearances and assarting (see Figure 2.2). In the fragile ecologies along the mountainous and drier northern shores of the Mediterranean, forests, once cut down, would not easily reestablish themselves. Also, in these regions fires could be devastating. Trading in wood was important, especially for ports, such as treeless Venice, which had to draw on timbers from the southern slopes of the Alps and the Dalmatian coast. It is very hard to say at what point the cutting down of Mediterranean forests had so degraded the environment that flooding and soil loss became problems in some regions. Certainly parts of the classical Mediterranean world had complained about disappearing forests and eroding soils, which were aggravated by overgrazing of sheep and goats. Lower population levels in the early Middle Ages presumably allowed nature time to correct these problems. We should be alert to signs of deforestation reoccurring in the period of growth after 1000. Surface coal seams were not present in the Mediterranean regions and therefore could not substitute for charcoal and wood, as they slowly did in parts of the north, such as England, by the end of the Middle Ages.

CROPS AND ANIMALS

The staple crops of Europe are familiar. In the north, the main spring crops were barley, often for brewing, and oats, for horses, and in poor areas, for people. Everywhere vegetables were spring crops. Peas and lentils were especially valuable because they could be dried and stored for long periods. The main fall crops were wheat and rye, for the staple bread, truly the staff of life, along with porridge, in these societies. Three-course crop rotation was common in the north by 1000 and by the thirteenth century had spread as far east as Poland. In this system, the peasants sowed one-third of the field in a winter crop, one-third in a spring crop, and left one-third fallow, usually for animal pasture. Three-course rotation generated a significant increase in productivity because now two-thirds of the land was under cultivation, as opposed to 50 percent under a two-course system, where half was cropped and half was fallow. Peasants knew that the land needed to rest occasionally, and they also understood that wheat crops grew better in soils that had peas or even clover on them in the previous cycle. So they rotated their fields and strips through this system, getting higher yields as a bonus, unknown in detail to them, from the nitrogen-fixing bacteria living in the roots of some plants. In some bottom lands, the soil was so good that it could be planted for years without fallow. Peasants were close students of their soils, and we should expect a lot of varieties in crops that depended on rainfall and soil qualities – which could vary over small distances.

Soils in the south, the Mediterranean lands, were not suited to three-course rotation, and the general pattern there was the ancient practice of planting in the fall, allowing the wheat to germinate and get the benefit of seasonal rains, and then a harvest around early summer before the great heat set in. A standard pattern in the south would be one-half of the land in a fall crop and the other one-half fallow, of course allowing for the ordinary production of fruits and vegetables. Olive trees grew throughout most of the Mediterranean forest lands on Figure 2.3. Grapevine cultivation in this period, a little affected by climate change, appeared increasingly deeper into the river valleys of northern Europe, along the Moselle and Rhine, for example. Olive oil was an important food staple in the south, but it was also used for lighting because there was little tallow or beeswax available for candles, which, when available, were usually costly in the south. Olive groves and vineyards, once established, could remain productive for centuries, and raiders and warriors usually left them alone. (Destroying trees and vines was a sign of brutal warfare.) Wine, like

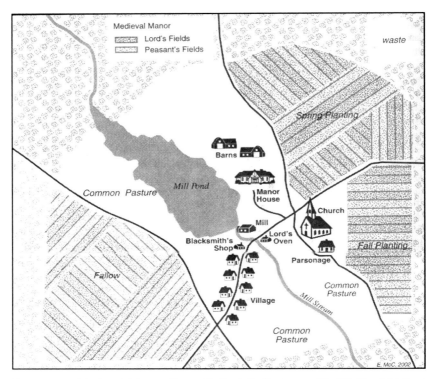

Figure 2.3. Medieval Manor (from Clifford R. Bachman, *The Worlds of Medieval Europe.* New York, 2009, p. 198).

beer and ale in the north, preserved itself and was a way to keep this pleasant carbohydrate, grape juice, available over the winters. Dried grapes in the form of currants and raisins were also appreciated. Wine was also essential for the Christian Mass, so it needed to be imported into those regions too cold to sustain viticulture – as far as distant Iceland and Greenland.

Specialized agriculture developed in some areas, in an almost infinite variety that is hard to catalog. Some new crops, for example, cotton and sugar, came from the east and were cultivated in the better watered areas of Cyprus, Sicily, and southern Spain. The Hospitaler Order of fighting monks obtained through gifts the initial capital to finance sugar production in Latin Syria in the thirteenth century. Fields of crocuses in parts of Tuscany yielded precious saffron. Picardy in northeast France became prosperous from vast fields of woad, planted for its blue dyestuff. Plantations of mulberry trees in parts of Greece and Italy supplied the only leaves that finicky silkworms would eat. These crops, and others, like hops for beer and flax for linen in the north, presumed a market in which some peasants could obtain their food supplies in exchange for marketable commodities. Some landlords, lay and ecclesiastical, also understood the benefits of cash crops. We will look more closely at some of these regional issues when we consider trade in Chapter 3.

The pool of domesticated animals remained basically the same in medieval Europe. Horses, cattle, pigs, fowl (chickens, geese, and ducks), sheep, and goats were inherited from remote antiquity. Peasants understood how to produce sturdy mules by crossbreeding horses and donkeys. Mountainous or hilly areas, north and south, were ideal for pasturing goats and above all sheep, whose wool, milk for cheeses, pelts, and meat provided so much to the diet and to the economy. Sheep in their millions became a decisive factor in the economy. By the thirteenth century, sheep vastly outnumbered the people in Yorkshire or Castile. Hilly abundant pastures in the north, and the vast expanses of grass in the central Mesta of Spain provided grazing and made the landlords, nobles or monasteries, wealthy. The prized Merino wool from Spain, which came from sheep brought there by North African Berbers in the fourteenth century, began to feed the nascent weaving towns in the south just as English wool came across the Channel to Flemish weavers and others in the north. The story of wool is but one example of the tight links between urban and rural economies.

Animals were ubiquitous – the warrior aristocracy fought on horses just as peasants needed them for plowing in the north. Peasants lived closely with these animals, shared characteristic illnesses with them, and slowly built up slight immunities to diseases that would kill those people not in close proximity to these animals. People and animals in a sense evolved together, and illnesses, such as influenza and smallpox, were also shared. All of these domesticated animals were smaller, sleeker, and wilder than modern types.

Peasants were not going to domesticate fish in the strictest sense, but fishponds in many areas allowed year round and easily obtained stocks of carp, trout, and salmon. Deepwater fishing for herring and cod required seaworthy craft not easy or cheap to build and maintain. Rabbit warrens too allowed for access to their meat and skins. Dovecotes were fixtures on big estates. Dogs and cats worked for lords and peasants alike in hunting game large and small. Europe still abounded in wild animals, and the wolf and the bear were formidable opponents. The warrior classes tried to monopolize hunting and claimed rights to certain noble animals, such as stags and swans. One of St. Francis's most engaging acts of charity was his solution to the problem of the wolf of Gubbio, whom the residents agreed to feed in exchange for being left alone. All these animals had an important part to play in the economic and indeed social histories of medieval people – lords, peasants, and townspeople alike.

PEASANT SETTLEMENT

Rural people settled where the land could be plowed or might yield something to eat, where they were safe, as on hilltops, where they had freshwater at a pond, spring, or creek, or at a place where roads or paths crossed. Sometimes villages were established outside of major fortifications or holy sites. Some of these places were ideal and had been settled for many centuries. Peasants rarely lived in isolated farmsteads, and the characteristic settlement was the village, or its smaller version, the hamlet. In these nucleated villages, the people lived together and walked out to their fields. Divisions are arbitrary here, but work usually defines the village – the vast majority of people were in farming of one sort or another – although, of course, there were mining or fishing villages too. A big village might contain three hundred people and begin to look like a small town; indeed, some evolved into towns. A hamlet (at least three families) might contain only five or six and were often satellites to the larger, nearby villages. These settlements had names, deriving from a bewildering array of traditions from old Roman, Greek, or Celtic place-names to the latest Newton or Neuburg. Villagers frequently moved small distances, often carrying along the old place names.

A major distinction is between the planned and unplanned village. Since the time of the Romans and subsequent tribal settlements, many villages were planned as colonies for veterans or ventures of one type or another. These planned villages are an important feature of the settling of new lands across medieval Europe from 1000 to 1300, especially in Eastern Europe. The planned villages often have regular fields and houses set out along streets or around a central green or square. In other places, it seems that people had always been living there, and villages and field patterns evolved slowly over time in highly local and distinctive ways. Blocks or strips of land, depending on soil types and crops, coalesced or were divided according to the vagaries of inheritance. A village might easily come into existence over the ruins of a Roman villa as farmers stayed on the land that they knew, just as newcomers settled down around a pioneer on some new land. The planned villages of the medieval colonization phase required a new profession, the locator. This person, working for a landlord, recruited peasants and set up villages on new lands – the Saxons moving deep across the rivers of central Europe are an example of this phenomenon. These German villages in places, such as Transylvania, were interspersed with Slavic villages that might be planned or unplanned. Every village had an economic and social history – a reason for existing that responded to the historical geography of particular microregions.

Villages and hamlets were flexible and durable features of European society; they existed long before the Middle Ages and in much of Europe they still endure. This flexibility meant that they changed over time. Hence, a snapshot of the village at any point in time fails to convey the dynamism of the village. Yet, some people continued to live outside them. In some difficult areas, such as the highlands of Scotland, we cannot be sure what forms rural settlement took. On Iceland, single farmsteads prevailed, with the "Big Men" controlling enough people and occasional slaves for their farm to resemble a hamlet. But mountainous regions generally favored dispersed single farmsteads and hamlets. Often transhumance was a feature of these regions as people and animals moved vertically by season, following pasturage from lowlands to highlands or across the steppes as the weather changed. In the lowlands, peasants lived in small, timber, or wattle-and-daub one-story buildings with two or three rooms for people and animals. This flexible structure allowed for expansion as family groups changed over time, and they could also be rebuilt or slightly moved with ease. This was beneficial because the land around the hut or cottage, called, in English, the *toft*, was greatly improved over time by human and animal wastes and might become the garden or a small field as the living space was moved. In mountainous regions or other glaciated areas with a lot of surface rubble, peasants built stone dwellings, which were durable and warmer in the cold months. In parts of Spain and Italy where their labor was especially threatened and valuable, peasants were moved by landlords into fortified villages where they might be controlled and protected more easily. Even before 1300 there were a few deserted village sites across Europe because, for one reason or another (usually thoroughly exhausted soils), the peasants moved on. But, in general, the pattern was for the villages existing around 1000 to endure, with many new ones springing up, mostly planned, during the processes of internal and external colonization.

Documents, such as manorial court rolls and even handbooks for confessors, reveal the social life of peasants inside these villages, and some things merit notice. Actual forms of tenure varied enormously. Much of the period from 1000 to 1300 witnessed efforts by peasants to regularize the ways they held land and might exchange, sell, or inherit it. We will look at these issues more closely when we bring the landlords into the picture. Throughout much of Western Europe the course and aftermath of the Tenth Century Crisis took the form of what some scholars have called "a feudal revolution" and others have stressed as its most distinctive feature – the rise of peasant servitude. In late tenth- and early eleventh-century Catalonia, the Mâconnais, and England after the Norman Conquest, the landlords increasingly burdened formerly free peasants with material exactions that diminished their economic and social liberties. This complicated process turned much, but not all, of the peasantry into serfs, and it was more successful in some parts of Europe than others for reasons we will explore shortly.

The fusion of a peasant village and a lordly estate, more common across continental northwestern Europe, became the classic manor (see Figure 2.3). The serfs on this manor practiced a three-course crop rotation. This idealized village had only one "Big House," and its ten huts sheltered perhaps fifty men, women, and children. No real place was exactly like this sketch. Not every manor had its own blacksmith or mill pond, but most did. The lord had first claim to the common pasture rights and was sure to locate his house upstream from the serfs. The surrounding forests were a valuable resource that could sustain increasing population, up to a point.

For the moment let us focus on the hallmarks of serfdom, what serfs owed the landlords – a compulsory labor service, a ground rent per unit of land, a death duty, some sort of payment or fine for marrying, and a head or poll tax. On the local level, there was almost an infinite variety of negotiated or coerced set of impositions that might not include all of these standard features. This seigneurial regime defined what the landlords collected from their serfs – a revenue stream, income, or what economists call "rents" because they derive from the power to demand them. Rents might include a bewildering array of other exactions concerning, for example, the obligation to cart the lord's wood or the duty to use the lord's mill or oven and to tithe to his church.

The overall effect of this feudal regime was to alienate the serfs from the fruits of their labors, to humiliate them by controlling, for example, whom they married or where they lived. In practical terms, the landlords compelled obedience to all these demands by running the local courts and when necessary fining or beating the serfs into submission. The role violence played in this regime should not be underestimated. Peasants were reduced into serfdom by force. Only a few slaves found promotion to this status as something of an improvement, and it did not end the beatings. Many words were coined or adopted to describe these serfs – the most common was the old Latin word for slave, *servus*, but also *villein* (a villager, rustic, inevitably a base person) and in one revealing old French expression, *homme de corps* – a man or woman whose very body could be subjected to work or be punished as the landlord saw fit. This seigneurial regime flourished in those parts of Europe suited to large-scale agriculture and where the lords were strong enough to enforce it. We will return to the important question of regionalism when we look at the lordly class.

Landlords owed protection to their tenants, serfs, and slaves. This security allowed farmers the time and incentives to study and improve their lands, animals, seeds, and tools. The great survey of manors in England ordered by William I in 1086/1087, the famous *Domesday Book*, was itself an astonishing bureaucratic achievement. That it survives is also remarkable. The Domesday inquest missed London and Winchester, but provides a wealth of details on mills, animals, and above all the conditions of land tenure. The book and inquest are two snapshots that intended to describe the kingdom on the eve of the Norman Conquest in 1066 and currently, and these records are descriptive rather than an effort to explain change and processes. Yet, its details by county clearly show that already by 1087 the king, the Church, and the warrior aristocracy owned the vast majority of the lands of England. Serfs (villeins) comprised about 40 percent of the population, small holders (cottars) about 32 percent, freemen 14 percent, and slaves still 10 percent of the population. These percentages varied according to the lands and their uses, as did the ratios of oxen to horses, the extent of forests, and other aspects of rural life.

A few local examples will show the flexibility of the feudal regime and how it changed over time. The manor of Halesowen in the English Midlands first appears in *Domesday Book* in 1086 as a huge entity, perhaps 10,000 acres, including a number of villages and hamlets. Slaves still existed at that time, but soon enough they all would join the mass of unfree tenants, serfs here called *villeins*. When the manor belonged to the crown in the thirteenth century, the terms for the unfree peasants included a substantial annual rent for their lands, six days to plow and ten days to sow for the lord, and one day's boon work, and they also had to mow grass and fence the gardens. The customary tenants also owed the lord a death duty or heriot (*mainmorte*) of their best beast, and their heirs had to pay entry fines, two years' rent, to take up the holdings. They also had to pay fines when their daughters married. The freeholder peasants, who comprised about one-third of the tenants, did not owe labor services but still had to turn up regularly at court. When the Premonstratensian Order of canons got this manor and built an abbey there in 1217, they doubled the entry fines and probably the rents as well. The canons also built a mill and required the tenants to use it, and they instituted some local tolls. All peasants owed suit at the manorial court, where petty fines regulated brewing, marriages, debts, trespasses, and a host of other customs. The labor services remained the same, and in 1327 these services were commuted to a money rent. These changes over time in one place reveal the chronology in which lords imposed on their peasants rules they thought benefited themselves.

Elsewhere, local circumstances resulted in different outcomes. For example, the famous Statutes of Lorris, a model contract that shows the favorable terms that the kings of France used in the twelfth century to attract peasants to new villages. Here the process of assarting included new settlements on royal lands, with the king as landlord looking for tenants. These new tenants came from somewhere – extra children from older villages, runaway serfs, or migrants looking for a better life. The king offered these peasants a simple modest money rent, a token part of the crop (rye) for lands, defined labor services amounting to gathering wood for the lord's kitchen, and carting his wine to Orleans – and this was required only of those people who had horses and wagons and who had been asked. The peasants owed suit at the king's local court, but they enjoyed defined rights there and were promised that there would be no new demands placed on them.

The statutes reveal a pervasive sense of peasant liberties – they were free to travel locally without tolls, sell their possessions, and, if they wanted, to leave the village. The king granted new arrivals the year and a day privilege, that is, if they lived in Lorris for that time with no one claiming rights over them, they became free members of the village. These economic and personal liberties reflect a regime that preserves only the mildest forms of serfdom at the same time as other peasants found their circumstances becoming harsher. Here peasants owed almost no labor services, no death duties, were free in their personal movements and decisions, including choice of spouses, and promises of justice presume that the king's officials did not beat people in Lorris. There, the peasants were no longer serfs and were very nearly free although they were landless at first. Whatever the king derived from places like Lorris was more than he received when the lands were vacant.

It is important to keep in mind the kind of mosaic panorama of landholding systems in the countryside. Manors, such as Halesown, or peasants, such as some relatively fortunate tenants of the kings of France, were known but were by no means universal throughout most of Western Europe. In the south, near admittedly little cities, such as Barcelona, Montpellier, Genoa, and Lucca, for example, system of public law, based roughly on Roman models, still supported the notion of a private property right in land. Where this right existed, it was possible to sell land, even if the owner needed the permission of his kin or some lord to confirm the act because they too had some rights or expectations over the property. For example, a small archive of documents, beginning in 1065, record the patient efforts of Ricard Guillem and his wife Ermessinda to buy vineyards, houses, arable land, and entire farms in the region around Barcelona. These charters reflect a solid legal context, a monetary system, and, above all, the clear right to own land and sell it without any lord's approval. Rights over land in the countryside were seldom absolute, and as we will see urban land had its own rules. Where land could be bought and sold, one might also lease it, under long terms set by Roman models, that is, twenty-nine years or even greater spans measured in lifetimes. These features, never absent in the north but more precocious in the south, are the hallmarks of a land market. Such a market can change the relationship between tenant and landlord or between buyer and seller. Markets could also be copied and exported.

The demeaning personal aspects of serfdom might be entirely absent where a market determined the ties between those who controlled the land and those hands were needed to work in the fields. Peasants in the valleys around Genoa saw nobles living in castles who usually controlled the best lands. The bishop in town and some powerful local monasteries also owned land, which was often leased out on favorable long terms and fixed, customary and low rents were paid to the powerful, often their kin, who then turned around and bargained with local peasants. These tenants often had their own lands, and in the valleys it was rare for a man or woman to owe labor – this was more common in the fertile plains and river valleys. The common theme is that the lords, the powerful, had most of the best land, and ran the local courts or interpreted the old laws and kept the best records of their rights. The thing to ask about the peasants in localities is: did they have to right to leave, to buy and sell tenancies, and to negotiate terms as individuals or a collective? If the peasants did not pay in their own labor, they needed access to markets to sell their surpluses to obtain silver pennies to pay their taxes and rents.

These local rules presume some pressure from the peasants, who could indeed negotiate their terms and in most places had a headman, some elder with respect who spoke for the villagers. Seigneurial regimes reflect a mix of coercion and bargaining – the same king of France eager to pursue his own runaway serfs was also in the business of attracting other tenants and looking the other way at their origins. Some villages in the twelfth and thirteenth centuries had communes, which were sworn associations of the members that stood in solidarity against the lords of the land. Rare notices of village chests survive and in these places the peasants kept modest amounts of cash and above all precious documents that secured their collective personal status and land tenures. Levels of literacy in these villages remained low, but there is no doubt the peasants understood the value of the written record over memory even if they could not read.

Christianity imbued these settlements with some economic and social practices. Tithing was easy to observe and enforce in the countryside, where priests and monks could count the sheep and have special barns built for their share of the crops. In Denmark, for example, the new practice of tithing (and manorial farming) granted thirds to the local priest, church upkeep, and the bishop. In other places the poor received the bishop's portion, and often lay people owned the tithes. In the eleventh century, paganism was waning fast and increasingly confined to the northeastern and southeastern corners of Europe, for example, the Turkic Cuman and later Tartars of the south and the still-polytheistic Baltic peoples in the north. So with some important exceptions, the peasantries of Europe were Christian. Throughout much of Castile and Aragon, Muslim peasant villages were a fixture of rural life in these expanding kingdoms. On Sicily these Muslim villagers were fated to be harassed and pushed out in one way or another during the thirteenth century. Some Jewish peasants survived under Greek rule in the east and under the Venetians on Crete, but it was becoming increasingly difficult for Jews to own and work farmlands across much of Europe because they did not fit into the emerging feudal systems of land tenure, and they were not wanted by lords or their Christian neighbors. One story of this period concerns heretical peasants – those who rejected the teachings of the official Church. These people were virtually nonexistent at the millennium, but in the twelfth and thirteenth centuries, for example, the Cathar faith attracted some peasants, and in some places, such as Languedoc and the Pyrenees, the majority. This change of belief did not alter farming, but it did profoundly affect the worldview of these peasants. Crusades and inquisitions destroyed these communities by the early fourteenth century, so force solved the problem of the heterodox peasant.

What, in practice, did it mean then to say that these peasants were Christians, beyond the facts that their lay and spiritual rulers wanted them to belong to the official Church, follow its rules, and pay its tithes? Lists of male and female names, gathered from 1000 to 1300, reveal that the great and various collection of Germanic, Celtic, and Romance names was shrinking down to a smaller set of familiar Christian names deriving from the set of prominent saints. So, many more Johns and Peters and Catherines and Marys appeared everywhere, and this was especially significant for the peasants because very few had any other name. What this meant in practice is harder to say, but we assume that the naming patterns reflect a general desire to internalize the values and good qualities of these saints and to seek their protection for the bearers. St. Francis (Francesco) of Assisi bore a new name, practically invented by his father apparently as a tribute to his prosperous trade in cloth with France. (Indeed, today children bearing the names China and India, for example, are not unknown.) So there were some new names, and in this spectacular case, the name Francis and all its variants appeared quickly in the vernacular languages across Europe.

One Dominican priest, Stephen of Bourbon, while hearing confessions in the thirteenth century diocese of Lyon learned of a mysterious St. Guinefort, previously unknown to him. He found out that peasant women preserved a story of this holy martyr who came to have special powers for healing sick children. Occasionally women left babies in a sacred wood overnight and later discovered that a healthy baby had been substituted for theirs, or indeed that no changeling or infant was there to be found. These practices scandalized Stephen who became even more stunned when he figured out that this saint was in fact a dog, a holy greyhound. Old and deep beliefs about the spirits in the woods and the powers of creatures remained deep in a peasantry ostensibly Christian for centuries. Stephen claims he had the dead dog dug up and its bodied burned – what can the peasants have made of this warning?

What did Christianity have to do with peasants and their lands? The subject is vast but here are a few highlights. The biblical injunction "to be fruitful and multiply" embodied an entire worldview about the natural world that encouraged procreation and an attitude toward land and its creatures that positively mandated exploitation of nature. This world was designed for people, and it contained everything they needed. Peasants, closest to the land, were an integral part of this system. They truly earned their bread by the sweat of their brows and were supposed to feed their so-called betters. They also tamed pockets of nature as they cut down forests, drained swamps, and experimented with grafting fruit trees and crossbreeding types of sheep. The Church also taught the peasants a family structure resting on the familiar nuclear type, and it encouraged marriage and procreation of legitimate children. Church rules about infanticide, inheritance, godparenthood, work on Sundays, baptizing children, and tithes increasingly prevailed. A substantial minority of peasants everywhere knew the Church as a landlord with meticulous records and a need for income. Not all peasant culture derived from Christian teaching, and on some matters older or secular habits prevailed. For example, a gender division of labor in village society stereotyped some jobs, such as plowing, for men and left women in charge of small animals, brewing, and other tasks. Yet, when harvesting the crops, delousing the children, or weeding the fields, all able hands pitched in, and there was almost no work that any peasant, man or women, indeed girl or boy, could not handle in a pinch. Peasant culture, as well as sermons, frowned on idleness, because it was a cause and symptom of poverty that left the Devil many opportunities.

FEUDAL SOCIETY

Feudal society hovers over the Middle Ages as the characteristic feature that most people remember. Social and economic historians have a long tradition of looking at this great time span as one when social ties among lords and peasants, as they evolved, shaped the typical and memorable features of a world standing between the classical past and early modern globalizing capitalism. Critics have maintained that this vision of feudal society is a mirage that is doing more harm than good and is an outdated mode of analysis invented by lawyers who made their living in the intricacies of feudal law. A concession to these critics is to speak about feudal society as opposed to feudalism, a confusing generalization unknown to the people in our period of study. "Feudalism," like all "isms," is an empty box into which people drop all their ideas and examples in order to generalize about the practices they study. Our path here is to focus, on the one hand, on relationships, and, on the other hand, on property. A feudal society presumes that relationships among people start from the premise of something we can call feudal, in fact, the fief. A *fief* was a piece of property held in exchange for some service we will consider later in the chapter. The holding of a fief creates an obligation and is hence social and more enduring than if it was simply the momentary tie between a buyer and a seller. Confusingly, scholars sometimes refer to this obligation as a *feudal rent* – military and other services from the warriors, cash rents, and labor services from the peasants to the warrior. For our purposes, a *rent* is a stream of income in-kind or in cash, agreed on or imposed by local custom. These feudal rents are not strictly market rents because the peasants had little bargaining rights and often no formal contracts. Force and the market determined their rent. Some peasants lived on lands that were parts of fiefs, but they did not possess fiefs – they lived in a lower class that did not hold property in this way. A class of powerful people controlled the land as in some way a fief, or as personal property, the *allod*, for which they may have owed some public obligation, usually a tax, sometimes military service.

By the eleventh century, the Latinized Germanic word *fevum* had supplied the Latin word *feudum*, which was a grant of land called a *fief*. Over this century, a vocabulary emerged that described the people who were involved in this relationship. The vassal held the fief. He was typically a *miles*, a warrior most effective on horseback, a knight, from a Germanic word for a type of servant, but not a humiliated one because he served in arms. This vassal received the fief from a lord, a *dominus*, who might himself be the vassal of someone more powerful. Only kings and emperors might claim to have no earthly lord. Often a ritual of homage served to symbolize and ratify the act by which the vassal became the man (*homme*) of another man, his lord. Homage might involve getting down on one's knees before a lord, or kissing his hand, or for a lucky vassal to be raised up and exchange a kiss on the cheeks or mouth with a lord. In a society that valued oaths, it is not surprising that soon enough in the eleventh century, an oath of fealty became common as well, by which the vassal swore to be faithful to his lord, who in turn swore to fulfill his part of the contract to his vassal. The fief was the cement of the system and what tied the fighting men together in a contract based on mutual military and other support in exchange for land. The more powerful the lord, the more vassals he had because his power rested on his mounted retinue, the men who would turn up to fight when he needed them. The vassal of a powerful lord could, in turn, count on a good lord to protect him when he needed protection. Mutual protection, by contract strengthened with an oath, to hold property and to fight – these were the hallmarks of feudal society from the perspective of the warrior class. In economic terms the warrior class was rent seeking, using their skills in violence to compel an income, a feudal rent, from the peasantry.

In exchange, the fighters offered to protect the peasants from even worse people.

Most scholars approve of the idea of a first and second feudal age, usually shifting sometime around 1050. This chronology is tentative and vague, but it does stress the dynamism of the eleventh century. In the first feudal age, beginning during the Tenth-Century Crisis, the characteristics of the regime slowly emerged in its heartland, in the north between the Loire and Rhine rivers. This regime required a class of professional warriors, increasingly defining themselves as noble, who in the first feudal age emerged on the local scene from very diverse backgrounds – some Carolingian counts, some local toughs, indeed some peasants with a sword and a horse and the will to dominate others. These people spent good money in the second feudal age having family trees drawn up to demonstrate their proud genealogies. But the crisis of the tenth century threw these men into prominence, and the order and military strength they created were the most important factor in resolving the crises of the invasions. Mounted warriors stopped the Magyars and Muslim raiders. Some Vikings who settled own in Normandy became lords and vassals, and their chief claimed to be a duke. Church lands often became fiefs because bishops and abbots too needed vassals. Kings used these fighting men on the church lands by demanding military service from the clergy.

The first feudal age witnessed the growing hegemony of a social idea, articulated by clerics, that the world was divided into three orders: the fighting class of warriors, the professionals who prayed, and the peasants who farmed. From the beginning gender, roles were distinctive in the division of labor in the orders. These three "natural orders" replaced an older vision of a Christendom divided into a clergy who prayed and dispensed the sacraments and a heterogeneous laity that had the duty to support and protect the clergy. Even at its inception in the tenth century, the idea of three orders was inadequate to the task of describing a real world in which women prayed and farmed. Merchants and small cities always mattered. From the view of the lordly class, they were the order that counted for the most. Although few in numbers, their extra children staffed the church and filled the best spots in the most prestigious nunneries and monasteries. Noble women cemented family alliances and passed down noble blood to their children. Lordly donations and swords protected the Church and led crusades in this world. For these services, warriors expected prayers and sacraments that eased their own violent selves into Paradise.

The first feudal age also witnessed the drawing together of some old social facts, such as the mounted warrior, the manor, and a subjected peasantry, into a system devised to maintain a warrior class. Kings, even heroic ones, had retinues too small to fight the Magyars, and so local strongmen drew together vassals who fought for them. Kings might have been individually weak, and they no longer had a fisc or any sort of reliable tax base to fund an army. Kings too needed vassals or the money to hire fighters. Even the army that William Duke of Normandy used to conquer England in 1066 consisted of both vassals who owed him service and would share in the booty, and men, true mercenaries, who wielded their lances for pay. Even now, at the cusp of the two feudal ages, silver also mattered, and William's wealth came from many lay and clerical hands from the peasants working the productive soils of Normandy, its counties and bishoprics – one of whom, the duke's uncle Odo bishop of Bayeux, fought at Hastings.

The feudal revolution of the eleventh century is the rise of a seigneurial regime throughout much of the countryside of Western Europe. The landlord exercised, through some local or manorial court, rights of justice, over a subjected peasantry that included free and unfree peasants. A chief (who may be the king),or as in Italy, a nascent commune, a free association of townspeople granted self-government, were the effective lords of the countryside. Just as these processes were taking shape, contradictory trends surfaced, which made all generalizations about feudal society perilous. For example, in one of the first known instances of this innovation, in 1058 the abbey of Nonantola in Italy began the process of ending serfdom by abolishing one of its most demeaning aspects – its serfs were not to be beaten. By the thirteenth century cities, such as Bologna in 1257, abolished all forms of serfdom – in the latter the names of the lucky 5,855 people were recorded in the *Liber Paradisus*.

Elsewhere, as in fertile Tuscany, over the course of the twelfth century many landlords commuted old money rents and services into rents-in-kind, usually in grain, over long terms. Rents in wheat, for example, protected landlords from inflationary pressures on fixed customary cash rents and provided a steady stream of a highly marketable commodity sensitive to market pressures. Oaths of loyalty still bound these peasants to the landowners, who in the thirteenth century began to experiment with the *mezzadria* (sharecropping). Under this system, the landlord leased a farm to a peasant family and often supplied the house, tools, and animals. The peasants worked and paid over to the lord a fixed share, usually one-half, of all of the produce the farm generated. This system spread the risk of crop failure between worker and owner, but it guaranteed the landowner food supplies and marketable commodities, such as grains and wine, that could be turned into cash. The peasants had the use of a farm that they would never be able to buy. They were at the mercy of the market for their produce and labor. Under fixed money or grain rents the peasants bore most of the risk; as sharecroppers they had different incentives and the opportunity to prosper. They were piece-rate agricultural laborers working for one-half of everything that they produced. In commercialized areas, such as northern Italy and Flanders, where increasing numbers of urban people needed to purchase their food, entrepreneurial landlords were wise to secure their incomes in kind rather than in increasingly debased fixed sums of cash. In these places, market forces were transforming serfdom even as in parts of eastern Europe, for example, serfdom was being imposed for the first time.

This dynamic to feudal society requires a patient attention to the issues of regionalism and chronology. In northwest Europe, the classic west and its frontiers, two systems of land use predominated: (1) the open fields plowed in strips and on the Atlantic coasts a *bocage* or (2) hedgerow style of farming enclosed fields called *crofts*. The Pyrenees and the Alps separated these methods from a general Mediterranean style of farming and village life (described below) showing elements of similarity throughout this vast region. More sparsely populated regions, such as the Slavic lands and Scandinavia (excluding Denmark), exhibited small village and dispersed farming and pastoralism. A good way to open up traditional Europe's horizons is to compare its rural scene to that of the Byzantine Empire. This great state still controlled most of the Balkans and varying parts of Anatolia down to 1204, when the Fourth Crusade wrecked the empire, sacked Constantinople, and created a Frankish or Latin feudal empire in parts of this region. This Frankish state ended in 1261 and the Byzantines recaptured their capital, but parts of the Peloponnesus remained in French hands for a long time, and valuable islands, such as Crete and Negroponte, were lost to Venice for good. In these areas colonial practices imported into the East, as in Latin Syria, created some feudal regimes in the countryside and reduced parts of the indigenous population to serfdom. The brief comparisons here to Byzantine agriculture concern the empire's prosperous centuries, which began earlier than the West's, and witnessed its heyday in the twelfth century, before the catastrophe of 1204.

What tenth-century crisis the Byzantines endured was quickly resolved by successes against the Slavs and Turks, and the empire entered its golden age under the dynasty of the Comneni. In the countryside, polyculture, the raising of a wide variety of crops, and pastoralism were the mainstays of rural life. This was the world of the olive and vine. Water mills were common and also used to irrigate land. Storing and distributing water were necessary in these relatively dry climates that received seasonal rains. In general terms, peasant villages and great estates were the norm. These estates were collections of rent-paying tenancies and seldom practiced demesne farming, though in some places by the fourteenth century peasants owed public labor services called a *corvée*. Managing these estates was a common theme in East and West. Specialized officials with manuals and records understood that land was capital producing after-tax income for its owners. The bishops and monasteries were great landowners as well, and we are especially well informed about the holdings of the great houses near Mount Athos in Thrace. Another interesting similarity between the east and west is that monastic records are a valuable window on agriculture. Small, peasant holdings predominated, and slavery in the countryside was waning in the twelfth century, as it was in the West. The size of farms naturally varied and depended on the local soils. The basic pattern of Mediterranean agriculture with its square open fields prevailed, where suitable, for cultivating the basic cereal crops: wheat, barley, millet, oats, and rye – all spring plantings. Notable special crops were fruit trees, the olive trees planted near the sea at low elevations where it did not freeze, and mulberry trees for the silkworms. Peasants understood that vines exhausted the soil, were very labor intensive, and required frequent replanting. Greece and Anatolia still had great forests, some owned by the state. Rural peoples supplemented their incomes by working at a variety of crafts including cloth, ceramics, and metal working. A pool of wage earners stood in reserve to help fill seasonal demands for labor.

The great mass of peasants called the *paroikoi* were tenant farmers who might have owned a few vines and other personal property but were renters and not serfs. They owed rents that were traditionally higher than the taxes paid by proprietors of the land. Only a minority of peasants owned their land outright. Irrigated and intensely cultivated patches of gardens (now called *huertas* after the Spanish model) produced good yields of vegetables, a major part of the diet. Another big distinction among the peasants was who owned animals. The more-prosperous ones had their own ox and could join together with a neighbor to form a plow team. On these light soils, two oxen were enough to plow, and this source of power made a difference in the lives of some peasants. One important feature of Byzantine land taxes is that they varied according to the quality of the soils. On the large estates where the owners also had the rights to the peasant taxes, this bonus amounted to one-half of heir incomes. These peasants had village communes, and in the eleventh century the local taxes were conceded to powerful landowners.

The empire was itself a great landowner and in the twelfth century the rulers adopted the pronoia system by which peasants living on imperial, fiscal lands paid their obligations directly to soldiers for their lifetimes. This system allowed the emperors to pay their troops on the local level and saved the trouble of collecting and redistributing this income. At first, the pronoia grant was strictly for the lifetime of the soldier, and it created a personal, economic relationship between the state and its soldiers. In the thirteenth century, necessity compelled some emperors to grant pronoia for two generations. Clearly, however, this system was not a feudal society in Western terms because the Byzantine State had laws guaranteeing property rights and land markets, a regular land tax systematically collected, and it did not need social forms, such as homage and fealty to secure military service. In fact, the empire supported a powerful army and fleet that were testimonies to the enduring importance of using taxes to pay warriors. The heart of this system was not the fief but was instead the extensive state lands that gave the emperors the income that they needed to pay for the military and the bureaucracy. Some estates, defined as military lands, also directly supported fighters, and occasionally church lands were required, in lieu of part of their tax-exempt status, to pay money directly to the military. This system also required a monetary economy and the state had for centuries maintained a reliable and prestigious gold currency, now called the *nomismata*.

The Byzantine agrarian economy was clearly part of the broader Mediterranean system that thrived despite a complex pattern of microregions and microclimates. Whatever economic and social problems the Byzantine Empire experienced did not result from its agricultural base, which seemed in good shape in these centuries and able to sustain a pattern of demographic growth similar to the West's. Byzantine agriculture achieved in these centuries improved yields, increased specialization, and rational ways or organizing and taxing land. Peasants were at the heart of this method of farming, and many of them also participated in a pastoral sector characterized by transhumance patterns common in the Mediterranean. As we will see when we consider trade and other economic matters, the Byzantine State was exceptionally effective in developing and implementing economic policies and a legal system for making them work. The state also supplied a sound currency that made this region among the most monetarized in the Mediterranean. The challenges this state faced from the East and West, from crusaders, Turks, and others, wrecked many of these accomplishments in the fourteenth century, when this region experienced the common calamity of plague.

DEMOGRAPHY

The survey of the agricultural base reveals a general pattern of increased scale and scope to farming that could have sustained an increase in the population. Analysis of skeletons from medieval Danish graveyards has yielded good evidence on individuals and their life expectancies – here a diverse and wholesome diet produced people about the same size as they are today. Studying people in groups and population movements, the science of demography, is difficult for the Middle Ages because the original sources are not good. Medieval people were aware of numbers and their uses, sex ratios, and ideas about multitudes, but they did not count themselves. Without a clear census of people, scholars have to scrutinize other sources for clues on population growth. Some records reveal the number of households in a specific city or region, usually for tax or rental purposes. Other sources occasionally count the number of persons in a household, so estimates of population usually reflect some debate about the proper multipliers: the number of households and their size. Crude birth and death rates occasionally emerge from some types of records. Royal and noble genealogies can yield demographic data about the great lineages that kept track of births and deaths, but these families are hardly typical. Civil and canon law, as well as court records, supply different opinions on the age of majority, the role of consent in marriage, and other issues, such as informal marriages. Wills can provide a sense of the household over time as living and deceased members were recalled, but these sources do not survive everywhere and are more common in the notarial, urban south in this period. Other indicators also provide some sense of growth: new settlements and parishes, the size of fleets and armies, extensions of city walls.

Some scholars argue that nineteenth- and early twentieth-century censuses from some rural, underdeveloped parts of Europe may be good indicators of the carrying capacity of the land and hence provide clues about medieval numbers of people. Considerable speculation and guesswork go into these estimates of populations and some scholars shy away from the enterprise and the mental effort required to imagine medieval societies' benefits from even sketchy estimates of population. For example, if England had more than two million people around 1087 and has more than fifty million today, even this rough ratio helps to provide some sense of how the landscape may have appeared in the past. With these problems and warnings in mind, let us consider the rural demographic trends, saving most of the urban problems for Chapter 4.

Good evidence from rural fourteenth-century Macedonia indicates that the population there was about thirty-four people per square kilometer. Conservatively using one-half that figure to project back to 1025 and the height in area of the Byzantine State for Thrace, Macedonia, Bulgaria, and Asia Minor, and using the lower figure of nine people per square kilometer for the less populated parts of Greece, Angeliki Laiou has estimated the rural population of the empire at eighteen million. In 1025, the largest city in Europe by a big margin was Constantinople at two hundred thousand, and allowing for other cities would put the empire's population at nineteen million. By the 1170s, when much of Anatolia had been lost to the Turks, the population was still probably about the same because of demographic increases over the previous century and a half. Before 1204 Constantinople may have reached as many as four hundred thousand, its medieval height. This numbers help to demonstrate how important the eastern Mediterranean remained in terms of people and their economic activities.

For the rest of Europe before the plague of 1348, the estimates of population vary considerably, but there seems to be a consensus about England's population, with two million at *Domesday Book* (1086/1087) and at its medieval height about 5.5 million in 1300, a near tripling of population. More reliable numbers from parts of France concern household size and these figures derive from patiently accumulating information from manorial, fiscal, and other sources. The best figure is the number of children per household with children – this excludes the single and childless who had to replaced if the population was to grow. (One-third of medieval couples had no surviving children, for complex reasons, including infertility, early death, and other factors.) Here are the French numbers on children per household: 1000–1050, 4.3; 1050–1100, 4.2–5.7; 1100–1150, 4.6–5.3; 1150–1200, 4–5.2. These numbers indicate a range of 0.3–.6 percent population increase per year, by no means an explosion but in line with the demographic trends noted at the beginning of this chapter. Urban figures are less common, yet for Genoa 1150–1250 a sample of wills

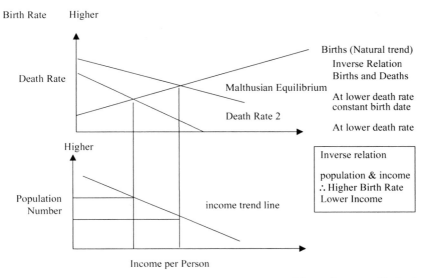

Figure 2.4. Malthusian Population and Incomes (adapted from Gregory Clark, *A Farewell to Alms*. Princeton, 2007, p. 27).

indicates 2.5 offspring for couples with children, far below the rural numbers. If reliable, this suggests, as most scholars assume, that medieval cities were not the engines of demographic growth and relied on rural migrants to sustain and increase their populations.

The reasons for this population growth are complicated. The standard Malthusian model (more land~more food~more people) posits a strict relationship between the food supply and population levels in a traditional closed economy. At best, food supplies expand by incremental arithmetic growth if all goes well, while uncontrolled population growth is geometric. Where the lines cross, the equilibrium means subsistence at this population level, but no more. The model suggests this grim paradox – raising the death rate increases the standard of living and that will eventually enable families to have more children – more pie, more people. Another way of looking at this dynamic is to assume a Malthusian equilibrium where life expectancy at birth is the inverse of the death rate. Hence, only by limiting births can life expectancy increase – here is another paradox: peace, good hygiene, and weather will reduce the standard of living and eventually the population as well. (See Figure 2.4) Gregory Clark, an advocate of the Malthusian model, also assumes that wealth alone is the most important factor in the Malthusian model because changes in its levels, the standard of living, influence everything else – consumption, lifestyles, and natality. This is true because the great mass of people, peasants, spent virtually all their income on food, clothing, and shelter, leaving to the tiny number of rich elites among the warriors and the clergy the opportunity to consume more. Yet, only the warriors put some of these resources into larger families; the clergy, monks, and nuns were officially celibate. Overall population trends depended on marriages and births among the peasants. Even a 0.5 percent annual growth rate over centuries can double and triple population figures and confound the dismal Malthusian predictions about the necessary link between births and deaths.

The numbers suggest that an increase in births provided the impetus behind population increases. The injunction to be fruitful and multiply had not been repealed, and farming needs children. Avoiding offspring within marriage was considered an immoral act, even as the Church stressed the values of celibacy and virginity. A greater emphasis on the infant Jesus was part of an evolving attitude toward childhood that cherished offspring and encouraged natality. Greater numbers of births appear likely. Without much data on death rates, we do not think that people were living much longer than they had before. Political stability (the benefit of feudal society?) and no lethal epidemics probably reduced death rates. General trends in agricultural productivity presumably led to dietary improvements for women as subtle as more amino acids from lentils and meat products became more widely available. Increases in the food supply and the teachings of the Church lessened the extent of infanticide, which in traditional pagan societies had fallen more heavily on women. One constant was that women, even healthy ones, continued to die from the complications of childbirth, though this leveled off at menopause and after that women lived a bit longer than men.

European societies knew that attitudes about the proper age at first marriage were a means to control births provided that there were strong social sanctions against illegitimacy. In some parts of Europe, particularly in the Mediterranean, we see evidence that delaying marriage for women and men was indeed a way to conserve resources and in practice control the number of children. Every year that a teenage girl did not marry lessened the number of children she might bear. Every year that she waited to marry increased the dowry her father had to pay and at a certain point made it less likely that she would ever marry. Peasant men needed to control some land and establish themselves before they were ready to establish a new household or burden their parents with a wife and new babies under the same roof. This marriage model, derived from southern sources, posits a relatively young age for women at first marriage, usually between fifteen and seventeen years of age, although the sources record plenty of younger wives. Men waited until their mid-twenties or even late twenties to marry. How common this marriage pattern was in northern Europe remains intensely disputed. Some evidence in the north suggests that women there married later but still younger than their husbands. But the demographic results from the models are interesting. The relatively young age of the women increased the child-bearing years and contributed to rural population growth in the twelfth and thirteen centuries. The age gap between spouses meant that this society would produce a number of widows, able to control property and serve as guardians and helpers to their children. Men were older fathers and may have identified with the carpenter St. Joseph, who was often portrayed as the elderly husband to a younger wife.

Many factors affected the age at first marriage besides a desire to control the size and shape of the households resulting from these unions. For example, higher rents and more crowded tenancies may have forced peasant men to spend more years acquiring the wherewithal to marry. Migrating to new lands made marriage easier. Maybe better diets were driving down the age of menarche (still a few years later than today's 11.5 years) and enabling women to bear more children over their lifetimes, even as pregnancy remained a risk to their health. Women had the ability to limit pregnancy by using safe and effective means of contraception – pessaries containing compounds acting as spermicides or ones interfering with implanting fertilized eggs in the womb. To what extent peasant women used these practices or abortion is unknown, but more children were assets to peasant families. Family size argues that peasant women were enduring multiple pregnancies during their fertile years. Even allowing for the terrible levels of childhood mortality perhaps 50 percent between birth and age ten, better-nourished rural women saw more of their offspring into adulthood.

Agriculture and rural life were the basis of a functioning European society and economy. Increased agricultural productivity fueled demographic growth and resulted from a rational exploitation of the land and its people. Entrepreneurship began in the countryside with people building up and rationalizing holdings. Landlords, warrior or monastic, should have encouraged these efforts, as the Lorris statutes indicate. The warrior class assumed the duty of protecting society from bandits and predatory neighboring lords and coerced the peasants into supporting them. States still existed and were occasionally able to defend peasants, whose own families were also a place of refuge and self-help. These behaviors formed, in the West, a complex, feudal milieu in which ties of obedience percolated through society.

All theories advanced to explain economic development, which is sustained growth over a long period of time, can shed light on medieval increases in agricultural productivity. There is no reason to assume that this growth was evenly constant and occurred everywhere in Europe. A new model for England posits slower growth from about 1000 to the mid-twelfth century and then a transition to a more rapid period of growth extending to the fourteenth century. Studies of Danish resources suggest a moderate population growth rate in the twelfth and early thirteenth centuries, still checked by famines, and faster growth for the balance of the thirteenth century. A favorable climate and the absence of great disasters, such as massive epidemics, storms, volcanoes, or earthquakes, helped more people to raise bigger crops. European agriculture was no miracle but instead depended on more secure property rights and social status that gave peasants incentives to improve their circumstances, even while supporting the lordly class living on their rents. Elites certainly had more luxuries and comforts during the twelfth and thirteenth centuries – all generated by hard work. European society had not escaped the Malthusian limits defined by the resource base on its numbers, but it had extended these limits by bringing more land under cultivation after the crisis years in the tenth century. We have no good way to measure whether the average peasant was better off in 1250 than in 950 – but there were certainly many more of them by the later date. Institutions as humble as a village commune served to improve the bargaining rights of peasants who were able to slowly erode the harshest features of serfdom. The unfettered market was not the panacea for all economic and indeed social ills. Self-sufficiency was a hallowed ideal but people lived in the real world of buying and selling. Commercialization was a two-way street and affected family size in the rural and urban areas. It is time to draw the connections between the stories of lands, lords, and peasants, and the revival of another aspect of the market – trade.

SELECT BIBLIOGRAPHY

Peter Biller, *The Measure of Multitude*. Oxford, 2000.

Thomas N. Bisson, *The Crisis of the Twelfth Century: Power, Lordship, and the Origins of European Government*. Princeton, 2008.

Marc Bloch, *Feudal Society*. Chicago, 1961.

Pierre Bonnassie, *From Slavery to Serfdom in South-Western Europe*. Cambridge, 1991.

Robin A. Butlin and Robert A. Dodgshon, editors, *An Historical Geography of Europe*. Oxford, 1998.

Gregory Clark, *A Farewell to Alms: A Brief Economic History of the World*. Princeton, 2007.

Philippe Contamine et al., *L'économie médiévale*. Paris, 2003.

José Enrique Ruiz-Domènec, *Ricard Guillem: Un sogno per Barcellona*. Naples, 1999.

Georges Duby, *The Three Orders: Feudal Society Imagined*. Chicago, 1980.

David Herlihy, editor, *The History of Feudalism*. New York, 1970.

Rodney Hilton, *Class Conflict and the Crisis of Feudalism*. London, 1990.

Gary Holthaus, *From the Farm to the Table*. Lexington, KY, 2006.

Nils Hybel and Bjørn Poulsen, *The Danish Resources c. 1000–1500*. Leiden, 2007.

Angeliki E. Laiou, *The Economic History of Byzantium*. Washington DC, 2002.

John Langdon and James Masschaele, "Commercial Activity and Population Growth in Medieval England," *Past and Present* 190 (2006):35–81.

N. J. G. Pounds, *An Historical Geography of Europe*. Cambridge, 1990.

Zvi Razi, *Life, Marriage and Death in a Medieval Parish: Economy, Society and Demography in Halesown 1270–1400*. Cambridge, 1980.

Susan Reynolds, *Fiefs and Vassals*. Oxford, 1994.

Jean-Claude Schmitt, *The Holy Greyhound*. Cambridge, 1983.

5

TRADE 1000–1350

HE TOPIC OF TRADE INCLUDES EXCHANGES RANGING FROM buying eggs or a field from a neighbor to the most exotic commodities crossing the Silk Road linking China and the West. Dazzling long-distance ventures, for example, the travels of the Polos of Venice, have too often obscured the local and regional trading networks and old markets for land that were the backbone of the economy. Erik the Red found Greenland just as our period began and Marco Polo had returned from China and dictated his adventures there by the late 1290s. Expanding horizons of Europeans and the vast profits from long-distance trade have masked the deep currents of humbler commerce in grain, salt, and wood. Still, an analysis of trade opens up Europe's frontiers and reminds us that this part of western Eurasia was not a closed system but rather increasingly depended on linkages to the wider worlds of the Middle East, East Asia, and Africa. The period from the tenth century to the plague witnessed the rise of the first world system of trading in which these disparate regions formed, to some extent, a common market that brought prosperity to its participants. Travelers, pilgrims, conquerors, scholars, and adventurers also frequented the routes that the merchants used and fostered communications among the big regions. Innovations and best practices spread quickly, from forms of contracts and systems of numbers, to gunpowder and the compass. Men and women on the roads and seas do not make a new economic system unless their contacts lead to changes of behavior and not just merely news from the wider world.

Trade, as the Florentine businessman Francesco Pegolotti defined it in the early fourteenth century, was business: the work of buying and selling. Because most merchants did not sell the fruits of their own handicraft, trade involved travel as merchants and goods circulated in local, regional, and international markets. A market is a place where business takes place in a protected setting. Markets are also places where people allocated resources based on supply and demand, which they studied closely. Pegolotti, whose own business experiences as an agent took him across much of Europe, knew that in his native Tuscany the market was *mercato*, and in other related dialects the *piazza*, the open setting where merchants displayed their wares. He credited the Genoese with bringing the Persian *bazarra* (bazaar) to Europe, and in other Eastern contexts the word *fondaco*, on Cyprus *a fonda* (as it was also known in Spain), denoted a protected place for businessmen to lodge. Another Arabic word, *sugo* (suk) also meant market from Andalusia across North Africa into the Middle East. In Greek, the Italianized *panichiero* was also a hostelry for merchants, and in Flemish *alla* (hall) was the same thing, a familiar word in all the Germanic-speaking lands. Great merchants and humble local retailers frequented these markets, and we will examine their urban spaces in Chapter 4. Here our main goal is to understand the rise and significance of long-distance trade.

A standard story about the rise of trade has for centuries dominated accounts of European economic development, and it goes something like this. Land, labor, and capital are the basic factors of production. A school of economic thought taught by the physiocrats contended that land was the basis of any productive economy, and we have put agriculture first partly as a result of that traditional privileging of farming. Land cannot move, however, and those observers struck by mobility as a powerful economic force have focused on labor – people and capital – a surplus in the form of goods or money that can also travel. Mercantilists believed that a society's wealth derived from a favorable balance of trade, and so they charted movements of labor and commodities, finding prosperity where surpluses accumulated. Because gold and silver surpluses testified to successful trading, this school of economic thought is also known as "bullionist." This approach also assumed that there was something about the human character that relished buying and selling, negotiating, and bartering, that thrived on the ambitions, relationships, and experience of business as well as the goods acquired in the process.

Mercantilism as a state policy found its name in early modern Europe, but its assumptions stretch back deep into the Middle Ages. For if a favorable balance of trade was the main way to explain the wealth and poverty of nations, then the monarch or ruling group's job was to negotiate or compel favorable trading terms with neighbors. Adam Smith (1723–1790) did not view trade as a zero-sum game in which some grew rich and others poor but the mass of wealth remained the same. Instead, he stressed comparative advantages by which each society or economy developed its market strengths and strongest products and traded for equally improved items from others. According to this theory, each society would use its resources in the most profitable way to excel at some production that would command market share. Advantages to consumers were derived from the great range of excellent goods that would become available to them, provided that trade was free and governments or interest groups did not succeed in rigging the terms of trade to benefit themselves and not consumers.

Smith's understanding of the benefits of free markets and rational choices by consumers to maximize their own comfort has become central to the standard story of how trade played the dominant role in the ways the European economy developed from the ninth century to the plague of 1348. If this theory is true, then any innovations that foster the smooth and fair functioning of a market economy will benefit trade and hence prosperity for the greatest number of people. Modern theorists have focused attention on institutions that secure property rights and reliable legal systems that bring the benefits of trade to those taking the risks on land and sea. Institutions, as defined by Avner Greif, are simply "systems of social factors that conjointly generate a regularity of behavior." In other words, we need to explore collections of motives, rules, and beliefs that shape how people behave and make choices about how they work, consume, and trade. Examples of these institutions range from merchant guilds and trading companies to treaties and merchant law and courts. The purpose of these institutions is to make behavior predictable, in order to minimize risk and allow rational people the chance to make plans or investments that will pay off in a future that they can envision. Merchants were not yet able to use mathematics to calculate risk, and they understood that uncertainties in the form of sickness or natural disasters might strike at any moment.

Game theory, really the study of human behavior in making choices, stresses how one's optimal behavior depends on the ways other people act. At equilibrium the results are best for all, which is exactly how Smith saw the benefits of free trade. But game theory is a bit more subtle and stresses how this equilibrium is not a unique solution but instead evolves over time and depends on the concrete historical context in which people make these choices. Economics is after all simply the science by which we study human choices about consumption. Society is the surrounding context in which people live and make choices. To find the roots of increased medieval trade and prosperity resulting from it, we will want to focus on how, where, and why some people changed their behaviors. Farming, praying, and fighting no longer constitute the entire set of choices.

Current models for understanding trade view it as a transaction – a socio-economic behavior that changes over time as the rules people make improve the outcomes. A consensus on transparency holds that these transactions benefit all parties when they occur in an environment that encourages honesty and predictability in making contracts. As we will see, medieval people spent a lot of time worrying about the language of contracts, the reliability and standards of weights and measures, the soundness of the currency, and other matters. These positive circumstances – enforceable contracts, clear numbers and quantities, and sound money – reduced transaction costs and hence made trade more efficient and profitable. They were especially important when traders ventured beyond their own group to trade with peoples who spoke different languages and believed in other creeds. In these long-distance trades, where trust was harder to maintain, self-interest could still drive very different people to strike deals. Game theory assumes that different cultures share the same rational self-interest that has been part of economic thinking for centuries. Institutions themselves are also actors that affect the behaviors of people inside and outside of the institutions. The guild of butchers made rules for their own labors. Their customs influenced consumers, young people hoping to enter the trade, and governments trying to protect the common good by securing safe supplies of meat, which was a task not always safely left to the guild. Institutions are not human beings, but the rules and rational people share one trait – predictable behavior. This aspect of culture will help explain, for example, why the guild of Christian butchers excluded Jews. Consumers looking for the best products and prices stimulated tensions between groups of butchers separated by their faiths.

MERCHANTS

The history of trade is the story of how medieval people exchanged commodities and profited by moving them from places where they were plentiful and cheap to where they were scarcer and hence more expensive. We have already looked at how peasants produced some agricultural products, and in Chapter 4 we will look at manufacturing and handicraft production. For the moment, we will be focusing on local and international markets for exchanging goods and the institutions and techniques that facilitated trade. We will enter these markets as medieval merchants and travelers did, as people behaving in certain new ways. There is a venerable tradition in medieval economic and social history that seeks out the first traders and tries to explain why the traditions appeared where and when they did. These heroic entrepreneurs have become staples in economic models seeking to explain the process of commercialization or the rise of markets and trade. Hence, we begin with people. This method of proceeding, however, cannot be separated from the problems of the primary sources.

A fortuitous survival of a mass of miscellaneous records in a storeroom of the Maghrebi synagogue in Cairo has provided amazing details on the networks linking Jewish traders from Andalusia (Muslim Spain) across Sicily and North Africa through Cairo to points east bordering on the Indian Ocean. Without the details provided by a few contracts and letters, we would have to depend on sketchy narrative sources to show that this trade even existed. What little we know about the dominant majority of Muslim traders and merchants from Rum in Christian Europe comes from these same Egyptian sources until Italian records begin to appear in sufficient quantities in the twelfth century in Genoa and Venice. Tantalizing references to merchants from Amalfi, as early as the tenth century, suggest that these intrepid southern Italians led the way in opening up northern Mediterranean trade in Egypt in the tenth and eleventh centuries. The loss of local records and the triumph of Amalfi's rivals makes this trade very hard to document. Still, we know that the Amalfitans were great merchants and travelers who made their way to Jerusalem in sufficient numbers as pilgrims before the first crusade of 1095 to justify having their own hospice there. Hints and fragments of information before regular runs of documents were kept suggest a revival of long-distance trade in the Mediterranean, North, and Baltic seas. Later, better sources illuminate this trade.

Because we are starting with the merchants, the inevitable question is: who were they? Both the items that they traded and the methods by which they could trust one another mattered. Their identities are worth considering first. The search for a nascent merchant class within the feudal milieu has inevitably focused on a few entrepreneurial lords and peasants. Some members of the lordly class made the not-always-sharp jump from raider or pirate to trader. Even some intrepid fishermen put to their boats to unexpected uses when the fishermen became merchants. These clues indicate that feudal society and those embodying its values were the obvious candidates to branch out into new activities. There was no innate hostility between feudal society and the rise of trade or indeed capitalism. Even ports and cities, islands of ostensible refuge for peasants and even lords, were parts of the system of growth and exchange on which trade depended from its inception.

The great Belgian economic historian Henri Pirenne argued almost a century ago that the career of St. Godric of Finchale was a marvelous vignette that explained how at least one merchant got his start from nothing. Godric began life in late eleventh-century English Lincolnshire as a poor peasant with no resources. However, his area of the coast, facing the North Sea, proved to be fertile ground for beachcombing. Godric began to gather up what scraps he could find from Viking and Flemish wrecks and whatever else was washing up on the shore. (Often this jetsam belonged to the king, but he was not there to claim it.) A lucky find enabled Godric to become a peddler who slowly traded his wares into a larger stock of goods. He eventually became a merchant with contacts and business across the North Sea. Now we know about Godric because he experienced a spiritual conversion that put him on to the path to poverty and sanctity and hence a saint's life from which these details come. His previous career, the proverbial rags-to-riches story, demonstrated how a canny sense of markets rewarded those with the ambition and luck to better themselves. Godric's story is unique. Behind every successful merchant family there was often some entrepreneurial founder of the family's fortune, and at least a few of them must have sprung from the most-populated social class – the peasantry. Of course, the story begs the question of origins – where did the Vikings get things to lose in a shipwreck? They might have been simple thieves but even that status presumes that that there must have been some wealthier victims in the vicinity to pillage. We naturally ask: where did they get their wealth? Hence, the seductive and generally pointless search for ultimate origins, but there is still some value in looking for the source of a merchant class, because they cannot all have been men like Godric. Yet, we can accept that the psychological makeup of some peasant farmers drove them to comb a beach rather than to plow a field. Some people, such as Jews, excluded from ordinary economic activities could become itinerant peddlers. Trading small plots of land taught peasants something about bargaining and value.

Robert S. Lopez, in the 1930s, used good records for medieval Genoa that enabled him to propose a hypothesis about how that city became an important trading center. These circumstances are not unique to Genoa but relate to all those places where feisty rural nobility looked for new opportunities. These nobles, a collection of people descending from the old Carolingian aristocracy and some new men, controlled the countryside, the local church, and marshaled what wealth local agriculture produced. They also enjoyed a small stream of cash rents in the form of silver pennies. This money presupposes the existence of local markets and fairs. Local alliances among nobles and private wars at times, in the absence of a strong local power, led to anarchy. Troubled times and fragmented power in a small port like Genoa meant that opportunities for trade existed. These potential merchants needed to find markets. They needed customer and suppliers. Agriculture and some booty from piracy provided the capital, and local sailors and fishermen had sufficient knowledge and timber to make small ships that were capable of voyaging across the Mediterranean. This story so far fits the scraps of information we have about tenth-century Genoa. We also know that by the time of the First Crusade in 1098, Genoa and other ports had sufficient naval power to bring supplies to the armies besieging Antioch. In the interval, a merchant class had appeared and taken over the city from its bishop and count – this too happened elsewhere. Modified versions of the story also existed elsewhere – in Venice, the local nobles, from the beginning, drew their wealth from the fisheries and salt pans of the Po River estuary, not directly from peasants. Yet, some take-off had occurred.

Trade cannot exist without markets, and no one thinks that there was enough local consumer demand or products in places, such as Amalfi, Pisa, or Barcelona, to account for the rise of commerce. We are postponing the discussion of commodities for the moment, but we need to consider right now questions of distance – where were these potential suppliers and customers if not in the ports? The initial items of trade found everywhere in the region consisted of mix of exotic high-price luxuries, such as pepper and silks, and humbler items of mass consumption, such as the salt necessary for the human diet and also the best preservative available. Our potential merchants were close students of these matters, and they had the resources to invest in the first bags of salt or spices to move from where they were relatively cheap to where they could yield a profit. For every beachcomber turned peddler, there must have been hundreds of men, with resources or skills and knowledge that other men and women investors would trust with their resources, to engage in this trade. The search for markets made these merchants itinerant, indeed, great travelers moving goods from A to B. They sailed the Baltic, North, and Mediterranean seas and found their ways up rivers and over mountain passes with whatever goods that increased in value by moving across these distances.

Scholars have known that these first-generation entrepreneurial types in Europe had one other obvious advantage. They had more prosperous neighbors – in the Muslim world stretching from Andalusia in southern Iberia across all of North Africa into the East, and an old and well-integrated market system in the Byzantine Empire centered on the Aegean. Although partly in Europe, these richer and more-developed areas opened up from the beginning European horizons to Africa and Asia. The Geniza records, among other sources, reveal that these people already had well-established commerce before the first intrepid person from Rum entered their markets in the tenth century. The nearest neighbors, of course, had advantages. Venice's links to Constantinople, forged in late antiquity, were never broken. Amalfi was close enough to what remained of Byzantine Italy to have similar benefits. But all distance is relative, and news of the wealth of Byzantium and the world of Islam percolated across seas and rivers, along with the goods and cash, to find interested raiders and traders as far away as Novgorod. Swedish traders, for example, were farthest from their wealthy neighbors, but the great rivers of eastern Europe flowed south to the Black Sea and potential lessons. The important point here is the advantage of having wealthy neighbors to serve as suppliers, sources of information, and even booty to jump-start their poorer neighbors.

Lopez's search for the origins of a merchant class led him to people who were as perfectly capable of pillaging Muslim shipping in search of capital as they were of squeezing the silver out of their peasants. At a certain point, the interests of the potential merchants resemble the story of the goose laying the golden egg. Too frequently, resorting to violence was not a long-term solution to the problem of gaining wealth. Eventually Muslim targets would disappear or become tougher to seize. Peasants might run away or fight back. Even bandits benefited from settling down and reaching agreements with local people. So these potential merchants were quasinoble pirates capable of envisioning a more regular future, in which taking a chance on peaceful trade was, in fact, less risky that pillage or extortion. In the north, the Vikings had learned the same lessons as their large treasure hoards of Muslim and English silver testify.

To look for the origins of the European commercial revolution on its prosperous fringes seems to beg the question about indigenous development on several levels. The explanations for the continued vitality of trade in the Muslim and Byzantine worlds are off of the table, out of sight, and are simply a preexisting condition for Europe's growth. These exogenous factors cannot be discounted – nor can they be the entire story. Having prosperous neighbors can be a trap to the economic development of the less-advanced region. If merchants and raiders simply prey on or colonize their unfortunate, poorer victims, then the latter cannot borrow or steal what they need to sustain endogenous growth. The Slavic and Albanian Adriatic coast is an example of this phenomenon – it became the early medieval "slave coast" because its most important resource, people, was pillaged for centuries by all its neighbors and then traded to the Muslim and Western and Eastern Christian worlds into this period and beyond.

Some clues indicate how these commercial relationships actually developed. Muslim merchants were completely unwelcome in Christian ports in the eleventh and twelfth centuries. Any that turned up out of innocence or bad weather would find themselves captives and their goods seized. In theory, Byzantine traders would be safe but in practice very few ever appear outside their eastern sphere of influence in the western Mediterranean. Westerners traveled south and east, and those too far away from the Mediterranean to go themselves ended up trading with those that did through intermediary mechanisms, such as the Volga River system or the Fairs of Champagne (more below). For whatever complex and fortuitous reasons, Western Christian merchants generally found a safe welcome as customers in Muslim and Byzantine ports. From time to time bad relations caused Western merchants grief, and they and their goods were seized – this happened to the Genoese in Egypt around 1100 as a result of crusader conquests in the Holy Land. But, in general, Western merchants were welcomed in the East because they had a reputation for paying high prices for second-rate goods and were therefore a bonanza to local merchants.

In reality, the foreign merchants brought rivalries and trouble with them. In 1171, the Venetians sacked the Genoese merchant quarter in Constantinople and also seized some ships and cargoes at sea. In faraway Acre, a rich terminus of the caravan trade across Asia, a vicious war broke out in 1257 between the Genoese and Catalans on the one hand and the Venetians, Pisans, and Provençals on the other. This War of St. Sabas involved other powers but was fundamentally a struggle over lucrative trading privileges in the East. In one disaster in 1258, the Genoese lost more than 1,700 men and many ships. Indigenous rulers in the East had to tolerate this violence and sometimes even compensate Western victims because force as well as self-interest determined the terms of this lucrative trade. At first Muslim, Byzantine, and crusader rulers tolerated Western merchants like geese that every year could be counted on to turn up in Constantinople, Acre, Tunis, Alexandria, and other places. This asymmetry in relations points to the important roles violence and the threat of violence played in the actual ways commerce developed during these first centuries of the commercial revolution. Privileged trade opened the door to concessions extorted at the point of a sword.

TECHNIQUES OF TRADE

Trade happened when a merchant bought low and sold at a higher price. Trade flourished when merchants figured out many ways to make markets function more smoothly. At every step of the process of buying, transporting, and selling commodities, merchants invented or transformed institutions and methods of doing business. Those in the Mediterranean had the advantage of seeing and borrowing whatever best practices they observed in the Muslim and Byzantine systems. Traders in the north, farther from these stimuli, devised many similar strategies, demonstrating that rational self-interest was capable of producing profitable trade in different settings. Starting once again with the people, we will follow these merchants along their trade routes in search of markets. Where traders stayed and how they made deals are central to understanding trade. Also, from the beginning merchants were concerned about their security and wanted privileges that provided optimum conditions for their businesses. Many of these privileges concerned customs duties and tolls – the easiest ways to tax trade. Rulers had an interest in siphoning off some of these profits, but too much skimmed would push trade toward more favorable places and terms. Where merchants ran their own affairs and decided tax questions, their policies reveal a nice understanding of the risks and benefits of ostensibly free trade.

Trade required a venue, a market, open periodically. Traders must have a place to stay and store their goods, as well as a means to travel safely and to avoid as much as possible paying vexatious tolls. Where tolls were reasonable and predictable, they were no real barriers to trade. If tolls became predatory, merchants could choose to go elsewhere and did. They also needed ways to learn these things – hence the value of guides and merchant lore. Merchants also required skills in numbers and written words that make records and contracts possible. Above all, they wanted a favorable climate that reduced as many risks as possible. Trade was a hard way to make a living, and crimes, such as theft, forgery, and piracy, could make things worse.

Two inheritances from late antiquity in Byzantium, the *xenodochium*, a charitable hostelry, and the *pandocheion*, a proper inn for travelers, provided easy and open access for merchants, pilgrims, and other travelers. Muslim merchants and rulers adapted these institutions into the versatile *funduq*, a secure place for merchants and their goods. These commercialized places catered to Muslim merchants and were fixtures in every city. By the eleventh century, the Byzantines were borrowing back in a sense these evolved institutions and establishing them for their own traders. At the very beginning of the revival of commerce, these funduq offered havens for Western traders as well. By 1000, Amalfitan and Byzantine merchants were present in these places in the Muslim world. In the twelfth century, the original sources on these funduq thicken. Pisa secured privileges for its merchants to use one in Egypt in 1154 and joined Venice and Genoa in securing safe havens in recently conquered ports in Latin Syria. This type of place, grander than a simple inn and warehouse, became a true merchant quarter, known in Italian dialects as a *fondaco*. A fondaco had houses, a church, an oven, cemetery, baths, and whatever else the travelers need to feel at home. In Muslim territories, Western merchants usually had to be content with more modest arrangements. In Spain, rulers of Castile and Aragon acquired funduqs in conquered Muslim cities, such as Valencia, and found them to be useful institutions for attracting and taxing foreign merchants. In turn, Catalan merchants acquired North African fondacos overseas in Muslim Tunis in 1253 and Bougie in 1259. In 1228, Venice began building a great fondaco for the German merchants in order to encourage them to come to Venice and trade. The emerging patterns support the already established asymmetries in trade arrangements. For whatever reasons, and we will explore them below in this chapter, Muslim states often found it prudent and profitable to grant these trading facilities to Western merchants. These Westerners also sought privileges in Constantinople and access to the Black Sea trade routes from the Byzantines. Christian states on the northern shores of the Mediterranean sometimes provided these facilities to other Western Christian traders, but never to Muslims or even Byzantines.

In the north, German merchants found a similar path to privileged trade and security. In the tenth and eleventh centuries, these Germans began to replace the Frisians as the most important continental traders. Two key events leading to this path are the founding of the port of Lübeck in 1159 and the privileges Henry II of England gave the merchants of Cologne in 1157. Lübeck became the model for a great trading town that served as the linchpin of the German Hanse, which began as an association of merchants. Cologne merchants active in the wine trade wanted a secure place, eventually called a *guildhall* in London, elsewhere a *kontor*. The period 1150–1250 witnessed the rise of the Hanse and

German merchants as a great trading route developed connecting the arc of cities from London to Bruges, Hamburg, Lübeck, Reval (founded in 1219), and Novgorod – all connected by waterways to hinterlands. Outside the German lands these merchants depended on the protection of foreign rulers to sustain their trading in the face of rivals like the Flemings, Danes, and Norwegians. (The Dutch stayed out of the Hanse and were not yet an important factor in northern trade.) Danish export trade in cattle and horses relied on driving these animals over land routes and required markets but not big cities. Another axis of this trade stretched from the Swedish island of Gotland and its main port Visby south through the German cities and then west to the Fairs of Champagne where they linked up with Mediterranean networks or east to Riga (founded in 1201) and points south toward the Black Sea.

The important development here is how the German merchants, who shared a common language but were increasingly left to fend for themselves by fragmented states and weak rulers, reduced their risks by seeking common privileges for trade as well as securing merchant quarters. Their famous Steelyard in London is a tribute to their importance to the economic life of England's capital, and a clue to what commodities mattered in this trade. In the north, German merchants thrived by a judicious mix of new trading cities and *kontore* in established ports. Unlike the Italians in the Mediterranean with their proverbial fierce rivalries, the German Hanse was at first a great confederation of merchants from many cities. In the later Middle Ages, the league of cities became the predominant feature of the Hanse, but this development was in response to challenges after the plague, a problem with consequences in the Mediterranean as well. The Germans faced English, Flemish, and Norwegian rivals in the west and Russians in the east, but all these powers were Christian, unlike the circumstances the Italians faced in the south. Yet, the common theme remained: a search for regular, predictable trade conducted under set rules in a secure environment. In many places, local merchants resented the Germans, but their access to capital and profits made them indispensable to local rulers and producers.

Merchants required markets, places where buyers and sellers could find one another. Retailers in small towns could provide some items, but even they needed to be stocked. Medieval consumers and merchants relied on fairs, which were periodic markets that attracted travelers to a safe place to conduct business. One of the oldest regular fairs in Europe was held under the auspices of the royal abbey of St. Denis, which twice a year sponsored the Lendit Fair in a field just outside Paris. Tracing its origins back to Carolingian times, this fair

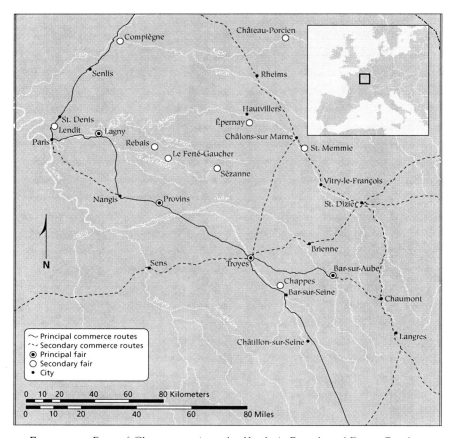

Figure 3.1. Fairs of Champagne (map by Keith A. French and Darin Grauberger, University of Kansas Cartographic Services).

gave the monks a regular income from fees the traders paid to have the abbey's reputation guarantee their peaceful trade. Nearby, perhaps in the late tenth but certainly over the course of the eleventh century, the counts of Champagne sponsored a series of fairs in the main towns of their region (see Figure 3.1). The four sites of these fairs became Troyes, the count's seat and an old Roman settlement, Provins, a castle and then a considerable weaving town, Bar-sur-Aube, a major crossroads, and Lagny, a monastic center. Six fairs running in through the year in roughly two-month cycles made the region attractive to merchants coming from Flanders and above all the Italians from the south. From the Fair of the Holy Innocents in January through the famous Lenten, May,

St. Jean's, St. Ayoul, and finally the fair of St. Remi before Christmas, these events gave merchants a schedule for traveling, arranging transport of goods, and setting up their stalls for selling.

A series of astute counts, notable feudal lords, and ardent crusaders, fostered these fairs because they rivaled Paris and brought prosperity and income to the local nobility and their townspeople. The count provided laws of the fairs, guardians, safe roads and places to stay, speedy resolution of disputes, and predictability in exchange for moderate fees. In 1209, the king of France also extended his protection to merchants traveling to the fairs. Many notaries, both local and traveling with the merchants, redacted contracts for the exchange, often on credit, of northern money and cloth for spices, eastern imports, and other luxuries that the Italians hauled north up the Rhone or over the Alpine passes. Lombards and later bankers from Cahors provided money-changing services and some credit while Jews were left with pawn-brokering services to lesser clients. The fairs became venues for settling international debts and credits. A new contract, the bill of exchange, developed as a contract facilitating the transfer of money by contract rather than by hauling around bags of silver pennies. At these fairs, Latin remained the written international language of contracts. French speakers, regardless of their ethnic origins, enjoyed advantages, and interpreters earned good livings.

The fairs thrived in the late twelfth and early thirteenth centuries, providing an important clearinghouse for goods and money between the Flemings in Bruges, the merchants of the Hanse, and the Italians from the south, sometimes organized, as in the case of Siena, into a corporate body that traveled together for safety. These successful fairs are another sign that feudal society was well suited to take advantage of geography and fairs to increase everyone's prosperity. This has all the hallmarks of policy. Two later developments made the fairs of Champagne less significant economic events. When the county fell to the French monarchy in 1285, the Flemings, long-term rivals of the French, were harassed and found trading there difficult. Also, the Italians, principally the Venetians and Genoese, were exploring the prospects for direct sea connections by galley service from the Mediterranean to a central place like Bruges. These sailings became regular by the 1290s. Also, merchant and banking companies found ways to establish permanent connections in the north through resident partners in places, such as London, and this made annual arduous travel less necessary. The fairs stopped mattering in the late thirteenth century and ended altogether in the aftermath of the Black Death. Other places, such as Lyon,

Avignon, Copenhagen, Augsburg, and Nuremberg, emerged at various times in the later Middle Ages as convenient entrepots for traders to meet. Local market fairs and lesser regional fairs continued everywhere trade occurred across Europe. The services, information, and goods that these events provided were essential to integrating the European economy.

CONTRACTS AND NUMBERS

A merchant class has appeared and traveled long and short distances to buy and sell goods. These traders also needed a system of law, and in Chapter 4 a look at town government and political economy will provide the best context for exploring the legal framework for commerce, work, and other economic activities. The focus here is to examine the art of the deal – how merchants made contracts and used these instruments to conduct their activities more efficiently. A vast amount of medieval business always occurred on a handshake and an oral agreement, depending on the reputation of the parties, to enforce the terms. Local business did not always benefit from elaborate written records. The deals that needed time to mature were the ones that could not rely on memory alone to enforce them. Some minority groups, such as the Jews, with no good recourse to wider legal enforcement mechanisms, always had to depend on their own relatives and coreligionists as the most reliable partners and traders. They had their own languages, notaries, and customs about commerce. Even among the majority groups, some business always occurred outside the formal and somewhat costly setting of written contracts. These documents, which become so ubiquitous over the course of the twelfth and thirteenth centuries, provide the main evidence for a revolution in the methods of commerce. The problem for economic historians is that we do not have a first example of any contract. Initial runs of documents, from the notarial cultures of the south and at first Genoa, reveal business practices already old before the first evidence that survives. Also, we know well that Muslim and Byzantine commerce also relied on written contracts that may have inspired their Western rivals to borrow these sensible practices.

The classic contract is the *commenda*, a partnership between two traders – one who traveled and one who stayed home. In its starkest terms, the traveling merchant took some capital (cash or commodities) from an investor to put to work in a common enterprise that may have had many partners. A traveler, off to Alexandria or the fairs of Champagne, promised to put this capital to work in the venture in exchange for one-quarter of the profit. He bore all of the risks of the venture, expenses came out of the joint capital, and his investor was liable for nothing except his or her own contribution. From the very beginning, especially where old Roman legal ideas still prevailed, women, especially widows, had the right to make contracts, and they appear early as investors. The efficiencies, incentives, and results all flowed from this simple arrangement. Investors, by finding multiple partners, could spread risk across ventures even as they often took contracts from others and ventured into the wider world. The traveler might have at first been without capital and what he offered his potential partners was perhaps the reputation of his own family and the ambition to make a start as a merchant. His one-quarter of the profit was of course elastic and motivated him to trade as profitably as possible by looking for the best deals and keeping his expenses low. Sometimes the contract stipulated that the traveler was to invest in a specific commodity, such as pepper, but more often the details were left to his best judgment of the market he found far from home. Upon his return, the merchant settled with his partners, who of course bore the risk that he might disappear in the sea or the Alpine snows, or abscond with their capital, or simply trade poorly and make little or no profit. Year after year, investors and travelers accumulated the knowledge necessary to invest wisely in the best travelers who went to the most profitable venues. In a Venetian variant of the *commenda*, called the *colleganza* (early examples date from the 1070s), both parties usually contributed capital and divided the eventual profits according to rewards for shares and the labor the traveler put into the enterprise. As with all these contracts, the deal was for one venture – a voyage from Venice to Thebes or Genoa to Alexandria. In a bilateral *commenda*, known in the original sources as a *societas*, both partners contributed capital, ideally in equal shares, but the traveler, working harder and bearing the main risk, took the greater share of the profit, which was typically two-thirds. This variant of the contract suited those partners who had capital and wanted to see it on the table.

Across the Mediterranean world from Lisbon to Caffa in Crimea, the parties went to a notary, a scribe skilled in writing down contracts into his cartulary or notebook. He knew how to frame the contract in the proper legal terminology, and his contract, suitably witnessed, was legally enforceable. Often the parties kept no copy for themselves and instead relied upon the notarial cartulary as the copy of record. Copies cost money, and the notary's formal record sufficed and was often deposited with some public authority after the notary retired or died. This explains why some early cartularies survive – the most famous is from the pen of the aptly named Giovanni Scriba of Genoa, whose work dates from the 1150s. The 1,306 acts of business in all forms in this collection include 335 contracts for overseas commerce, the vast majority *commenda* or *societas* agreements. Another type of contract, the sea loan, appears in this cartulary. The traveler, in an example from 1157, going on a trading venture to Sardinia, borrowed fifteen lire and promised to repay twenty lire one month after his safe return. This important condition made the loan legally acceptable in Genoa because of the risk involved – if the traveler never returned for whatever reason, his heirs did not have to pay. The lender received a specific sum for this service, regardless of how profitable the voyage was. In practice, Genoese and other merchants overwhelmingly preferred the first two types of contracts because they were true partnerships and did not raise any vexing moral questions about interest on loans – which is discussed in Chapter 5.

These contracts are a burst of information about trade rivaling the Geniza records for Egypt. Giovanni Scriba's cartulary contains evidence of a sophisticated method of making contracts that was already up and running for many years before the first surviving examples. No indigenous economic traditions in Genoa can account for this method of making contracts. Genoese traders did not learn about contracts from reading old Roman legal texts about them. What little we know about Byzantine partnerships suggests that joint liability always remained a feature of those contracts. Byzantine merchants pooled investments but continued to share liabilities for the original investments. Old Muslim legal sources confirm the pattern found in the first surviving *qirad* contracts from the Geniza records that this flexible form of partnership shared risks, profits, but not liability. Whether the Arabs found or invented this style of contract remains uncertain. It is likely that Western merchants learned by watching somewhere in the Mediterranean this method of raising capital, and it suited flexible entrepreneurs and those pioneering new businesses. The surviving records show merchants using unilateral and bilateral *commenda* contracts to make deals with peasants about investing in herds of goats or sheep.

As commerce developed, best practices spread across the Mediterranean world. The earliest surviving notarial records from Barcelona, Montpellier, Marseilles, Palermo, and other places all contain the basic forms. Travelers to the fairs in the north brought these practices with them, but the rarity of surviving commercial contracts from the north makes it hard to state exactly what form they took. Merchant law and court records suggest that partnerships prevailed and joint liability was a feature of companies, not deals. From the beginning the notarial cartularies contained notices of other types of contracts – straight sales of goods or land, quitclaims by which a party acknowledged receipt of what was owed, simple loans with artfully concealed interest payments, and wills (a contract with the living heirs among other things) that provide a snapshot of a merchant's activities and investments. Keeping an eye on the fortunes of the *commenda* contract is the best way to note changes in the circumstances of trade. Whenever the percentage of this form, as opposed to all other types of business, begins to decline, it is usually a sign that more investments were slipping into longer-term arrangements, such as companies, and that some investors were employing agents overseas rather than forming partnerships with itinerant merchants. Activities at the fairs of Champagne during the thirteenth century probably facilitated the development of a new form of contract: the bill of exchange whereby a person borrowed money in one place, say, Siena, and promised to pay at a different time, six months, in another place, Troyes, and in the currency prevalent there – livres. Money changers, and their partners and agents, were in the best position to make and deliver on these contracts, which facilitated trade and removed some of the risks of transporting cash. These bills also became a way to advance credit and charge interest for what was in effect a concealed loan. A bill written on a person's reputation, rather than secured by pledges or guarantors, was risky. The best way to share risk, the insurance contract, first appeared after the plague and will be examined later in Chapter 6.

These contracts presume the ability to calculate numbers, to add up the total capital and figure one-quarter of the profit. Merchants had old tools to aid their mental skills, including the abacus, whose base-ten system of beads gave a visual tally, as did tally sticks with their notches and even checkerboard patterns of piles of coins for those who needed to see their sums. Leonardo Fibonacci of Pisa (c. 1170–c. 1240) in the early thirteenth century wrote a book on numbers, the *Liber Abaci*. One of the few personal details he supplies is that as a boy he spent time in the Pisan customhouse in Bougie in North Africa. There he may have first seen or learned about the marvelous new Arabic numbers, borrowed from the Indians and including the mysterious *zepher* as the Arabs called zero. Around this time, Arabic numerals began to appear in commercial documents, and they were a vast improvement over Roman and Greek systems of alphabetic numerals.

Fibonacci's work was a practical introduction to the world of numbers for merchants and traders. He explained the basics of mathematics, as well as the proportional or fractional way of determining values and weights of merchandise in different systems of measurement. Because barter, in his view, depended on a mental notion of price, that is, a number of some kind, merchants needed to be able to think abstractly about values, sizes, and weights. Fibonacci was a mathematical genius, and his practical math problems evoke the world of buying and selling from Constantinople and the crusader East to what is modern Algeria. He managed elementary algebra without the modern notation and explained to whoever cared to know how to find the cubic roots of numbers. There may be more math problems here than the average merchant could ever solve, but the text is a tribute to the love of puzzle solving that was also central to the merchant's occupation. Besides knowing how to figure exchange rates between currencies, the merchant also needed to introduce time into his calculations. Markets rewarded the ability to mentally picture what something would be worth in six months, even to think of time as quantifiable, such as money. There could be no reward for risk without the curiosity and ambition to succeed. Numbers gave ambition a practical goal and rewarded problem solvers who understood the new system of Arabic numerals percolating westward along the trade routes.

Both the honor-based cultures in the Mediterranean and the feudal ideals prevailing among the nobility and their imitators in parts of Europe stressed the literal sanctity of contract. Even in the cartulary the oath to fulfill the terms of a *commenda* was as serious as the vow between lord and vassal. Of course, both worlds had their embezzlers and traitors and forgers and liars. Laws and courts existed to enforce contracts but to resort to them was to lose time and money. Better by far to rely on reputation, good faith, and culture to make honoring contracts second nature to all. These qualities became proverbial tests of character.

THE DEAL

Trade requires that buyers and sellers find one another, and cities and fairs were obvious places for these encounters to occur, where strangers might meet. As Luca Pacioli (c.1445–c.1514) later observed in his classic text on accounting, a merchant needed cash, a good accountant, and accurate records and ledgers. A good reputation also enabled a merchant to obtain credit, without which it was not easy to conduct business. This broader context, a place and the financial wherewithal to be in business, made trade possible. Merchants faced other obstacles to making a deal. If the parties did not speak the same language, which was likely far from home, they needed interpreters and multilingual notaries to make deals. Whether in the customhouse in crusader Acre or on the docks in Alexandria, Constantinople, or Visby, wise travelers knew languages or reliable interpreters. Common trading languages developed in big spheres of commerce – in the north because of the Hanse German was useful; in the Mediterranean French, Greek, and Arabic all rivaled for the best lingua franca. Farther east, Persian and Mongol were assets and in the big arc around the northern parts of the Black Sea one Slavic tongue helped merchants and travelers communicate in the others. Simple manuals and word lists, which were primitive dictionaries, helped to teach literate merchants what commodities each region supplied and how to communicate with the locals. Young men also served apprenticeships with experienced merchants and learned trading firsthand. The lore of commerce, picked up in travels and ports, encouraged merchants to seize opportunities that came their way, and few specialized in particular items. But having invested the time to learn routes and languages, merchants built routines of business as they specialized in markets as far away as Famagusta on Cyprus or Bruges on the Flemish coast. Ship captains and pilots and muleteers and drovers knew the sea lanes and paths from one place to the next.

Merchants at first relied on notaries as specialists in contracts, which, for traditional reasons, remained in Latin everywhere in the Christian Mediterranean West through the thirteenth century and in most places long beyond. Notaries knew the rules, but as they listened over a career to thousands of negotiations and contracts, they also became a good source of information about the economy. Their professional reputations depended on preserving their customers' privacy while at the same time recording their business in writing before witnesses. This was a neat balancing trick. Notaries went to where business occurred – the fair stall, the church porch, the covered market, or a warehouse or funduq. Death-bed testaments brought notaries into the home, but commerce was more public. Efficient notaries were in most places members of a guild with rules and charged according to a scale. This reduced transaction costs while making contracts valid and reasonably transparent. Money changers facilitated the exchange of different coins, and some of them eventually turned their benches (banca) into the first banks. For a long time, these companies were private banks deriving their capital from partners rather than depositors. Goldsmiths and jewelers could also provide a safe place for leaving valuables and even arranging credit. Coins were a store of value and a means of exhange. Money as an abstraction helped people see a connection between the present and the future, between borrower and lender.

Other professions contributed to the infrastructure for trade, or the institutions that made it more profitable. Innkeepers or the staffs of funduqs housed and fed traveling merchants. Transporters of all types moved their goods. Town criers shared the news and auctioneers helped to set prices in an extremely transparent setting. For those merchants who had a hard time finding the right customer or supplier, local brokers made it their business to bring such people together, usually charging about 1 percent of a transaction for such services, which could amount to very respectable incomes. Synergies developed among these professions. Innkeepers could point one in the direction of carters and muleteers. Brokers knew the interpreters; the notaries in the ports knew captains with space for cargo and crewmen. Some of these trades required a long apprenticeship – it took time and learning to become a notary. Others required capital, if, for instance, one wanted to buy an inn. A good talker with a nose for news might set up easily as a town crier, broker, or auctioneer. All of these activities provided entry into the merchant class and explain the great social mobility within the group. Many, of course, began to inherit their status through the great merchant families who dominated business and politics in some towns. But the rags-to-riches stories, Godric, and many others, had more than an element of truth about them. The routines of trade left some widows and working women the chance to participate and use their minds to make money by investing in or running an inn.

COMMODITIES

Having looked at the people involved in trade and some aspects of how they made deals, we can now consider the last subject of what goods they traded – the commodities that constituted the lifeblood of commerce. Anything whose price might be increased by moving it in space could be an item of trade, from huge constructions, such as an entire ship, to the delicate and almost weightless crocus stigmas that yielded valuable saffron. The commodities by themselves could fill many books, and so we must pick and chose good examples of things and places that illuminate the broader picture. Europe's many microregions and microclimates contained a wide array of resources that might be traded, and its people had generic skills, such as turning hides into leather. Europeans also wanted things from outside of their world, whether herring and cod from the nearby North Atlantic or cinnamon, cloves, and pepper from the East Indies. Natural products, mainly the results of farming and pastoralism, constituted the bulk of medieval trade in every sense. These goods range from cereals, to wood, minerals, wool, fur, and living creatures, such as horses and slaves. Considerable labor can go into the elaborate efforts to extract salt from seawater or take tin from the ground. The result, a bag of salt or an ingot of metal might be directly consumed in the case of food or become part of a manufacturing process that mixed tin and copper to produce bronze, brewed beer from barley, or made cloth from wool. Every step in the process of production added value – even the apple picked off of the ground was worth more simply by being collected. Nevertheless, there is some benefit to dividing all commodities into two big classes – more or less natural products, and those that result from skilled human labor being directly applied to raw materials. Merchants, of course, traded in all types of products, but there is a difference between selling timber or oars, and rules about selling them to friends or enemies. The value-added commodities provide one of the great purposes behind urban development and will be analyzed in more detail in Chapter 4.

The story of commodities can become a bewildering map of arrows as things move around Europe – wools comes out of England, wine from southwestern France, silver from the Harz mountains of Saxony, finished wool cloth from the manufacturing towns in Flanders and northern Italy, and flax from Egypt – the list is endless and ultimately baffling. A few admittedly extreme examples can clarify the basic issue of commodities. We must ask, as those who came to live in a specific place came to ask – what do we have here that can be traded for what we do not have or what we really want? Self-sufficiency was a delusion that even those monks and nuns claiming to be dead to the outside world never realized.

Let us start with Iceland, virtually at the end of the known world, in the period of the Free State from about 1000 to the 1250s, when the island had been settled and its best lands taken. Iceland is a good case because it had no cities and its merchants tended to leave for other places, such as Norway. Merchants from Norway, in fact, dominated the island's external trade and indirectly connected it to the Hanseatic networks. On the island, farmsteads exchanged goods they needed, but there was a basic general need to import staples – barley, wheat, timber, and linen. The settlers had the money they brought with them to the island – the silver was Viking plunder. But there was no silver to mine on Iceland, and gradually all the cash might flow out to pay for imports. In fact, Iceland remained a silver-poor society that frequently had to resort to barter or payments in-kind in a useful monetary equivalent, such as standard units of homespun wool cloth. What the Icelanders had to export above all was their wool and woolens, which were famous for their high lanolin content and hence somewhat waterproof quality.

Iceland, like everywhere else, had some special valuable exports to send elsewhere: sulphur, white falcons, and walrus ivory. There would never be enough of this stuff – or narwhal tusks to be passed off as unicorn horns, to pay for what the Icelanders needed, so wool ruled for centuries. In the early fourteenth century, some amazing Icelandic entrepreneur found a way to make stockfish, the famous dried cod that soon became the island's most valuable export. This is what trade in commodities amounted to on Iceland – so much imported metals, spices, luxury cloths – all the many things imported in exchange for what Icelanders had – from pastoralism and fishing. Finally, Iceland is an unusual place because it is basically a last stop. To the west, there was more fishing and even more isolated Greenland, but that was it. Island economies and trade tend to force the places to become entrepots of a carrying trade, like the role Cyprus played in the eastern Mediterranean, or to have the economy drift into a kind of colonial emphasis on the most profitable extracted product – silver from Sardinia or wheat from Sicily, in this way, resemble the commercial function of stockfish on Iceland.

Muslim Spain, gradually reduced to Andalusia in the south as a result of the conquests by Castile and Aragon in the thirteenth century, was not literally an island, but its circumstances are a useful counterpoint to Iceland. Andalusia was prosperous, had important cities, a sophisticated economy, and commercial links to the wider world of Muslim trading stretching from North Africa to Egypt and beyond. Andalusia had resources to export – olive oil, dried fruits, copper, mercury, ambergris, leather, and important to the Muslims, supplies of timber for their tree–poor parts of the southern Mediterranean. Silk was important in the earlier centuries but became less significant as an export in the thirteenth century as more competitors surfaced. Muslim Spain continued to import Egyptian flax and began to take in more wool in the thirteenth century. Trade in foodstuffs everywhere existed on the local level, but in order to travel long distances, food had to be salted, smoked, pickled, or dried. So, like other regions, Andalusia occasionally sold or purchased rice and wheat and exported dried figs and raisins. The frontier between Muslim and Christian Spain was not impermeable, and some trade continued across it, as merchants from Provence and Italy also came to trade. Genoese traders helped foster the shift of trade from the southern to the northern shore of the Mediterranean. Iceland was a last stop in trade except for what trickled in from Greenland. Andalusia was a great crossroads attracting gold across the Sahara and then to eager northern markets, and pulling down furs, from as far away as Rus, that became highly prestigious and sought after luxuries for residents of the Sierra Nevada and Morocco.

Sardinia was a poor island with little to offer the outside world except some wheat, mediocre cheese, and above all silver. Local squabbles prevented the indigenous population from benefiting from this resource, and more prosperous foreigners, first the Pisans and Genoese in the twelfth and thirteenth centuries, and later the Aragonese merchants, used violence to seize the island and loot its resources. This impoverishment happens to some islands, even ones originally economically complex, such as Ireland and Sicily, that became the targets of wealthy merchants interested in cheap commodities. Silver is a useful example, however, because its value as a commodity was its function as money, a well-respected medium of exchange by coin or weight. Mining silver directly increased the money supply and made some regions magnets for luxuries. More silver helped keep the money supply in pace with population growth and prevented prices from increasing faster than they did from 1000 to 1300. As Table 3.1 shows for England, estimates of English money in circulation (mostly silver, gold negligible before 1331) kept pace with population increases. Also, the political power controlling supplies of silver could turn this cash into power through war or other means.

Originally, in what became central Germany, first the area around the Harz mountains in the 960s, then Goslar around 1025, and then farther east to Freiberg from the 1160s and south to Bavaria and the Tirol (see Figure 3.2), repeated new discoveries of silver supplies fueled prosperity in Saxony and beyond. The cycle is interesting – a burst of fresh wealth from new mines soon exhausted medieval technology's ability to pull silver from ore. Nevertheless, a boom followed the new source of supply. The Tirol silver strike began to pan out after 1300, and signs of a bullion famine first appeared. But exactly when European trade began to flourish, from the mid-tenth century to the early fourteenth, German silver became an important basic commodity in this world's trade. This silver and coined money soon enriched merchants from Magdeburg and Cologne and sustained trade in every direction – east to Poland, north

Table 3.1. *High Estimates of English Currency Data (from Martin Allen, "The Volume of English Currency, 1158–1470,"* Economic History Review *54 (2001): 595–611, at 607).*

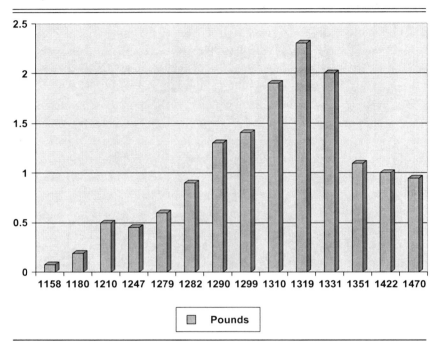

to Scandinavia, and west to Frisia and England. This silver helped to finance the Hanse merchants and pay for their imports of wine, wool, and cloth, which in turn strengthened more distant markets. By connecting to the fairs of Champagne, this silver also linked northern and southern markets. Exploring for veins of silver itself became an important profession. The mines at Kutná Hora, discovered in 1298, eventually made the kings of Bohemia rich and powerful. This last great discovery in Europe's silver boom was capable of exporting 22–24 tons of silver annually in the 1320s and 1330s and helped to maintain silver supplies in the face of diminishing yields elsewhere. These silver boom towns and others, such as the aptly named Argentiera and Iglesias on Sardinia or Freiberg in Meissen and smaller ones in Tuscany, England, Scandinavia, and elsewhere, became ideal places for merchants to peddle their luxury imports. Wealthy miners and mine owners eagerly purchased silks, spices, wine, fine woolens, and other expensive items.

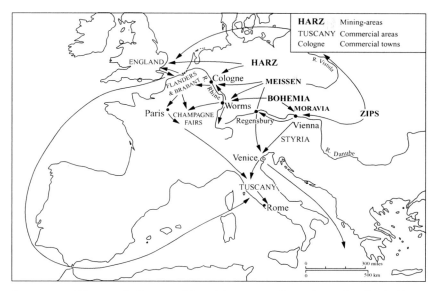

Figure 3.2. Thirteenth-Century Silver Movements (from Peter Spufford, *Money and Its Use in Medieval Europe.* Cambridge, 1988, p. 137).

Pepper is the classic spice but just one of the 288 "spices" Francesco Pegolotti listed in his famous manual on commerce. A spice might be anything small and valuable, such as the familiar pepper, cinnamon, ginger, cloves, to chemical like alum, dyes, such as indigo, drugs, such as hashish, and even items not springing to mind, such as incense, gemstones, and sugar. Even bulkier items, such as cotton, originally made this list because it was expensive, originally transported in small, valuable quantities. Sugar and cotton eventually became bulky items of commerce shipped east in bales and sacks from Egypt and Syria. Pepper came from so far away that by the time it reached Alexandria it had increased remarkably in price so that even when it got to twelfth-century Genoa, or farther, it could substitute for money. Some expensive manufactured goods, such as soap and beaten silver, also counted as spices. Some spices, such as honey, wax, and hazelnuts originated in Europe, but the ones people wanted the most, such as pepper, were from far away. At a "zero boundary," transportation costs might make a spice so expensive that no one could afford it, but this did not happen anywhere. Southerners made and lost fortunes selling spices in northern Europe, where few of them originated.

Wool is the classic natural product. Moving this fiber from the backs of sheep to the backs of people was a major trade everywhere. Clothing was a necessity. Silk and cotton were for long only for the rich, and linen, skins, and furs had their costs and disadvantages. Weaving cloth and cutting it to make clothing were major trades to be investigated later. Vast herds of sheep enriched lay and monastic landlords, but even peasants could keep enough sheep to make the venture profitable. The incomes of the great Cistercian abbeys in Yorkshire and elsewhere sustained consumption and building projects that benefited the local economies. Cistercian grange policies cleared off lands (from woods and people) to create vast grazing areas. In well-watered places the herds remained relatively fixed, but in the semi-arid conditions prevailing in Castile, moving the flocks and their herders was necessary – hence transhumance. Big herds first appeared there in the eleventh century and the flock owners needed the coastal ports to sell much of the crop overseas. In the late thirteenth century, Alfonso X formalized the Mesta Real, a national guild of livestock, primarily sheep owners. The big entrepreneurs needed secure pasturage and rights to move the flocks across private lands and jurisdictions. The king derived regular taxes from the privileges that he granted and the resulting trade. The pastoralists carefully crossbred local and imported stocks to produce the justly famous superfine wool of the Merino sheep, a new, hardy animal that was well suited to the environment.

Castilian wool supplied local weavers in cities, such as Barcelona, but was exported mainly to centers above all in northern Italy, though some made its way via Basque ports to Flanders. Likewise, highly prized English wool exported by Italian, Flemish, and German merchants kept weavers busy in Bruges and Florence. The opening up of the sea lanes from the north to the Mediterranean made an international trade in wool easier. English weavers, like the ones on Iceland, competed to export actual value-added cloth, and, of course, English merchants wanted to be in the lucrative business of exporting their island's most valuable commodity. The interests of monastic producers and Italian merchants combined to use an old way of doing business, the forward contract, to make the wool trade more routine. Big producers had large building projects, taxes, and other expenses that benefited from a predictable and secure income years into the future. The Italians wanted to assure their customers on the continent adequate supplies of raw wool. The forward contract allowed the parties to make multiyear deals at fixed prices. Up-front payments in advance helped producers and were a kind of loan, and the prices sometimes included a discount that was in effect an interest payment. Only a small amount of fine-quality English wool was sold by forward contract. The complex international market for wool brought the English Crown, producers, and customers into tighter relationships. This trade illustrates the issue of economic policy, in the sense that states looked to commerce as a source of revenue to pay for their characteristic activity – war. Trade wars also occurred – witness the classic rivalries among Pisa, Genoa, and Venice. Here merchants directly paid for the ships and weapons involved in protecting their livelihoods. In fact, the merchant fleet was the war fleet, the city government the creation of the long distance trader, and the line between trade and piracy often a fine one.

The main centers of the fur trade were Kiev, Novgorod, and Kazan. Kiev exported ermine, sable, and beaver furs down the Volga and Don trade routes to Byzantine and eventually Muslim customers who paid in silver but also in luxuries, such as spices and silk. In the eleventh century, Novgorod began to monopolize northern and eastern supplies of fur. Novgorod also became an entrepot for exporting massive quantities of gray squirrel pelts, in barrels of 5–10,000, eastward to Hanseatic customers. Its merchants obtained cloth, salt, wine, herring, and silver. (Kazan controlled the trade routes to the Muslim Tartars dominating land access to the Black Sea.) In the fourteenth century, Moscow, closer to Siberian supplies of luxury furs, especially sable, began to challenge Novgorod. The issue was who would serve as intermediary between hunters and peasants (in some places paying rents in squirrel skins) and the customers for royal ermine and humbler furs. River routes connected Siberian and Scandinavian supplies to the Black and Caspian Seas. Zones of influence and trade routes shifted – eventually a land route across Poland-Lithuania served Western Europe. Despite all of these changes, the fur trade persisted because fur never went out of fashion.

But let us return to wool as a prime example of the intimate connections between commodities, trade, state finance, and violence. In England, the crown in 1271 required a license for all who exported wool. The king needed the revenue and favored some traders, typically, at first, his foreign creditors. In 1275, Edward I started a customs duty (export tax) of 6s 8d per sack of wool, yielding him some £10,000 for wars and paying off his creditors, the Ricci-ardi of Lucca. The ability to impose this tax testifies to the strength of wool exports. Foreign merchants paid the duty on top of the prevailing price, but producers were confident that their product was still competitive in the inter-national market for wool. In the 1290s, the king temporarily tripled the duty to

£2 per sack to pay for his wars in France and Scotland. Beginning in 1313, he established a royal monopoly or staple on wool exports, which required, in this instance, all wool to be exported to St. Omer to be sold from there and taxed accordingly. The later experiments with the wool staple need not detain us here – the point is the role of wool in what constitutes royal or public finances and indeed economic policy. Basic necessary commodities, such as wheat and wool, enabled states to squeeze peasant and merchant alike. The way to tax wheat was to burden the peasant proprietor – not to put unpopular duties on bread. Likewise, taxing clothing was impractical, but passing on the costs of war to foreigners was irresistible. International trade in commodities, such as wool and salt, made these policies possible.

Urban society required a closer look at the old question – who benefited from the rise of trade? Rural producers supplied commodities and markets. Peddlers and fairs might have satisfied local needs for exchange. One of the great medieval social and economic transformations was the rise of substantial cities across much of Europe. Agriculture and trade provided the context for exploring this important development.

SELECT BIBLIOGRAPHY

Janet L. Abu-Lughod, *Before European Hegemony: The World System A.D. 1250–1350.* Oxford, 1989.

Martin Allen, "The Volume of English Currency, 1158–1470," *Economic History Review* 54 (2001): 595–611.

Adrian Bell, Chris Brook, and Paul R. Dryburgh, *The English Wool Market, c. 1230–1327.* Cambridge, 2007.

Jesse Byock, *Viking Age Iceland.* London, 2001.

Olivia Remie Constable, *Housing the Stranger in the Mediterranean World.* Cambridge, 2003.

————, *Trade and Traders in Muslim Spain.* Cambridge, 1996.

Philippe Dollinger, *The German Hansa.* London, 1970.

Steven A. Epstein, *Genoa and the Genoese 958–1528.* Chapel Hill, 1996.

Paul Freedman, *Out of the East: Spices and the European Imagination.* New Haven, 2008.

Avner Greif, *Institutions and the Path to the Modern Economy: Lessons from Medieval Trade.* Cambridge, 2006.

Robert S. Lopez, *The Commercial Revolution of the Middle Ages, 950–1350.* Cambridge, 1976.

T. H. Lloyd, *England and the German Hanse, 1157–1611*. Cambridge, 1991.

Janet Martin, *Treasure of the Land of Darkness: The Fur Trade and Its Significance for Medieval Russia*. Cambridge, 1986.

Francesco Balducci Pegolotti, *La pratica della mercatura*. Edited by Allan Evans. Cambridge, MA, 1936.

John H. Pryor, *Business Contracts of Medieval Provence*. Toronto, 1981.

Carla Rahn Phillips and William D. Phillips, Jr., *Spain's Golden Fleece*. Baltimore, 1997.

Kathryn L. Reyerson, *The Art of the Deal: Intermediaries of Trade in Medieval Montpellier*. Leiden, 2002.

Peter Spufford, *Power and Profit: The Merchant in Medieval Europe*. New York, 2003.

4

CITIES, GUILDS, AND POLITICAL ECONOMY

HE GRADUAL URBANIZATION OF EUROPE AFTER 1000 IS ONE OF the most important themes in medieval economic and social history. Yet, the rise of cities should not be overstated. Even by 1500 only a small percentage of Europeans, perhaps 15–20 percent, lived in them. Cities were always thoroughly imbedded in their regions and depended on networks of smaller towns and farmlands to sustain their livelihoods by producing a surplus. Cities are places where strangers are likely to meet because anonymity was possible there – unlike a hamlet. They are also places where people would starve without regional and long-distance trade. Merchants and artisans and lords and the Church, were the engines driving the prosperity of these cities. Their incomes and need for security provided the means and the reason to pay taxes. As centers of wealth, cities attracted the attention of others, kings, feudal lords, and church officials, who also needed money to pay for war and cathedrals and much else.

"Political economy" is an old-fashioned name for the intersection of politics and economy. In a late medieval context, the paramount issues were fiscal – taxes, customs duties, public debt, and the money supply. All governments faced these issues, but cities incubated the ideas and practices that made it possible to raise money for the common good, and to consider what economic and social circumstances were most likely to favor commerce and manufacturing. In other words, cities were places that needed economic policies, where people thought about markets not simply as naturally occurring phenomena, but as human institutions that wise people could manipulate to their own advantage.

Cities reflect the human tendency to form groups, to band together for mutual support and protection. Guilds, and later companies and firms, show the same impulse to cooperate as a means to compete with others. Feudal society, clans, and even big families accomplished these goals in parts of the countryside. Some lords founded cities as part of their efforts to control people and profit from them. No inevitable tension existed between subordinating the peasantry and favoring the rise of cities. These developments in practice worked well together. At a certain point, however, the townspeople wanted rights not granted to serfs, and then tensions occurred. Local movements succeeded (or not) in establishing various systems of urban self-government – the commune. Inside the cities, groups also coalesced around individual trades and professions. In many places the bakers, for example, formed an association known as the *guild*, a self-help organization dedicated to fostering the trade and those masters, employers, who dominated it. These three topics – cities, guilds, and political economy – help illuminate an urban society where other new features, such as wage labor and a gender division of labor, were appearing.

CITIES

There are many ways to define cities – by size, social, political, and spiritual functions or by legal status. In the simplest terms, we are looking at settlements where most people are not farmers, and where the population has reached a certain size. A town, conveniently a small city, might have as few as one thousand people at the beginning of urbanization. The most populous cities in Europe, Constantinople before the sack of 1204 and Paris before the Black Death, may have reached as many as two hundred thousand people, and the major cities, such as Florence, Venice, Naples, and Palermo, topped out in the early fourteenth century at over one hundred thousand. Hundreds of places counted in the range from small towns to the urban giants. The general trend follows the demographic facts considered in previous chapters. Swelling numbers of people from rural birth rates fed the population growth in cites. Most observers conclude that the cities were unhealthy environments and unable to sustain their own growth and instead depended on migration to grow. Migration from outside of Europe did not contribute to population growth – in this narrow sense, Europe remained a closed system. Yet, it was not immune to African and Asian economic and social trends.

Medieval settlements required a certain amount of surrounding land to supply food and fuel. Intensively cultivated garden plots around some urban areas supplied townspeople with daily necessities. The practical limitations of transporting wood and foodstuffs created zones between the central places and their nearest neighbors. Naturally, the size of the rural zones varied depending on the quality of local soils, the ease of water transport, and other issues. Some regions of Europe, the Low Countries and northern Italy, were able to sustain a larger number of cities than others because of their good lands. A few great cities, such as London, Paris, and Constantinople, drew on such a large hinterland that their sheer size suppressed the growth of other cities within the zone the central place needed for food and firewood. Calculating how far peasants and mules could travel in a day or two to sustain cities of certain sizes has produced an array of grids and maps showing the likely positions of central places across Europe. If we also note the prior existence of ancient cities and durable geographic features, such as ideal ports and good places to cross rivers, we can establish a logic to the size and number of Europe's cities. No historical geographer could have predicted the institutional factors that conferred permanent advantages on Rome or why some particular cities, such as Bruges, grew at the expense of less-lucky neighbors. European agriculture and fuel supplies could sustain an urban population that remained even by 1500 in many places less than 10 percent of the population, and even in the most urbanized regions less than 25 percent.

As many cities, so many stories. Each urban society and its region merits study. Because we must generalize in order to make sense of so many particular places, it might seem best to set up types and examine the typical port, the standard industrial or university town, or royal capital. This model has merits, but no city was quite like another. For example, Ghent and Florence were wool cloth towns, but their institutions, culture, and much else were totally different. Guilds will pose similar problems – in no two places were their growth and roles really the same. So, we must proceed by learning enough about a few cities so that as you come across more examples through study or travel you will be able to fit them into an increasingly complicated pattern of urbanization in later medieval Europe. Two regions, the Low Countries and northern Italy, will dominate this analysis because they contain many large cities and became the most urbanized areas of Europe. They also led the way in Europe's most important industry – wool cloth production – but this business alone did not by itself drive urbanization – for Icelanders made plenty of cloth and had not a single town.

One thing all cities had in common was that they had permanent markets. Many old cities had bishops because the church's organization reflected ancient patterns of settlement at desirable spots. Some cities coalesced around a castle, bridge, good harbor, or some natural advantage that made the place safe. Every city (except Venice) and even some villages built walls for self-defense. Those little places that had clung to existence during the early Middle Ages and survived to about 1000 were most likely to thrive and grow. A few new important cities were purposefully created after that date, as was Lund, what became the city of Denmark's archbishop. In the ideal world where everyone prayed, fought, or farmed, people needed new words to describe urban people, and we will settle on the burgher, the bourgeoisie, and the cittadini. Very quickly, cities reflected older inequalities, and some men placed themselves above others. This tendency required those who ran cities to distinguish between the inhabitants – anyone who happened to live there, and the true burghers – property owners and citizens with some material stake in the city's life. Outside of the city walls, the growth of suburbs (*faubourgs*) help to chart the pace of urban growth and illustrate the need for new circuits of walls. City air made men free from serfdom. Where women and slaves would find their liberties remained unsettling questions.

Bruges (see Figure 4.1) in the 1120s was a small city of perhaps 1,000 people tucked up the Reie River close to the sandy coast of Flanders. This city thrived where roads and waterways intersected. Its substantial stone castle protected the inhabitants, who were mostly merchants, builders, traders, and boat people. The city had two big parishes but no bishop – it was not an ancient site though Roman ruins were in the area. At this time the North Sea was retreating but floods remained a menace and probably encouraged people to cooperate on vital matters like ditches and dikes. Bruges castle also functioned as a community headquarters for the region and an administrative center for the count of Flanders. Its location, a big open and covered market square just outside of the castle gate, was also a reason for its modest economic success. Houses and shops surrounded the commercial and administrative center. Bruges was a place of opportunity and provided employment to notaries who kept the count's financial accounts. The city did not fit well into the existing social rules of traditional, feudal society of lords and peasants, and so it was filled with flux and tensions. On March 2, 1127, some conspirators killed their count, Charles the Good, while he was praying. The ensuing crisis encouraged an able and temporarily unemployed notary Galbert to record the aftermath as local powers and groups struggled to assert authority over Bruges. His vivid story is one of the few contemporary accounts from anywhere in Europe that describes how violence and local competition shaped urban development.

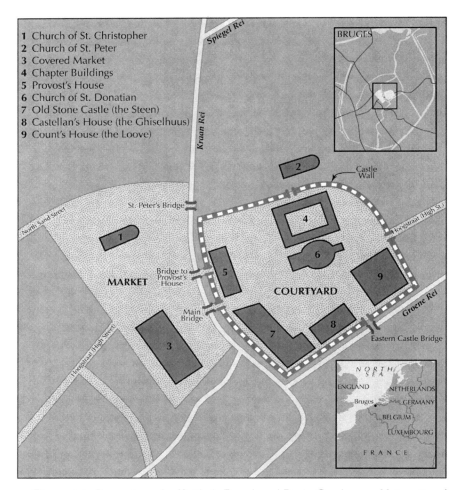

1 Church of St. Christopher
2 Church of St. Peter
3 Covered Market
4 Chapter Buildings
5 Provost's House
6 Church of St. Donatian
7 Old Stone Castle (the Steen)
8 Castellan's House (the Ghiselhuus)
9 Count's House (the Loove)

Figure 4.1. Bruges (map by Keith A. French and Darin Grauberger, University of Kansas Cartographic Services).

Charles died without immediate heirs, and the townsmen, the burghers, took advantage of a power vacuum and formed a sworn association whose first purpose was to choose their count. The kings of France and England had stakes in what happened to Flanders and were not likely to yield to common people. These burghers did not hope to name the next count by themselves, but they did expect to be consulted about the issues that mattered most to them: security, the common good, and caring for the poor. These concerns constitute a sophisticated political, economic, and social program. Their neighbors in St. Omer received a charter from the new count that together with Galbert's account makes clear exactly what the burghers wanted. Their leaders, the aldermen, (elders) were recognized as the town's officials and the count promised to protect them. Security issues extended to personal status – the townspeople were not serfs to anyone, although not all of them counted as burghers. As a sign of free personal status, no one paid a head tax. Landowners no longer owed dues on urban land, and these freeholds became everywhere the mark of urban status – the burghers – householders who owned their building and had at least a traditional right to the land under it. Finally, merchants wanted the right to have their customary laws – a way to settle commercial disputes that did not resort to trial by combat or ordeal but instead rested on fairness and reason. This merchant law could draw on the common legal past of Europe, containing the rudiments of a commercial law drawing on Roman and other traditions. What mattered most were rules about enforcing contracts and arbitrating disputes among parties that did not expect to carry every problem to a court, with its expenses and uncertain outcomes. Merchant law became a common law across Europe.

How the burghers defined the common good focused on their desire to work and trade without being impeded by outside exactions. The St. Omer charter promised to free the members of the commune from all customary taxes and to exempt them from some vexatious tolls. The merchants wanted to travel safely but also without having to pay whatever power set itself up on a bridge or road to skim off some of the benefits of trade. Lords and the church (which owned some traditional tolls) saw trade as a revenue stream to tap while the merchants saw these toll keepers as predators. Urban people became close students of tax policies and were inclined to use tolls, customs duties, sales taxes, and monopoly income on necessities, such as salt, to pay a commune's bills and provide for basic services, such as walls and courts.

In order for local markets to function well, merchants needed sound money – a silver currency of reliable fineness not subject to the profit-making schemes of the count. Rulers understood that the right to mint coins was profitable because of the small traditional payment, a royalty, owed to coiners. Even more profits could be obtained from stretching out the available silver with other metals literally to make more money. Some communes eventually manipulated their money supply, but they at least knew why and the commune profited. In St. Omer, the count conceded his mint to the commune in exchange for a substantial annual payment and the promise that the burghers would maintain good money for the common good. The right to mint money everywhere remained a keenly contested privilege, and the most successful monarchs were, as in the case of England, able to impose a common and reliable coinage on their cities. Florence introduced its famous gold florin in 1252 as a deliberate policy to strengthen its bankers and their currency as an international means of exchange. Its commune also expected to profit from minting gold.

Finally, the burghers in Bruges had claimed that they wanted to take care of the poor. They knew that the tithe that they were supposed to pay to the local churches was in theory intended to be divided into thirds to support the clergy, the material fabric of the buildings, and Christ's poor – the deserving widows and orphans. The burghers could reasonably claim that supporting the liberties of the church was in the interest of the poor. They also intended to focus their own charitable donations on these poor souls, using the church to administer these donations and grant spiritual benefits to the donors. Everyone understood that the best antidote to urban poverty was employment for those hands able to work at a trade. The burghers expected the "common good" to favor local prosperity that, in turn, allowed the able-bodied poor the chance to work for the burghers. Their guilds were partly intended to regulate competition among the members on thorny issues, such as training and wages. The issue across these emerging cities across Europe was the poor. The common teachings of the Church encouraged an ethos of charity often disbursed by lay religious confraternities. A wage economy, something that was fairly new, also operated in a moral framework in which the laborer was indeed worthy of his (and certainly her) hire.

The communal conception of the common good, resting on an oath binding Christians, from the beginning excluded Jews from full participation in urban society. The circumstances of Jews were complicated and apparently none lived in Bruges. Elsewhere, in Castile, Aragon, and Muslim Spain where Jews were most numerous in Europe (still less than 5 percent of the population), their continued existence depended on the good will of sovereigns taking money from the Jews in exchange for protection. After 1000, as landholding became more difficult for Jews, they became, especially in Christian Europe, an increasingly urban population even as some towns, for example, Genoa and Venice, were hostile and permitted none to settle. No Jews had lived in England until some came over with the Normans after the conquest of 1066. The fates of Jews ands other minorities in medieval society will receive extended discussion in later chapters. For now, it is enough to observe that their small numbers play no apparent role in the communal movements, the rise of guilds, or indeed the economic development of Western Europe. Increasingly confined to economic activities inside their own communities and unpopular trades, such as pawnbrokers, rag merchants, and tax collectors, Jews became (along with others) convenient scapegoats for those who questioned the rise of new institutions and a market economy. Older scholarship picked up on these medieval complaints and exaggerated the role Jews played in these developments, especially after 1000 when a Christian merchant class appeared to take charge of local and long-distance trade. In Byzantine and Muslim lands, the Jews certainly endured second class status, but they remained free to engage in some professions and trades denied them in the Christian West.

In the German Empire, that vast but ill-defined state stretching from the North Sea to the vicinity of Rome, imperial free cities, such as Cologne, Mayence, Worms, Speyer, Strasbourg, Basle, and Ratisbon, started as episcopal towns. The bishop provided a cloak of authority that spread over the burghers' claims to self-rule in the eleventh and twelfth centuries. (The well-intentioned bishops of Mainz and Speyer were not able to prevent massacres of local Jews during the crusading fervor of 1096.) Pisa was an ancient Roman port with a continuous existence since antiquity. Pisa's commune, beginning in 1081, received from the emperors a series of charters allowing self-rule. Its system of government, revealed in exceptionally detailed records, in 1162 depended on a board of five consuls (later between five and ten), chosen by the previous group, who appointed the other officials and judges and enforced the law. A council of forty senators assisted the consuls, and other groups made lists of citizens and their property in order to prepare galleys to protect the port, especially during the sailing season from April to October. Overseas trade was the lifeblood of Pisan prosperity, and it also served as the entrepot for Tuscany's commerce coming down the Arno River. These consuls and senators were not Roman survivals but instead took their venerable names in order to attach their new free status to traditional job titles with no current relevance.

Pisa's consuls conducted a foreign policy and were generally loyal to the German emperors (hence Ghibellines) and expected to be supported in their colonial ambitions on Sardinia with its modest agricultural wealth and silver mines. The consuls as collective chief executives settled disputes, directed the constructing of city walls, and regulated the city's relations with its powerful archbishop. Pisa also had a famous law code, the usages or customs of Pisa, in its oldest form dating from 1161 but reflecting centuries of practice as well as a deep understanding of even older common Roman law. This law code largely concerned shipping and contracts and above all stressed that equity should prevail in commerce. Pisa experienced a rather typical institutional progression. The old commune extended its authority over the nearby countryside but ran up against similar ambitions in its nearest neighbors Lucca and Florence. By the early thirteenth century, the city had a podesta, a professional city manager, always a foreigner, chosen for a one-year term who was supposed to ensure impartial courts and defend the city against its many enemies, especially the Genoese. In 1254 the Pisan popolo, the merchants and major employers in the guilds, took over the commune and established yet another authority, the captain of the people, as a remedy to the defects of a clear, experienced local executive. A great naval defeat in Pisa's port in 1284 led to Genoese naval supremacy in the Tyrrhenian Sea and the beginning of hard times for the commune, which began to fall into the hands of a series of local strongmen, the signori. The late thirteenth-century commune had a more ambitious political program than its predecessors. It supported with money the local hospitals, hermits, monks, and nuns, and helped to clothe the new orders of friars, the Franciscans and Dominicans, active in urban ministry. The commune even paid a bounty to eliminate the local wolves, offering 2 lire alive, 1 lira dead, and five solidi for cubs. All these decisions reflect local choices made by ruling groups, however defined, valuing their autonomy.

Bonvesin della Ripa, a member of a new religious order, the Humiliati, in 1288, wrote a short work on the marvels of Milan. His book, a pious panegyric on his hometown, described a city that had a podesta but in Matteo Visconti a noble captain of the people in the process of establishing a durable family dynasty over a free commune. This remarkable source situates the city clearly in its region – populous Lombardy with its exceptionally fertile lands. Located at the confluence of two rivers, Milan had according to Bonvesin an ideal climate and plenty of freshwater from wells and springs. He was attuned to the local environment and understood natural resources and advantages. His choice to divide the book into eight chapters reflects his gaze and priorities. The contado, and Milan's housing, people, abundance of goods, power, fidelity, liberty, and dignity interested Bonvesin in that order. A close observer of Milan, Bonvesin supplies many numbers, some more credible than others. For example, he wrote that the famous hospital of Brolo could house 500 poor and sick people and take in another 500 when necessary, and that it supported 350 babies out with wet nurses – this seems reasonable. He claimed that there were 200,000 men in the city and Milan's large contado, which included many towns, some significant like Monza, and 150 villages with castles. He thought there were seven hundred thousand people in this region, and two hundred thousand in Milan proper. The problem is that he had no real basis for this guess, and was probably on the high side, as he was when estimating the one thousand five hundred notaries active in Milan. More believable is that there were seventy schoolteachers, and he must be right that there were precisely six trumpeters.

Good and bad numbers all serve Bonvesin's larger point that the markets and fairs, plus the region's natural abundance in crops, such as wheat and cherries, guaranteed that any healthy person could make a living suitable to his or her station. He thought Milan was at full employment but recognized that many could not work – hence the need for charity. Bonvesin was briefer on the other topics but they mattered as part of how he conceived Milan. Spiritual power made Milan rich in religious treasures from St. Ambrose's time in the fourth century. Political power partly derived from the large and prosperous trades practiced by blacksmiths and armorers – Milan made enough weapons for itself and for export. Milan, a Guelf town, had suffered for its loyalty to the papacy and had resisted tyrants – the German emperors. Bonvesin, as a good member of the Humiliati, devoted to piety and cloth weaving, found the city's main dignity to come from its Christian faith. He tried to be balanced and noted Milan's defects – it lacked civic peace (like many cities) and without a port it had no sea power – hence, its interest in Genoa just south over the maritime Alps. Having no university meant that Milan did not have many foreign inhabitants. Bonvesin saw this as a blessing because these foreign students probably would have corrupted the local people. Above all, his praise of Milan reveals a strong sense of civic patriotism in an age when larger entities did not yet command this type of loyalty, when indeed Germany and Italy remained geographical expressions.

Cities provided a good environment for intellectual activities. Great university towns, such as Bologna and Paris, became centers where professors lectured and wrote books on theology, canon, and civil law. Salerno's medical school helped facilitate the transmission of Arabic and Greek science into western Europe. Not every city had or wanted a university, however, and the popes eventually asserted their authority to charter an official school whose degrees were recognized across Europe. Ambitious building projects like cathedrals employed artists and architects as well as masons and carpenters. As kings became less peripatetic and settled down, their courts became centers for musicians and poets to make livings and enhance the intellectual climate. Schools in cities turned out increasing numbers who could read and write as their trades demanded. Notaries, for example, were literate and stimulated a market for books and literature in Latin as well as the vernacular languages. Urban culture rewarded the reasonable and literate members of society and attracted learned men to teach in its universities and take care of the legal and spiritual needs of the inhabitants. Jews were excluded from universities and maintained their own Hebrew language, yet some of their scholars knew Latin. Also denied access to the universities and those professions inside and outside the Church that required degrees, some women nonetheless learned to read and write in cities, whether in the urban convents or in the family. Urban economic life granted some of these women, often widows, a chance to run wool shops as opposed to merely spinning thread or weaving cloth.

Communes emerged in the Low Countries and northern Italy, and found some imitators in southern France and Germany as townspeople banded together to foster their self-interest. Home rule did not guarantee economic success and being the capital of a national monarchy with a close interest in its governance did not harm London and Paris. By the end of our period of study, Pisa had become a wrecked and malarial shadow of its former economic prominence, Bruges had yielded local supremacy to Antwerp, and the great age of Seville, Bristol, and Lisbon was just beginning for the Atlantic ports. In general, the long-distance traders, in position to earn the biggest profits and provide jobs for allied trades, were the first to see the benefits of ruling their own cities outside the models of monarchy and rural lordship. These people, however, soon divided along wealth and status lines into the big people, defined as the really rich and powerful, and the little people, the great mass of respectable middling folk. During the thirteenth and fourteenth centuries, many communes experienced civic strife as parties of the people, sometimes allied with an aristocracy or a king, fought for control of urban institutions that seemed to guarantee economic success or failure. A new institution, the medieval guild, provided yet another way for people to divide into groups defending the interests of the employers in a trade or profession. These guilds, often existing on uneasy terms with other centers of authority in urban society, helped to determine the roles people might play in the wider world.

GUILDS

Guilds were usually spontaneous and local organizations devoted to fostering the welfare of the employers in a particular craft or business. As with any institutions, guilds had rules, beliefs, and norms, often codified in written statutes. Sometimes these associations needed the sanction of a higher power. In other places city governments or other authorities encouraged the development of guilds in order to more closely regulate the members' activities. In some cities, such as Bruges or Venice, the commune seems to have originated in effect as a merchant guild, a coalition of the long-distance traders who often ran local affairs for their own benefit. These institutions, which gradually developed rules and traditions, benefited the members in several ways. Above all, the guild was supposed to make the business or trade of its members more secure and profitable. As an institution the guild fostered what Sheilagh Ogilvie has called "cultural efficiency," a social framework where human constraints affected the ways employment and production evolved. In other words, guilds were a way to settle disputes about resources, in this case, the buying and selling of raw materials, finished products, services, and labor.

Religious confraternities permeated rural and urban medieval societies. A guild was also usually a confraternity in the sense that its members, bound by a common oath and faith, often had a patron saint, worshipped together in their chapel, buried their members, and spiritually bonded as a group who happened to be in the same trade. (For these reasons, they excluded Muslims and Jews from membership.) People excluded from guilds are telling signs of broader economic trends. For example, we should be alert to changes in rules about membership that privileged relatives of current masters. Artisan and craft guilds usually included this spiritual purpose but also organized people according to their trades and professions, which often had patron saints, such as St. Joseph for the carpenters.

Because membership in a guild carried benefits, the masters, who were full members, were interested in regulating entry into their business, maintaining standards of quality, and managing to some extent the competition among them for business. As employers, the masters were competing to train and recruit labor. The apprentice and journeymen and journeywomen system, by which young people obtained a technical education and learned to make candles or wool cloth, could exist outside of a formal guild structure. The masters hence had a quasipaternal or maternal relationship with the student, who was supposed to be educated and often fed and housed in sickness and in health. Often this relationship resulted in a lifelong tie that was sometimes buttressed by marriage to a master's offspring. Hence, the guild was a spiritual and social club as well as means to recruit labor. An organized trade was in a better position to manage the delicate balance of not stealing one another's employees while at the same time expecting a solid level of training among the workers. Guilds fused social and economic functions into a comprehensive way of life for its members and subjects.

Guilds first appeared in the Christian West along with the rise of cities in the eleventh century and the evidence for this rise thickens in the twelfth century. Guilds were partly the result of a pervasive tendency for such groups to form among medieval people who valued solidarity and sought to reduce risks by cooperating. Two aspects of this impulse toward self-help must remain at the center of our analysis. First, these guilds counted as full members only the employers or, at least, the self-employed. One needed his or her own shop or oven or tools to be an independent producer for customers and the markets. Those who worked for others for a daily or piece rate wage were subject to the guild's rules but were not among those who made the rules. In some parts of Europe, for example, Germany, the guild (Zunft) remained an important part of city life into modern times. These later associations played a role in inspiring the trade union movement among workers who often called their early (and illegal) bodies by the same names. But the medieval guild was in no sense a union devoted to fostering the well-being of the workers, and there is no line of descent between the medieval and modern ways managing employer–employee relations. In the later Middle Ages, journeymen and journeywomen (or *compagnons*) occasionally had their own shadowy and often illegal associations, but they were not able to bargain collectively with the employers.

The second aspect of this impulse toward self-help is more complicated, but it puts the questions surrounding European economic development into their proper context. Ancient Roman cities had groups called *collegia* or *corpora* (literally bound by a common rule or oath, or a body of people) organized along professional, trade, or craft lines. Under the empire, these institutions functioned as charitable associations of the members and also provided a convenient way for the state to regulate vital activities, such as the grain trade. These ancient guilds perished along with other sophisticated parts of the Roman society and economy and so there is no line of continuity between these guilds and the ones that appeared in the medieval West centuries later. This result is not surprising because the impulse to coalesce in such groups required only suitable circumstances to occur again. Yet, when medieval people searched for a Latin legal vocabulary to describe the new guild (this a Germanic word), they often went back to ancient labels and so the *collegium, corpus, universitas,* and *scola* all reappear, and some guilds will even have officials called *consuls.* This vocabulary also shows that the medieval university followed the guild model with its master educators in the same profession regulating the terms of their work and product – the qualifications of the students! Also, the examination to prove competency or approve a masterpiece became a guild tradition, and some apprentices obtained journeyman status this way. The type of people behind the communes and guilds agreed on traditional titles, but they left behind a false trail that suggested continuities between ancient and medieval institutions where there were none.

Any argument about the links between ancient and medieval institutions has to take into account what happened in the Byzantine and Muslim worlds. In the Byzantine parts of Europe and especially in Constantinople guilds continued to exist, uninterrupted since antiquity. These guilds were corporations or legal persons with the right to own property, have rules, and manage competition and relations with the government, particularly over taxes. These guilds also controlled training and remained social and charitable clubs. For the eleventh century, the original sources are not good, but these guilds continued to exist in a more competitive market as Western merchants began to appear in Byzantine ports to trade. The structure of the labor market remained complex and interesting with journeymen and women, apprentices, and slaves all at work, some in state monopolies and imperial workshops turning out high-quality luxury items, such as silk cloth and tapestries. A high level of technical skill among the silk workers prompted the famous episode in 1147 when Roger II of Sicily brought silk weavers and embroiderers from Thebes and Corinth to Sicily to start an advanced production there. Forced migration is one classic way to transfer technology.

The fine details of how the imperial bureaucracy attempted to control the price of bread, and still allow for the expenses and a reasonable profit (4.2%) for the bakers, show that until at least 1100 the continuities between the ancient and Byzantine guilds seem tight. Training and traditions also account for the high reputation that Eastern handicrafts enjoyed throughout the Western and Eastern trading networks. No evidence suggests, however, that guilds as far away as London and Paris needed these Eastern models for their own spontaneous institutions that served some similar needs. During the various crises, the Byzantine State experienced in the twelfth and subsequent centuries, the guilds seem to have withered away and were replaced by nothing indigenous. Instead, foreign merchant quarters and even artisan quarters appeared in the major cities and trade seems to have diminished local production in old staples, such as silk and ceramics. The larger story of how the emperors managed their political economy so poorly is not the issue here. Two basic conclusions remain – these Byzantine guilds were not the models for Western ones, and they did not survive, for whatever reason, to foster internationally competitive urban industries in the Greek-speaking East.

About 1000, Muslim rulers still controlled most of Iberia and its important cities, Sicily and of course North Africa and nearly all of the Middle East. As inheritors of another region of the late Roman economy and society Muslim rulers seem to have preserved public authority, which suited their purposes. Market inspectors supervised the bazaars, collected taxes, and maintained the moral order by suppressing the many types of fraud. Trades had an identity and sense of common purpose and often coalesced in neighborhoods or along a certain street. But they lacked any formal organization, and no one has found in Arabic sources any traces of guilds in Muslim cities in the eleventh and twelfth centuries. For instance, no crafts had rules about formal training in apprenticeship. A Sufi fraternity of silk workers in thirteenth-century Damascus was apparently a purely religious club. In Muslim cities, the markets and a strong central authority regulated the trades and professions without guilds. This result suggests that Western merchants would not find anything in these Muslim cities to stimulate a desire to go home and form guilds.

Just as every city had its unique history, so too did every guild have a particular path to development over the period 1000–1300. The story of a typical guild distorts these varieties in time and space so it is better to concentrate on some general issues. A charter from 1149 granted some weavers in Cologne corporate status. These workers specialized in making mattresses and pillow covers, so this group represented a stage of an already evolving division of labor as weavers honed their particular skills. A division of labor indicates a more efficient operation and one that fostered a tight solidarity among people with a special skill. This charter shows no signs of a gender division of labor in this trade or in Cologne, but we cannot doubt that women worked at these trades, were excluded from being masters in a guild, and were paid low wages.

In Worms, the fishermen in 1106 obtained the corporate hereditary right from the count and bishop to control the fish market. These authorities had the spiritual and secular power to sanction a guild, and the public responsibility to ensure the quality of fish. The fishermen wanted to limit their numbers in order to make sure each could make a living at this trade, and they also wanted their sons to have a claim on a share of the market. In this sense, the guild was a monopoly. The members wanted a monopoly to exclude interlopers from entering the trade and presumably taking the fish the members saw as their own. At this stage, the fishermen were not a cartel – they had not agreed to fix prices or set quotas on the catch. Most of the time guild members in many trades continued to compete against one another on quality, freshness, or other aspects of reputation that over time established a good position in the markets. In Pavia, where a commune existed since 1164, the consuls had to settle a dispute between the guild of fishermen and the monastery of Morimond over rights to fish. Rivers fell under public jurisdiction, but rights over fish could belong to other associations besides the guild.

In 1152 in Toulouse, the consuls of the city government set the maximum profits of the millers and bakers. This was a pervasive trend across urban societies everywhere in Europe – a public authority's concern for the food supply and fair prices. Throughout England, Henry II began setting up local assizes of bread and beer. These courts were supposed to regulate the price and quality of beer and the weight of standard loaves of bread. In order to accomplish these goals, authorities also had to set prices for wheat, barley, and oats. These complex price controls were difficult to enforce but show the needs of consumers were in theory understood.

The common good of the trade was the business of the guild. Most observers concluded that when this narrow interest conflicted with the broader public good, people could not count on the guild to do the right thing. In the thirteenth century, however, the Church taught that guilds were not conspiracies against the public good, and so they had a right to exist. Vigilant city officials had to supervise trades involving bread to make sure there were adequate supplies at affordable prices. Producers and retailers of grain might not agree on what prices were fair. Very few people believed that the markets alone would guarantee this result, especially for the poor. In cities, such as Toulouse and Venice, the public authorities may have taken the lead in organizing some guilds in order to regulate their activities more efficiently. Certainly in Venice the commune, controlled by the old families engaged in overseas trade, closely supervised all guilds and had a strong role in formulating the trade's rules. In the major royal capitals, such as Paris and London, the state also remained active in supervising the trades ostensibly in the name of the common good but in practical terms to keep the peace and prevent food riots and other disorders.

As a sworn association of employers, guilds often had statutes, private laws, devised by the members, or sometimes imposed on them, that set the limits on who could enter the trade and how they should practice it. These statutes survive from across Europe and where city governments took a close interest in guild activities, for example, in Paris and Bologna in the thirteenth century, the statutes survive in important collections. In some communes, such as Florence, where membership in a guild gradually became necessary for participation in political life, guild statutes for the major and wealthy employers were serious matters. Later copies of rules tend to make older ones irrelevant and disposable. For example, the Florentine guild of money changers was already old and prestigious before its first surviving statutes of 1299 – which were speedily revised in 1300, 1313, and 1316. Guild members liked to tinker with their rules, especially with an eye toward how their sons could enter the trade and the circumstances under which their wives and daughters had rights to manage shops and do business.

Another major concern of masters was apprenticeship – how long it needed to be, who was eligible, how many apprentices a master might have, and how the apprentice might prove his or her competence. Apprenticeship remained the most common form of technical and vocational education across medieval Europe. The daily routines of apprenticeship have left almost no traces in the surviving records. Most apprentices lived and worked with their masters, and received food, clothing, and shelter. The number of years required to learn trades was set by statute and custom and were often long. To learn to be a goldsmith in Paris took ten years, the same for a silversmith in Genoa. Normal terms of apprenticeship in both cities expected a student baker to serve five years. Did it really take so long to learn these trades, or were the rules intended to keep young people from competing with day laborers? Did masters simply want more work from apprentices at little or no pay? Apprenticeship contracts reveal a nuanced system of training in which the student often promised to perform all services inside and outside the house. In practice, this meant learning the trade as well as being a domestic servant. An apprentice learned about the hierarchy of labor in all its forms, that technical knowledge of a craft and going to the well for water were both work.

Nevertheless, the lore and technical expertise of some crafts took a long time to acquire. A spinner needed to understand the wheel, keep it repaired, and produce consistent thread. The apprentice repeated manual skills until the master's supervision was no longer necessary. Masters also passed down all the knowledge of the trade, from testing the fineness of gold with touchstones to measuring the strength of thread. In these teen years, the apprentices also learned lessons on discipline and cooperation in the workplace. Some apprentices needed to learn rudimentary numerical and writing skills. In whose interest was it to make a goldsmith in just one year?

The main obligation of the apprentice was to learn his or her trade and to acquire good work habits and loyalty to employers. Occasional paternalistic rules prohibited apprentices from gambling, drinking, and sex. A training wage might contribute to the apprentice's family wage and allow the master some years of work at a low price. Journeymen and jouneywomen working for a daily wage received less attention in statutes because employers were the bosses, period. Masters did not like the idea of competing against one another for employees and were quick to raise objections to having their best workers lured away. Setting wages across a trade by statute was impractical and hard to enforce – because other issues, such as meal breaks, lodging, and holidays always intruded to make it complex to figure out exactly what counted as compensation.

The ordinances of the drapers' guild in Chartres from 1268 reveal a nice mix of public and private concerns. This big guild included an alliance of trades in the cloth business including wool combers and carders, weavers, finishers, and dyers. In Chartres, anyone could join this guild upon paying a modest entry fee, and the rules compelled no one to join. Still, it would be hard to be in the cloth business and remain apart from this guild. The drapers were mainly concerned about maintaining the quality of their local cloth – known by the town's name, not the name of an individual producer, and so they banned the sale of inferior cloth and investigated and fined anyone who made it. Trade marks for specific towns developed to signal customers about quality. Sales of cloth took place at a public market so infractions were easy to spot. In Chartres, both men and women might rise to the status of master. In this town, the guild remained open to newcomers and unusually to a broad range of employees, but the common oath bound all to the high standards of quality and the dominance of the masters, whose monopoly was subtle but effective.

The *Livre des métiers* is a collection of regulations for the guilds of Paris compiled for the prévot or city manager Etienne Boileau in the 1260s. The 101 trades included represent a wide cross-section of work in Paris and reflect a minute division of labor – three separate guilds made buckles, divided according to the raw materials used. Most officials (*preudhommes*) of the guilds were appointed by the king's prévot or in some cases his appointee – for example, the king's baker had the right to name the officials of the bakers' guild. The statutes set the terms of work: how many apprentices and valets (journeymen and women) a master might have; who could enter the trade – sons, daughters, strangers and at what fees. Strict rules determined whether or not the laborers could work at night – depending on if the trade was noisy or required good light. The statutes also set the length of apprenticeship, but the years varied depending on whether the apprentice paid for training. For example, the wool guild expected four years of apprenticeship and a payment of eighty sou (four livres) or seven years without payment. The calculations here included the costs to the master of feeding and housing unskilled labor in the early years versus the value of an unpaid and experienced apprentice at the end of his or her term. Women predominated in some guilds – they comprised the majority of the work force in many aspects of the silk trades and also had the status of masters capable of training apprentices. Even if the guild excluded women from actually running the trade, it was important that skilled women were able to pass down their knowledge to the next generation of women, and even in some cases train men. In a few guilds, such as the makers of silk caps, women served as officials (*preudesfemmes*). A handful of guilds, such as the lapidaries in crystal and stone, excluded women completely – the usual excuse was that the women did not know enough to carry on the profession, but this ignorance, if true, resulted from their exclusion.

The 1292 taille in Paris, a tax assessed by hearth, gives a broader view of occupations outside the guild system. This source names 172 occupations and notes women working at many jobs – for example, copyist, artist, juggler, and dancer – for which there were no guilds. Women also worked as drapers, money changers, and in other professions that had guilds. Many women worked as domestic servants or as peddlers and wet-nurses, which were unregulated occupations. Women predominated in some jobs – most of the food trades, caring for the sick, and, as we would expect, in all phases of the silk business except actually running the main retail shops (see Table 4.1). Licensed professions, such as notaries and lawyers, excluded women, and women were absent from the ranks of porters and sailors, who performed heavy work and also toiled outside the guild system. The *Livre des Metiers* and taille records indicate that

Table 4.1. *Women workers, Paris, 1292 (data from David Herlihy,* Opera Muliebria: Women and Work in Medieval Europe. *New York, 1990, p. 146).*

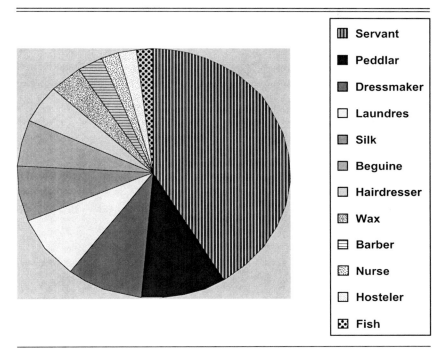

- ▥ Servant
- ◼ Peddlar
- ▨ Dressmaker
- ☐ Laundres
- ▨ Silk
- ▨ Beguine
- ☐ Hairdresser
- ▨ Wax
- ▤ Barber
- ▨ Nurse
- ☐ Hosteler
- ⊠ Fish

even in a city like Paris with many guilds and a sophisticated division of labor, numerous occupations, some quite remunerative, thrived outside this framework, in the general market for labor. The statutes reveal the ideal world of work as men envisioned it. Occupations of heads of households in the taille show women at work inside and outside the household at a much wider range of occupations than the statutes would suggest.

For parts of southern Europe, notarial records that survive from the midtwelfth century, contain written contracts for apprenticeships and the work of journeymen and journeywomen. The terms of apprenticeship were wisely committed to writing to make the contract enforceable and to ensure that the master and parent understood the responsibilities – the master's to teach a craft and the apprentice boy or girl's to learn it. Sometimes the parent had to pay the master to take on a pupil. In other trades, it was common for the master to pay the apprentice a small daily wage on top of lodging, food, and clothing in the later years of the term, when he or she knew enough to actually help the master. Work contracts, usually for some term of months or years, set a daily wage that sometimes increased over time, although, in some trades, a piece-rate system, so much money per woven cloth, prevailed. No sources reveal the actual negotiations over the terms of individual employment, and even these workers were the lucky ones to have a written contract and some security of employment. Much urban work, especially in the great ports, remained casual, seasonal, and relied on an oral agreement.

The guilds and the emerging urban economies fostered a system of regular wage labor, an entirely new phenomenon. Paying apprentices and lengthening the term of service had the effect of keeping them out of the competitive labor market and probably dragging down the general level of wages. Because wages were usually customary or negotiated on a case by case basis, the journeymen and jouneywomen tended to earn a salary that modern economists call "sticky" – stable, lagging behind other price changes, and not likely to increase for any reason other than experience – and even these raises were customary. The general level of prices and wages in the twelfth and thirteen centuries remain elusive, but, in general, they were increasing until the late thirteenth century, while prices were fairly stable.

In this context, what was up for grabs was the length of the working day, and how many days people worked, because there were many holy days and paid holidays were very rare. These were serious matters: in Provins in 1279, an effort to increase the working day by one hour prompted a rebellion by the wage laborers who killed the mayor in the ensuing revolt! Daylight placed some natural limits on certain trades not worth conducting by expensive can-dle or oil light. Still, in 1322, ostensibly for the common benefit, the king of France allowed all trades in Paris to work at night – this was certainly a favor to the employers who could now get more labor for the same pay. Freezing days occasionally stopped much work in northern European cities. Nearly all work ended on Saturday afternoon, and honoring the Sabbath was widespread. In Tournai, employers experimented with paying a higher daily wage on Monday, probably to lure people back to work after their day of rest. Most observers conclude that medieval workers, from the masters down to the newest appren-tice, worked to the limits of human endurance and their health; in other words, long hours on the days worked. How quickly they worked remains unknown and must have depended on their nutrition and the watchful eyes of their masters.

Records of employers in the construction trades working on cathedrals, castles, hospices, city walls, and other projects provide good evidence for wage rates for builders. Master stonecutters and masons as contractors often worked for a high daily wage. Valets, Knechts, compagnons, or builders' helpers were common laborers who earned about half of the master's wage, and the boys who were lucky to get unskilled task work. Masters and workers collected their salary on a weekly basis, and sometimes their pay was seasonally lower in winter when they were lucky to get work at all. These men, and some women, along with their colleagues in the butchers' guilds, were often big and tough people with tools that could easily double as weapons. When urban people revolted against a commune or some other authority, such people often appeared in the lead. Women, especially sensitive to the price of bread – as mothers and low wage earners – were often the first to protest high prices, shortages, or price gouging that they often blamed on the bakers.

The emerging market for urban labor encouraged employers to band together into guilds to foster their own self-interest and create a safety net of sorts to keep them from slipping into poverty. Inevitably, some masters simply failed in business or became too ill to work, and the charitable aspects of the guild might prove to be a real benefit. But the best antidote to poverty was work. The impulse of the masters was to limit their numbers and divide up the market so that all might prosper within reason. For the workers, the only safety nets were a paternalistic master, one's kin, or begging for charity. This circumstance encouraged a full-employment economy because the alternative was to starve or join the ranks of the shame-faced poor who existed because the Church or the better off or the commune fed them. From the beginning, the fear of poverty encouraged everyone who could to reduce their risks by acting in solidarity with others – by forming a commune or guild. Wage labor was salaried and free and evolved in a social context that was still quasi-paternal and feudal. Apprentices swore an oath to obey their masters, who usually retained the right to beat or correct unsatisfactory pupils. Employer–employee relations were marked by hierarchy and subordination, learned as apprentices and reinforced by the discipline of the daily wage. Employment at the will of the employers allowed some women an independent existence and the chance to learn rewarding skills and live outside of male domination. Children as young as five or six years old entered apprenticeship in another household and acquired another father or mother who was a role model to be obeyed and studied. This system of employment allowed some to advance from humble origins to the rank of prosperous master in a guild. Most people spent a lifetime working for others until they died or became too old to work and hoped to be lucky enough to have children who would see them through old age. Much work remained outside guild rules, especially in the countryside. Domestic servants were the single most numerous type of workers. Their work was vital to a functioning household. Here women predominated and received the lowest wages, and in parts of southern Europe were joined by enslaved domestics, wet nurses, or objects of sexual exploitation.

POLITICAL ECONOMY

This venerable subject concerns the policies governments make in order to promote the general economic and social welfare of the people, however defined. Economic and social thought, the subject of Chapter 5, contributes to the context in which policy makers decide which paths to follow. Our focus here is on the actual decisions and what the deciders intended and what actually resulted. Every state or commune had a direct stake in the economy because money remained the sinews of war or power. Military campaigns consumed vast amounts of money, and those fighting wars needed huge sums at once – because no one saved for future wars, and few were willing to fight for free or on credit. (Holy wars are a partial exception here because many participants were willing to fund their own efforts and those of their followers – but they faced the same issues of raising money for expenses.) Because the period from 1000 to 1300 began in violence and constant strife marks the subsequent centuries, the basic task of political economy is to explain how governments found the money to pay for war. National monarchies had various expedients. The old idea was that the king should at least live on his own estates and on traditional forest rights, taxes, and gifts, and that he was entitled to military service from men who had sworn to be vassals. The Church lands also often provided warriors and the Church contributed vast sums to holy wars and other enterprises deemed vital by the monarch demanding aid. The need for money to fight wars resulted in imaginative efforts to impose general taxes in the German empire, France, England, and the Latin Kingdom of Jerusalem. These taxes often introduced novelties, such as self-assessment, and the idea that it was best to tax commerce rather than capital assets – itself an early hallmark of medieval political economy.

Before 1300, state budgets are very hard to determine but everywhere monarchs spent the vast majority of their resources on war. Taxes were a last resort.

Kings experimented with various ways to fund their activities. Everywhere rulers manipulated the silver content of their coinage in order to stretch the supply of money at their disposal. Compulsory recoinages swept in the good money and often turned out debased silver money. Philip IV of France financed his wars against England and Flanders from the 1290s by debasing his kingdom's coinage, to literally stretch his resources. In England, the monarchy squeezed the Jews to skim off the profits of their credit business and when the Jews could yield no more, they were expelled from the kingdom in 1290. The expulsion of about one hundred thousand Jews from France in 1306 was a large windfall for the monarchy, and they later paid vast sums to be readmitted to the kingdom in 1315 (only to be expelled again in 1322). Then the monarchs turned to foreign borrowing, and generations of bankers from Lucca and Florence made loans to English kings in return for access to the wool market and other entice-ments. Eventually royal defaults helped to destroy most of the Italian creditors and their banks – the most famous is the collapse of the Bardi and Peruzzi in 1346. French kings similarly lured the Sienese bankers into huge loans and eventual ruined them through default. Cities were islands of wealth and much of medieval history consists of efforts by rulers to devise new ways to acquire some of this urban wealth. Burghers were often eager to pay for new privileges but resented serving as cash cows for seemingly endless wars. Where the cities were independent, the ruling classes had the challenge of figuring out how to tax themselves, while not ruining local prosperity.

War drove many economic developments. Fiscal-military states of all vari-eties came into being to pay for wars increasingly fought by mercenaries of one type or another. Every polity had tax policies largely devised to pay for wars. The strategies concerning what taxes to impose reveal the workings of the political economy even when we must tease them out of tax codes or customs duty schedules. One kingdom's experience is instructive. Louis IX of France took the cross in 1244 and for the next four years assembled money and men for a projected invasion of Egypt, which came to disaster in the Nile delta at Mansourah in 1250. The king, after his costly ransom, went to what remained of Latin Syria and remained there till 1253, spending additional sums in fortifying ports. Louis's own expenses for the crusade have been credibly estimated at 1.5 million livres, including the 208,750 livres paid in cash for ransoming the king and his closest followers. The monarchy's regular annual income amounted to about 250,000 livres, and most of this went for ordinary domestic expenses, including his modest bureaucracy that collected the taxes.

In order to wage war, Louis was looking for about six years' income. The most important point is that he found this money, in France, which was able to afford the expedition. Such vast sums spent on failure and lost or consumed overseas naturally raise the question of opportunity costs – what might France have done with these resources if they had not been spent on holy war? For Louis, there was no more important goal for a good king of France than to recover the Holy Land, so he did not ask this question and instead went to war.

Louis demanded, and the pope agreed, that the Church should contribute what eventually amounted to a tenth of its income for four years. The Church was by far the largest collective landowner in his kingdom and received its own tithes and charitable donations. The Church, as a set of institutions with good records and accounts, eventually contributed an estimated 950,000 livres to the enterprise, covering nearly two-thirds of the king's expenses. Louis's bureaucracy went to work and increased regular tax income. Jews were particularly hard-pressed – money lenders were expropriated and expelled. The monarchy also reduced ordinary expenses by limiting building projects and cutting some wages. Towns were asked to make special gifts for the crusade above regular taxes, and it seems that they contributed about another 274,000 livres. The mid-thirteenth-century economy was still the age of ready cash, so these sums reflect cash expenses made from the kingdom's stock of silver coinage. A lot of this coin left France for good – whether it enriched the markets of Cyprus where Louis established his forward base, or the Mamluk emirs of Egypt who obtained his ransom in 1250. Louis remained solvent until 1253, when a government crisis back in France forced him to return home and begin to borrow from Italian bankers to cover his immediate expenses. The royal need for revenues in the long run benefited peasants who found the kings' needs an ideal opportunity for purchasing their personal liberties. Townspeople paid customs and tallages and made ostensibly voluntary gifts to fund wars, which often gave local markets and manufactures a burst of business. In the case of a crusade, much of the king's wealth and the large additional sums spent by his followers ended up overseas. The lessons of political economy suggested that the drain on the kingdom was admittedly affordable but still costly in terms of what else might have been done with the money.

Generalizations about political economy are perilous so let us look closely at one commune, Genoa, which originated in 1099 as a result of the city's vast mobilization to send a fleet east to participate in the First Crusade. From the beginning, warfare required a political structure capable of fostering the consent and policies needed to raise money, men, and ships. The rules for the consuls of the commune in 1143 reveal the range of taxes the city employed. Genoa imposed a head tax on foreign merchants (not their own) and a 0.5 percent tax on their sales. Favored Genoese merchants paid very low customs duties – the 0.3 percent on pepper was typical. The merchants who ran the commune understood that customs duties distorted trade and if too high would drive trade elsewhere and benefit rivals, such as Pisa. The commune had a tax on land and commerce called a *collecta* that was only for the crisis of war. A gabelle on salt was a lucrative tax – really a state monopoly. Genoa needed to import nearly all of its salt. It was an easy commodity to tax, and people needed salt to live and to preserve food. Everyone understood that it was a regressive tax in the sense that all paid the same high price for salt. The commune also imposed tolls on the mountain passes in the north, and these tolls were more lucrative because Genoa remained upper Lombardy's easy access to Mediterranean trade and so this trade could sustain modest taxes. When necessary, Genoa could borrow money from merchants in other cities, such as Piacenza and Rome. Finally, the city had in 1138 received the right from the German emperor to coin its own money, and so it had the ability to take profits from the mint – but these needed to be carefully weighed against the undoubted benefit of a sound local currency.

Wars with Pisa in the 1160s made a *collecta* necessary, and the tax was set annually according to the need for money – it was often set at 6d. per lira on imports and 12d. on exports – the higher figure amounted to a 5 percent tax, not an unreasonable price to pay for what was, in effect, a trade war with a hated rival. By the early thirteenth century, the *collecta* had to be imposed to redeem regular taxes that had been sold far in advance to pay for immediate military necessities. At one point, the salt tax was already pledged for the next twenty-nine years. Mortgaging future revenues in times of crisis was wise policy in the face of crushing needs for immediate cash. The problem was that Genoa could not control the timing of these crises. In 1214 the commune, under a *podesta* (a professional manager) since 1190, tried to stop selling future taxes but this proved hard to do – in 1234 a costly fleet sent to aid the Muslim sultan of Ceuta in North Africa resulted in the salt tax being sold for another ten years.

In 1257 during a great war against Pisa and Venice, largely fought over trading rights in the eastern Mediterranean, Guglielmo Boccanegra became captain of the people and faced financial disaster and naval catastrophe. So much future income had been sold that the government was paralyzed, but it could not afford to expropriate the creditors – who were its leading citizens and merchants. Instead, Boccanegra's government seized all revenues from the creditors, but in a remarkable innovation it divided all the outstanding public debt into shares of 100 lire that were to pay 8 lire a year. This astute policy recognized that the debt could never be redeemed, so the creditors were promised a reasonable rate of return (8%) on their capital for ever. Just as important was the immediate rise of a market for these shares, which were allowed to be sold, bequeathed, or even donated to charity. So the creditors had a column in a great book recording the debt that listed their shares and, in theory, a steady, fixed income. Again, everyone understood, especially Boccanegra who spoke for the middling people of Genoa, that average people paid many of the taxes, especially the gabelles that funded the interest payments mainly collected by the rich.

Disputes about debt and the level of interest payments, and of course more debts for future wars, continued to divide the Genoese commune for centuries to come. At least in a commune these matters were debated and settled, which allowed for the occasional revolt. Political economy was invented in Genoa and places like it to pay for wars that the merchant elites deemed vital to their own survival, or for holy wars that the broader masses saw as furthering the prospects of their own spiritual salvation. After the revolution that installed Simone Boccanegra as Genoa's first doge in 1339, the new regime had to reconstruct its finances after mobs burned the existing tax records. Shares in the old compere fell well below par, ranging from 22 to 70 lire a share off the nominal price of 100 lire. Taxes dedicated to paying the interest on special loan funds no longer yielded sums adequate to pay the announced returns and so the market in these securities discounted them. To note one final detail, when Genoa went to war with Venice in 1350 over access to valuable Black Sea trading routes, the regime imposed a forced loan of 300,000 lire to pay 10 percent to finance the fleet to send to the eastern Mediterranean. The wealthy sacrificed capital to pay for a war that benefited their commercial interests, and secured shares that would, at least for a while, pay a high premium, to be shouldered as usual by ordinary people.

In the 1180s, Italian communes concluded a series of agreements with the Muslim rulers of the Balearic Islands. These documents are lessons in political economy as understood across the boundaries of language, creed, and ethnicity. Control of the seas and trading routes in the western Mediterranean was important to all parties. Genoese and Pisan negotiators retained Arabic documents, sometimes with an interlinear Latin translation, ratifying the truces that regulated these mixed relationships. The Muslim ruler of Majorca and its dependencies promised the Genoese, for example, that he would not attack them on land or sea, a term the Genoese reciprocated. In a revised treaty from 1188, the emir also exempted the Genoese from all customs duties in his state, the right to have a merchant quarter (fondaco) including permission to use a local bathhouse and oven one day a week. In turn, the Genoese granted the Muslims no trade benefits in their territories but promised not to aid any effort to conquer the emir's lands. The lesson of political economy here was that the prospect of violence occasionally drove enemies to make agreements it was in the interests of both to keep. The more powerful party, in this case Genoa, was able to extract trading privileges for its merchants that would over time make the commune more wealthy and powerful. Muslim emirs in turn made sure that Pisa and Genoa would not help Barcelona and the kingdom of Aragon to conquer the Balearic islands – a feat that they would accomplish in the next century.

Ideas about political economy appear in every negotiated or deliberated treaty, customs duty, excise tax, or general call for revenue from the people or privileged bodies, such as guilds or the Church. Warfare had many causes, but was sometimes a contest for resources, be they material or indeed spiritual, like Jerusalem. From the point of view of monarchs or their own elites, cities appeared to be barns of money where stored wealth might be tapped in times of emergencies, however defined. Organized violence remained the principal task of government and hence the impetus behind the need for revenues, hence taxation. As the technologies of warfare improved, and better armor and ships required ever-increasing expenditures, the needs for aggressive war or self-defense preoccupied medieval people at all levels, whether they were collectors or payers of taxes. Medieval economic thought developed to guide those making decisions about political economy, the common good, and the legitimacy of the search for lawful, moral profits. Turning to this subject will permit us to take a closer look at some of the themes raised in this chapter – especially work and the profit economy in markets that still respected the calculus of salvation.

SELECT BIBLIOGRAPHY

Manlio Bellomo, *The Common Legal Past of Europe 1000–1800*. Translated by Lydia Cochrane. Washington DC, 1995.

Francesco Bonaini, *Statuti inediti della città di Pisa dal XII al XV secolo*. Florence, 1854–1870.

Galbert of Bruges, *The Murder of Charles the Good Count of Flanders*. Translated by James Bruce Ross. New York, 1967.

Steven Epstein, *Wage Labor and Guilds in Medieval Europe*. Chapel Hill, 1991.

Bronislaw Geremek, *Le salariat dans l'artisanat parisien aux XIIIe – XVe siècles*. Paris, 1968.

David Herlihy, *Opera Muliebria: Women and Work in Medieval Europe*. New York, 1990.

Rodney H. Hilton, *Peasants, Knights, and Heretics*. New York, 1976.

William Chester Jordan, *Louis IX and the Challenge of the Crusade*. Princeton, 1979.

Ira M. Lapidus, *Muslim Cities in the Later Middle Ages*. New York, 1984.

René de Lespinasse and F. Bonnardot, *Les métiers et corporations de la ville de Paris: Le Livre des Métiers d'Etienne Boileau*. Paris, 1879.

Robert S. Lopez, *The Commercial Revolution of the Middle Ages, 950–1350*. New York, 1976.

Sheilagh Ogilvie, "'Whatever Is, Is Right'? Economic Institutions in Pre-industrial Europe," *Economic History Review* 60 (2007): 649–684.

Henri Pirenne, *Les villes et les institutions urbaines*. Paris, 1939.

Bonvesin de la Ripa, *Le meraviglie di Milano*. Milan, 1997.

Richard Unger, "Thresholds of Market Integration in the Low Countries and England in the Fifteenth Century," in *Money, Markets and Trade in Late Medieval Europe*. Edited by Lawrin Armstrong, I. Elbl, and M. Elbl. Leiden, 2007.

5

ECONOMIC AND SOCIAL THOUGHT

MEDIEVAL PEOPLES LIVED IN COMMUNITIES, PARTICIPATED IN markets, and thought about these activities (and others) every day. People did not often write down their thoughts, so we can study them mostly from what they did – what economists call revealed preference. The most articulate members of society did record a great deal of practical moral advice about how society and the economy should function after God expelled humanity from Paradise. These writers, a diverse collection of theologians, lawyers, merchants, and diarists, usually considered the practical affairs of this world to be secondary to the more important issues surrounding salvation and justice. Hence, we have no medieval economists or sociologists to consult because these disciplines had not yet been invented. What we have are theological works, sermons, business manuals, canon and civil laws, commercial treaties, and many other documents that supply the raw materials from which we can reconstruct, or sometimes simply imagine, economic and social thought. Although the thinkers were primarily interested in issues they considered more important, this fact need not stop us from examining the mass of evidence we have on many important topics. In brief, most of what passed for intellectual life in the Middle Ages did not concern social and economic thought. Scholastic professors, monks, and nuns inside and outside the universities dominated official thought. Nevertheless, even these people occasionally thought about matters we recognize as social and economic.

Medieval thinkers who discussed the economy from the vantage point of religion would have agreed with the American poet and essayist Wendell Berry that humans do not make value. Everything worthwhile derives from the Great Economy, nature, and its divine laws. Judaism, Christianity, and Islam conceded that people needed food, clothing, and shelter, and the activities that satisfied these wants did create real things vital to survival. Nature was abundant, but human needs were always running up against the problem of scarcity. What the Great Economy assumed was that people could and should maximize their happiness while multiplying their numbers and somehow minimizing their consumption. This morality surrounded the world of markets and work and challenged people to live according to its precepts. Some, such as St. Francis, adopted voluntary poverty as the ideal life precisely because it reduced consumption to its starkest level. Others found happiness in consumerism.

Nevertheless, markets and family life, among other activities, compelled people to think about justice, equality, and God's commandments. Many theologians were concerned that a belief in the infallibility of markets arose from the need to justify immoral market outcomes like usury and slavery. Some ordinary people found it more convenient to believe that slavery and interest on loans resulted from natural and orderly markets rather than from human evil. The Great Economy encouraged people to beware of abstract values and their false appeals. Finally, violence at every level of society continued to shape markets and economic outcomes. Everyone understood the role of warfare and the regular violence required to maintain slavery and a subordinated peasantry. Medieval theologians, in theory, rejected violence personally while having to find ways to justify holy wars and executing stubborn heretics. In theory, markets were places where needs rather than force determined outcomes, but, in practice, this was not always the case.

The Church was a practical and wealthy institution in this world. Despite St. Francis, it would continue to be so. Theologians therefore had the burden of justifying wealth. Their teachings emphasized that people had the duty to make last wills and testaments to benefit their souls through charity and to remember their heirs by legacies. The Church was also in the "sin removal" business, as Simon Cameron has explained. This business generated a considerable income and the church hierarchy needed doctrines that justified this outcome and all the secular profits that helped the war against sin. Whether the broad theological message constituted a benevolent incentive to emerging market capitalism or an obstacle to it remains one of the most contested issues in medieval social and economic history. Surely any peace and stability that church doctrine fostered became a public good that, in turn, encouraged economic development.

As usual, we must select those matters and people whose issues and thoughts merit analysis. Concerning the economy, the world of markets, and work, thinking about property was a major problem. What in this world was private

and what was communal, what to be shared? How was property to be shared –
what were the obligations of wealth and the debts owed to the poor? These
questions assumed, of course, that outside of Eden property was not all to
be held in common or to be shared equally. Property takes many forms, but
money crystallizes value and might become an end in itself, indeed the root
of all evil. What was the proper role for money and the search for it? As we
have seen, trade and labor gave people the necessities of life and, in turn, raised
questions about fair prices and wages. Every era has its characteristic debate or
problem that preoccupies generations of thinkers and ordinary people. In the
later medieval economy, the great issue, at least in terms of the amount of ink
spilled on it, was *usury*, the lending of money at interest. Modern scholars have
rightly continued to focus on usury because its evolving definition and moral
context reveal the best and worst of medieval thought.

The great social fact to consider was the family as a moral and emotional (and
economic) unit of society. How people entered families though birth, marriage,
and adoption reveal the values people placed on human relationships. Death,
the great equalizer, altered but did not end family ties. Gender roles within the
family preoccupied medieval thinkers, mostly male and surrounded by a web
of patriarchal and paternalistic values they seldom challenged. The normative
family was Christian and European for such Western thinkers who in our period
of study began to think seriously about the divisions in the human family, the
races with unalterable characteristics. Jews and Muslims under Christian rule
preserved distinctive social values and challenged their own thinkers, as well
as those from the majority communities, to consider the proper definition and
place of minorities in this world. One of the antidotes to poverty, charity,
required an elaborated ethos to convince people to take care of the poor, who
needed to be carefully defined.

Two topics, fairness and sumptuary laws, will enable us to keep a good
balance between economic and social thought. Both approaches in abstract as
well as concrete terms concerned a search for justice. Everyone thought that
societies and markets should be fair, but they did not always agree about what
exactly made a fair outcome. The supposedly legitimate difference between
master and slave certainly raises this problem. Who had the power to define
a just outcome and make his or her decision stick? Finally, toward the end
of the Middle Ages, as prosperity increased and divisions between rich and
poor became more apparent, some societies tried to control by law how people
displayed wealth. These rules, called *sumptuary laws*, set limits on public and

private consumption sometimes down to minute details on what kind of jewelry could be worn in public and how much money could be spent on dowries and wedding banquets. The impulse to control the use of wealth (as opposed to the means of acquiring it) reveals a lot about social values. Sumptuary legislation forced medieval people to synthesize their own views on how social values and economic realities intersected on an issue they thought vital, and today is hard to remember.

ECONOMIC THOUGHT

Medieval thinkers inherited from ancient Christianity and Judaism a strong and apparently unalterable rule that the lending of money at interest was morally wrong – a sin. The Quran and the sayings of Muhammad strongly deprecated the taking of interest on a loan. Usury violated the moral values of a neighborly agricultural economy, tempted people into sin by allowing them to take advantage of the needs of brethren, and even violated God's time by corrupting it into a period for a loan that rewarded a creditor who did not work for this profit but simply waited for it. Jesus said, "Borrow and lend freely, hoping for nothing in return" (Luke 6:35) – what could be more clear than that? In the early Middle Ages usury meant avarice – a lack of charity. An emerging profit economy required tighter definitions. The Second Lateran Council of 1139 flatly prohibited usury, soon enough defined by the canonist Gratian as anything taken beyond the principal. Such a gain was stealing and a sin and should be returned. At the end of the century, Pope Urban III again prohibited any gain from a loan as a sin against justice. The injustice clearly applied to those who paid usury as well as those who took it. Figure 5.1 shows a virtuous cycle of production, in which work and resources result in growth through investment and sustainable consumption – all without interest. Figure 5.2 indicates how money lent for gain created a usurious cycle in which money increased without work by the lender. Lending freely was a social and moral good but seemed to relieve distress and not encourage growth.

Across religious lines these issues became more complicated – it was still wrong to demand usury from a coreligionist. Usury paid by a Christian debtor to a Jewish creditor was not immoral from the Jewish perspective. The Church had a hard time convincing Christians who were desperate for credit, and not receiving any free loans or gifts from their fellow Christians, that paying interest to a Jew or a Muslim was a sin. A Christian taking interest from a

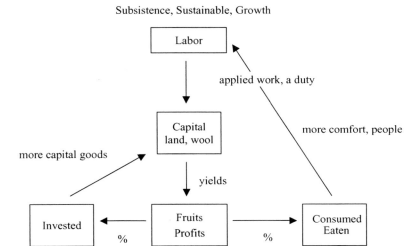

Subsistence, Sustainable, Growth

Figure 5.1. Virtuous Cycle.

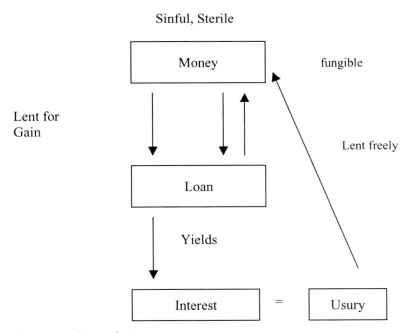

Sinful, Sterile

Figure 5.2. Usury Cycle.

Jewish debtor was also wrong and hard to explain away. Because societies increasingly restricted economic opportunities for Jews, it is not clear where the Jews obtained capital necessary for extending credit. Centuries of careful savings precariously accumulated in the hands of a religious minority with few opportunities for investment. In practice, the surviving contracts from the twelfth century reveal in Christian society sophisticated credit mechanisms and loans. These contracts evaded obvious taking of interest and surrounded these activities in the fictions of partnership and ostensibly free loans for sums plainly higher than the actual amounts transferred, hence concealing the real charge. Outside of this developing market economy was a group of urban and rural people needing immediate cash for survival. Some nobles lived beyond their means, monasteries and bishops engaged in vast building projects, and others also needed money not for investment but to sustain consumption. Increasingly, some of these people turned to Jews for loans because the taint of usury did not seem to apply in these cases. Also, the Jews would loan money to people, or accept items in pawn as security, that the regular credit methods regarded as too risky. Of course, such loans had high rates of interest and made the lenders unpopular.

Western canon lawyers and theologians after Gratian in the later twelfth and thirteenth centuries continued to think about usury. In the Byzantine tradition, the empire permitted the lending of money at interest and sometimes laws regulated the rate of interest. Roman legal traditions had condemned enormous damages to borrowers – usually 50 percent, but the law had assumed the existence of credit and interest. Common legal practices and ancient traditions in the eastern Mediterranean respected the commercial life and assumed that markets could be moral places where the pursuit of wealth, but not for its own sake, could be honorable. Greek theological objections to usury emphasized that members of the clergy should not lend money at interest (or presumably borrow). Higher prices for sales on credit seemed another way to disguise interest and were deemed usurious – and were explicitly condemned in Muslim thought. Gain for gain, in other words a mutually beneficial arrangement, was morally acceptable. Hence, renting a property or selling one's labor for a salary was not troubling because both parties gained something with the cash involved simply lubricating the deal. Money itself, basically coined silver, struck theologians dimly aware of Aristotle as sterile, that is, it should not reproduce itself. Again, in the eastern Mediterranean, Greek and Muslim writers remained aware of ancient economics and definitions of money.

William of Auxerre's *Summa* (1210–1220) made the clear connection that usury was also a sin against natural law because it sold time. Because money was sterile and the usurer did not work for his profit, gain might only result for the time between the original loan and the larger repayment. Albert the Great (c. 1200–1280) buttressed these arguments by stressing that usury took advantage of the needs of a neighbor and was without risk, hence the divine prohibition of it. Sinful in both natural and divine law and banned by popes, usury and those who practiced it were damned in western Christendom. Muslim theologians like al-Ghazali (1058–1111) remained suspicious of what they saw as the paganistic Aristotelianism that sometimes colored the thought of great philosophers, such as Ibn Sina (Avicenna, 980–1033). Al-Ghazali approached the economy from the perspective of *maslahah*, the common good and welfare of the believers. He understood markets, trade, supply and demand as all promoting wealth and hence fostering Muslim values. Self-sufficiency, defined as more than subsistence, provided the wealth necessary to maintain one's family and to be charitable. This Muslim conception of ethical markets remained hostile to usury and encouraged partnerships among merchants, even across religious barriers. Byzantine thinkers also knew that the ancient ideals of autarchy and self-sufficiency were illusions. Embedded in all of this thought remains an awareness of the microregions of the Mediterranean and the necessity of exchange in order for people to survive in ungenerous and unforgiving climates. Among Byzantine and Muslim peoples who thought about such matters, unclean money was what was taken from the poor under whatever circumstances – including but not limited to usury.

Thomas Aquinas (c. 1225–1274), the great Dominican theologian, incorporated the best of scholastic thought and the newest Aristotelian texts into his authoritative teachings on a wide variety of topics, including usury. Muslim philosophical and theological works were just recently becoming available and they had already speculated on the connections between Aristotle's ideas and the demands of a pure life according to God's will. Thomas was a moralist aware of these traditions and preoccupied with salvation, not an economist pondering market mechanisms. Aquinas thought deeply about money more as something potentially wicked rather than as a neutral means of exchange. Not everything he believed commanded immediate universal agreement, but his thought represents the general university consensus. According to Aquinas money could not be sold, therefore the laws of supply and demand did not apply to it. (Remember that he is thinking primarily about coined silver.) Money did not deteriorate in its use. Aquinas was not thinking about ordinary wear on coins but the abstract principal that the use and value of the coin remained the same as it changed hands. Hence, money was not a commodity nor did it deteriorate in use – it was fixed in value and not a fungible like wine, which if you loaned to a thirsty person who drank it, was gone. This idea of a fungible, derived from Roman law, divided material things into consumables and things that might be repeatedly used and depreciate naturally over time, like a house. As Diana Wood has clearly explained, if one borrowed a loaf of bread from a neighbor, no one expected the borrower to return the same loaf (now eaten): a similar loaf would suffice. Now the loan of money was the same for the borrower who simply passed the coins that he or she now owned to another hand to satisfy some need and could not return them, so the same amount was enough to clear the debt. To demand more was the sin of usury, defined as robbery because money was barren.

Aquinas lived during the 1250s when gold coinage reappeared in Western Europe, first in Genoa and Florence but soon in the northern kingdoms as well. He understood the complex relationships in a bimetallic money system and increasingly sophisticated accounting procedures that utilized moneys of account – ghost sums existing in a meaningful way only on paper in a ledger. His system of thought required the belief that the use and value of money were the same – and ancient philosophy ratified the concepts. The intention to profit on the sale of a horse was morally legitimate but planning to profit from advancing a loan was a sin. Even leasing a horse was acceptable because the exact animal was returned (not a fungible), but its use in the interval made a fee morally unobjectionable. Of course, someone might charitably lend an unused horse for free to a desperate rider, but in ordinary life all sorts of things were properly rented or leased. The owner of an enslaved wet-nurse might lease her to another family who needed the breast milk, and then return the slave to the owner and rightly pay for the milk.

Older ideas like the legitimacy of taking usury from an enemy of one's faith remained prevalent. An area of ambiguity remained unresolved – was it legitimate to take interest for a delinquent loan or in the case where the thing returned was damaged, like a lame horse? From the 1250s on, new ideas entered the debate. A loss occurring to the lender justified a fee for this damage, as in the case of the lame horse or even the late loan. The concept of an opportunity cost also appeared as some theologians wondered whether the cessation of profit to the lender during the period of the loan (possible gains from other activities) justified interest. Possible profits the borrower might make from the

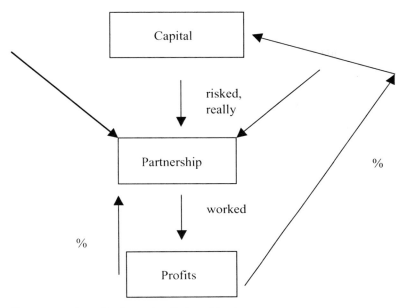

Figure 5.3. Licit Profits within Rules of Justice.

loan entitled the lender to a share in Byzantine thought by the twelfth century. For this reason, Western and Muslim theologians preferred that such people become partners jointly sharing risk rather than be borrower and lender. Profits from a partnership were legitimate because of the risks involved, and this rule extended to family banks in the business of extending credit. Figure 5.3 shows how partnerships earned legitimate profits, some profits were consumed and the rest were plowed back into the business.

By the fourteenth century, considerable ambiguity and hypocrisy surrounded the moral issue of usury. In the West, "usurer" was an epithet to hurl at unpopular individuals and ethnic or religious groups. Economic and political crisis in the eastern Mediterranean prompted Byzantine theologians to concur with their Western colleagues and rigorously condemn usury. The profit economy everywhere thrived on credit and interest, and secular governments and indeed church officials at all levels needed to borrow money and expected to pay for the privilege. Most theologians approved of the paying of interest for shares in a public debt, but some doubted the moral propriety of profiting from these arrangements, which were certainly risky to the investors. If the interest on a loan looked like a gift, few questioned its propriety. Many merchants were troubled by some of their activities and returned in their last wills some usurious gains or donated money to charities, thereby hoping to cleanse the money as well as their souls. Sometimes the theologians questioned such morally tainted wealth but in general the Church accepted these donations. Some Christians increasingly viewed Jews who took usury as being engaged in an activity so morally repulsive that the government should ban it and expel the practitioners.

Aquinas's contemporaries and the following generation of scholastic thinkers put together a medieval synthesis about the economy. Although not every thinker agreed with every subtle argument, the general outlines commanded widespread approval. Basing their work on the commandment not to steal, theologians defended the right to private property. An absolute commitment to the sanctity of private property also remained central in Jewish and Muslim teachings. Admittedly, there was no private property in Eden, but after the fall in a world of scarcity, such necessary evils (like sex) were indispensable to human survival. Merchant life too increasingly received a vigorous defense. Traders solved the problems of abundance and scarcity, and their labors benefited the common good. Uncertainty always troubled markets as wars, natural disasters, and disease disrupted the most prudent planning. Risks could be calculated in a rough way and were worth taking as fair bargains. Without these risk takers society would be poorer, hence there would be less to spend on charity, and the poor would starve. Hence, the early medieval opinion that a merchant could not be saved was quietly shelved. Scholars still vigorously condemned usury as a sin against justice. Christian merchants seldom fell into the category of manifest usurers.

Ibn Taimiyah (1263–1328) was an iconoclastic reformer and theologian who eventually died in a Mamluk prison. He wrote a book on public duties in Islam and tried to define how proper religious practices, drawn from the *shariyah* (common Muslim law), affected the economy. The relevant duty here was *hisbah*, the obligation to promote social or common good. An official known as the *muhtasib*, common throughout Muslim societies, was supposed to supervise markets, morals, and even religious practices like Friday prayers. He was to oversee proper weights and measures, suppress fraud, arbitrate disputes, provide services to the markets, and guarantee fairness there by enforcing Muslim law. From the beginning of our period of study Byzantine officials, often known as eparchs, had similar jobs and the posts were also common throughout Western cities. The distinctive feature of Muslim practices as envisioned by Ibn Taimiyah is the way that the *shariyah* provided a complete moral context for the economy and simply needed to be enforced. So the fundamental facts remained that people had a right to private property, that usury was immoral, and that fairness should prevail. All peoples had the right to benefit from this moral context and those peoples of the book had the privilege to trade, to make a living, and often to settle disputes internal to their communities according to their traditions. Muslims and Jews seldom enjoyed these economic rights for long in Christian lands.

The voluntary poverty of the Franciscan and Dominican friars was a serious challenge to the ethics of a market economy sanctioning profit and wealth. St. Bonaventure (c. 1217–1274), a distinguished theologian and eventually head of the Franciscans, concluded that private property had been necessary after the Fall of Adam and Eve to prevent strife. Without clear title to things, people would inevitably resort to violence to satisfy their wants. Yet, the Franciscans believed that it was better for them to have no property. They were becoming divided about whether their order should be absolutely poor or allow the pope or some authority to hold the property their piety would inevitably attract from donors. This idea that wealth was somehow tainted could disturb those who spent their lives seeking it. For Albert the Great (c. 1200–1280), the great German theologian and Dominican, private property did indeed help keep the peace. But he added to the defenses of private property the idea that it was efficient, that the responsibility and concern for lands and goods guaranteed a measure of fairness and smooth exchange, efficiency. Scholastic thinkers were increasingly aware of Aristotle and his ideas on *economia*, household management at first but soon enough a broader conception of a society as a collection of households. Aristotle helped these theologians articulate something they already knew – that humans were social beings. People satisfying their mutual needs without fraud or violence were normal activities, sanctioned by natural as well as divine law. Efficiency was an economic value, but the idea of a moral economy attracted theologians whose primary interest remained sin. Sufficiency was necessary for all, and efficiency should help guarantee that fair outcome for all.

Henry of Ghent (1217–1293), a professor of theology at Paris, emphasized the role of justice in exchanges and had a good sense of market theory. He also understood, as did many contemporary governmental officials and merchants, the difference between the nominal (official) and intrinsic (price of its metal) value of money. The spread between these two values (like the profit margin in a bill of exchange) became a means by which authorities and employers could take money that did not strictly belong to them, another species of theft. As other theologians stressed, a broader conception of the market affected the arguments Richard of Middleton (c. 1249–1302) made in favor of free trade between regions, hence across national and communal frontiers. The Church could be expected to define the common good as Christendom, and if the activities of merchants were praiseworthy, they did not stop at borders. Finally, Peter Olivi, a Spiritual Franciscan later condemned for heresy (on matters not relevant here) wrote a number of works on markets and usury. San Bernardino of Siena in the fifteenth century mined these and other works and popularized (without credit) some of Olivi's insights. As examples of how subtle late medieval theological observations about markets might be, two details merit notice. Olivi understood markets and saw that prices were a signal to suppliers when there was money to be made. This idea is very close to later notions of an invisible hand of collective self-interest regulating supply and demand. Olivi also saw that capital could be made profitable by industry, the application of effort, and intelligence. Hence, he saw wealth, or capital, as profit in waiting (in our words) along with labor one of the two factors of production.

One later theologian, Antoninus, archbishop of Florence (1389–1459), began life as a poor boy and advanced by merit as a Dominican theologian and pastor, revered in his hometown and later canonized. He knew Florence well, and as we will see, we can know even more about the social and economic life of these Florentines, the best documented in Europe. Antoninus had to rely not on tax records but his own insights for understanding realities of economic and family life in Florence. He knew his field and flock well and built on their great theological and practical traditions, writing his own Summa. Antoninus defended a moderate and just profit as morally legitimate. People needed an income to sustain their families and aid the poor. Yet, the Bible records that the first merchants were Ishmaelites, and Antoninus goes out of his way to note that Muhammad was first a merchant. Merchants trading with Muslims struck Antoninus as enemies of Christians, though he knew well that plenty of Florentines and others were in this business. A long line of popes had excommunicated and punished such merchants, and Antoninus also knew the great tradition from John Chrysostom to Aquinas denigrating the mercantile life. Although this pious archbishop was a friend to capitalist and worker, he also lived during a period of great Ottoman triumphs in the Eastern Mediterranean, and he was deeply hostile to Christian trade that strengthened Muslim states.

Usury prohibitions controlled the supply and terms of credit as well as complicated the relationships between Christians and other creeds. Once the debate moved beyond any payment of interest to a question of what constituted a fair return to the lender for the risks incurred, usury came to mean a rate of interest people simply thought was too high, one that violated justice. Because for most of the period under review Europe's money supply consisted mainly of ready cash and only at the end in a few paper instruments like shares or bills of exchange, this money supply was relatively fixed according to supplies of gold and silver. States might affect the money supply by debasing the metallic content of the currency – but bad money did indeed drive out good and prices soon rose to reflect the changed realities. Borrowers always favored low rates of interest and officials in government and the Church may have recognized at some level that low rates of interest could encourage demand and keep the economy prosperous – they may have been proto-Keynesians.

JUST PRICES

Because thinkers, lawyers, buyers, and sellers recognized justice as the standard for economic dealings, they were drawn to considering how a number of coins, a price, could be fairly attached to a thing. Special types of prices always concerned people. A slave as valuable property raised issues ordinary commodities did not. The price of labor, a wage, was also different than the cost of eggs. In both cases, the slave and the worker were according to Aristotle's talking tools, but they also might shape the bargaining surrounding their price or wage. Slavery and wage labor also raised moral questions about prices that engaged theologians. Theorists and merchants knew that bargaining involved deception because people asked for more than they would actually take while others offered less than they were prepared to pay. Bargaining is a search for information about prices and costs time, but its deceptive aspects worried theologians and others. Jewish, Christian, and Muslim theologians concluded that justice resulted from the decisions in marketplaces provided that buyers and sellers operated in good faith without fraud. As Ibn Taimiyah defined it, a just price was the market price in a moral context. Beyond individual consciences, what people or institutions would guarantee fair markets – unless they somehow regulate themselves for the best outcomes? Obviously, the state or commune could appoint market officials to oversee the markets, but who could rein in the kings or emirs when they manipulated the currency or rigged the terms of trade? Preoccupied with concerns about justice, the theologians also applied a "one-half rule" to fair wages and prices – so long as bargaining produced a price within 50 percent, one way or the other of the usual market price, no one was deceived. This legacy from Roman law joined another tradition, certainly practiced at times by Byzantine emperors and other rulers East and West, that the ruler could set prices by edict. Legal and religious traditions sanctioned free markets and bargaining, but the prince could make law or prices out of his own mouth.

In the early fifteenth century, the Greek writer George Gemistos Plethon closely observed the economy of southern Greece and conceived plans on how to fight the Ottoman Turks and restore the prosperity of this area. He was the outstanding economic theorist of his era – a nice parallel to Leon Battista Alberti, considered below as a social commentator. He understood what we call "political economy" but clung to the idea of the autarchy of the state, an idea traced back to Plato. His conception of the state, sustained by tariffs and sumptuary laws, seemed to favor barter for imported necessities like weapons, but even that is a trade policy. Plethon recognized three factors of production – labor, capital, and the security to be provided by the state – he means the military to fight the Turks. His theory of taxation assumed that after putting aside seed and animals to maintain flocks, all income should be divided into three parts – one part to reward labor – the peasants exempt from military service; one part to capital as rent – assuming peasants did not own land (if they did they kept two parts); one part to the emperor for the army – whose members were tax exempt. Taxes were to be paid directly in-kind to the military on the basis of specific peasants assigned to their support – this was a common strategy for supporting contemporary Turkish and other military establishments. This is a poor, rural economy under duress, stripped down to its abstract basis of agriculture and self-defense. Plethon conceived a policy to foster survival.

Bernardino of Siena (1380–1444) was a theologian, archbishop, and, above all, a noted preacher whose sermons distilled for lay audiences church teachings on many subjects. Sermons are a good source for insights on economic history because their points intersect exactly on those issues that troubled, or were supposed to concern, the laity. The sermon was not an economics lecture; it was a call to a better life. A preacher like Bernardino, however, took up practical concerns of ordinary people and tried to extract from the scholastic tradition and in his case Olivi's suspicious texts something relevant to daily problems. For example, Bernardino preached that the best price should be justified and limited, and hence the best price is fixed. But that conclusion begged the question because someone had to fix the price, based on conjecture and public opinion. People had different opinions of the just price, and Bernardino put forward a nice example for his mercantile audiences on Florence and Siena. He posed three estimates for the value of ten pieces of cloth – a pious price at 50 ducats, a sensible one at 50½, and a stiff price of 51 ducats (all to the buyer). All these prices were just and well within the one-half rule, but clearly 25 or 75 ducats would be out of bounds.

Prices varied in the marketplace according to law, custom, and discretion. Bernardino had a habit of noting possible objections to his views, perhaps faint echoes of lay opinions he heard in the confessional or on the streets. Someone might say, "I can sell my things for what I want and no one can compel me to do otherwise" – let the market prevail. Bernardino said this view violated justice. A merchant might then say that everyone wanted to buy cheap and sell dear, so prices inevitably rested in part on injustice and deception. Bernardino knew this and mentioned the 50 percent rule as the zone for licit bargaining, what amounted to tolerable deception about how much one was really prepared to offer or to take. Bernardino knew that human frailties like ignorance, lack of skill, dire wants, and insanity either interfered with or limited perfect bargaining. Not for Bernardino was the standard economist's "assume perfect competition" – even though it would have meant an end to all bargaining. Bernardino said in effect that only happened in Paradise where material things no longer mattered. In this imperfect world, scarcity normally prevailed, and only an appeal to justice could limit avarice and the role of power in the marketplace. In a final timely point, Bernardino returned to the issue of value and asked a telling question – what is the value of a medicine that saves one's life? He responded that it should be priceless but argued in subtle terms therefore for a fixed price that did not take advantage of a desperate person's needs and hence violate charity. This is how theologians thought about the economy.

The saintly Antoninus addressed in his *Summa* the special price of labor. Theologians were naturally drawn to the Bible where Jesus said "For the laborer is worthy of his meat" (Matthew 10:10) or "For the laborer is worthy of his hire" (Luke 10:7). Antoninus drew on over a millennium of biblical exegesis and canon law based on these lessons as well as the famous parable of the vineyard owner, which also involved defining fair payment to workers arriving first and last. He concluded that wages existed to provide for oneself and family according to one's station in life. Hierarchy and subordination remained facts of life. Yet, Antoninus favored a subsistence wage because then people could live virtuously (and efficiently) in a moral economy. If a weaver desperately took less money for his work than people usually made because he was poor and needed to support his family, Antoninus thought the employer should pay the usual or subsistence wage because the laborer is worthy of his hire by right of justice (and/or productivity?). Antoninus has opened the door to defining a subsistence wage (already viewed by some Muslim theologians as not enough for a pious and charitable life) not just for an individual but for supporting a family. In our terms, he was stressing the male head-of-household wage as subsistence and did not consider a broader family wage, including anything the wife and the children may have earned. Employers had another point of view and Antoninus thought about the legitimate claims they had. The guild system in Florence had no place for self-employed weavers, and Antoninus knew this. In discussing the carpenters, where masters worked too, he thought that the rules for profit in their trade should be the quantity of labor (or what they owed the workers), the effort of the work (industry and skill), and the custom of the country, another way of talking about the usual market price. Employers were not supposed to take advantage of their employees by holding back wages or paying in debased coin, but they too were entitled to a just profit.

Economic thought from Christian, Jewish, and Muslim perspectives concerned the functions of material wealth in this world. The right to private property was the bedrock on which all other assumptions about wealth rested. Every ethical system, be it the *shariyah* or scholastic theology, encouraged benevolence. Economic liberty in the marketplace created the paradox of inequality with the rich required to aid the poor through charity. The markets provided economic incentives driven by the basics of supply and demand in land, labor, and capital. Old ideas about autarchy and the corrupting influences trade with suspicious foreigners yielded to a practical world in which merchants brought the benefits of trade to consumers. The rise of wage labor granted a bargaining power in markets provided that no one intended to deceive. Bargaining implied free consent but Muslim, Jewish, and Christian practices continued to condone a trade in slaves and admitted other compulsions into the economy. Inequalities and troubles compelled some borrowers to seek credit. Ethical systems remained suspicious of any effort to take advantage of the needs of others through taking interest on a loan. This precept, like a rock in a stream, diverted a need for credit into other directions. Sometimes the Byzantines set a maximum rate of interest, or a despised minority group was pushed into the pawnbroking business. Coreligionists practiced partnerships and reluctantly did business with those not sharing a common creed. Risks, damages, opportunity costs, and other concepts carved a proper place for public and private credit markets to function.

Amid these economic ideas, merchants and bureaucrats devised forms of contract, trade agreements, tariff rates, and tax policies that embody their own practical thinking about how the economy might work. For example, in 1371 the rich Genoese merchant Francesco Vivaldi for patriotic and charitable reasons gave the commune 9,000 lire in shares of the public debt – the interest on which was to serve forever as a sinking fund to buy up more shares into the distant future. By 1454, this original gift's income had purchased shares worth more than 900,000 lire. Some lawyers and theologians might quibble about the paying of interest on the public debt, but in fact in Genoa even religious institutions owned such shares. The rich were supposed to be charitable, and what better way to help one's city than to relieve its debts and hold forth the prospect of eventually reducing taxes? Vivaldi understood political economy, the effects of compound interest rates over time, and the concept of the public good. By 1467 his legacy completely extinguished the targeted funded debt, and a grateful city put up a statue to his memory.

SOCIAL THOUGHT

Social thought comprises a vast set of writings and opinions. Once again the theologians and lawyers dominate because they were more likely to record their views and encourage imposing them on others. Ideas about what society was, who was a legitimate member, and how people enter and leave societies preoccupied people who never expressed their views except in the ubiquitous last will, a legal act by which Christians, Muslims, and Jews attempted to shape social life beyond the grave. Rules about inheritance and wills reveal deep beliefs about the family and how to maintain it – the best place to begin an analysis of social thought and how it changed during our period.

Demography supplies the raw facts about births, marriages, and population increases. Social thought is what medieval people believed the activities behind these numbers meant. The thoughts of ordinary people are so hard to find. By the twelfth century in Western Europe, theologians had succeeded in establishing that consent made a marriage. Abduction, often thinly disguised rape, and arranged marriages were by no means ended. Around 1140, the canonist Gratian compiled in Bologna a book that harmonized and standardized papal and theological teaching on many issues, including marriage. This work, commented on and extended across Europe, serves as a baseline for examining subsequent developments concerning the family. As long as a man and woman expressed their desire in verbs of the present tense ("I do") to be married, church and society recognized these unions as valid. Marriage need not occur in a church before a priest nor even have any witnesses – these would come in handy later if anyone raised questions about the legitimacy of the marriage. Marriages that occurred in churches often took place in the doorway or on the porch, and only in the thirteenth century did the exchange of rings become customary. In Christendom, the Church remained the ultimate arbiter of marriage because its rules prevailed everywhere, at least in theory. This Church taught that marriage was a sacrament – a divinely sanctioned act or ritual conferring grace on its partners. At the same time, the Church that recognized the pope as its head suppressed clerical marriage, common in the earlier Middle Ages, and required celibacy for all those in holy orders (another sacrament) as well as those in monastic life. Hence, social attitudes about marriage remained complex – it was still better to marry than to burn, but holy people did not marry. In the world of Islam, a rigorously defined clergy did not exist, and among Jews and Orthodox Christians in Eastern Europe, rabbis and Greek priests were allowed to marry.

The settled position on Christian marriage by Gratian's time required a monogamous heterosexual union that lasted until one of the spouses died or entered the religious life. Divorce or annulment were possible in theory if, for example, the husband or wife committed adultery or if the original consent was somehow defective – violating rules for example on the age of consent. Only closely defined circumstances, such as proved impotence, justified a divorce, and Gratian was part of a trend that favored keeping marriages together as a social and spiritual good. Church officials would go a long way toward excusing impediments to marriage if the unions had already happened, because they viewed marriage as a foundation of Christian society. Marriage helped the partners avoid vice, it enabled people to have legitimate children, and it provided companionship and an emotional unit. These basic assumptions carried many implications in theory that did not always resemble practice across Europe.

The Church taught that extramarital sex of any kind was a sin and a crime. Increasingly strict rules about the proper circumstances to have sex are summarized in Figure 5.4. Canonical rules about intercourse may seem bizarre or a cynical manipulation of the fear of Hell. Another way to look at

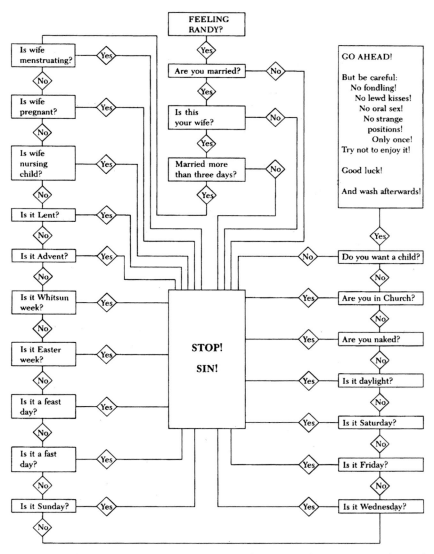

Figure 5.4. Sexual Decision-Making Process (from James Brundage, *Law, Sex, and Christian Society in Medieval Europe*, Chicago, 1987, p. 162).

the rules is to see them as an attempt, however fumbling, to subdue lust and to protect the innocent. The Church encouraged exogamy by a strong incest prohibition that Gratian defined as extending to seven degrees of kinship – out to distant cousins. Illegitimate children faced many obstacles in society so social pressures of all types favored legitimacy, especially because it established rights of inheritance. Medieval marriages were supposed to provide companionship, especially in the absence of children, in a harsh and uncertain world – and many childless couples adopted children and raised them "for the love of God" – as a charitable act.

Gratian harmonized previous legal opinions by neatly defining marriage as based on both consent and sexual consummation. A slight division existed among thinkers in the two leading universities of the West. In Gratian's Bologna, lawyers, while acknowledging the primacy of consent, continued to stress the old idea, widely held in secular society, that sex made a marriage. In Paris, lawyers stressed the importance of consent and the emotional assent to the union that consent implied. Consent raised a host of issues about mental states and a proper age that subsequent generations of lawyers continued to debate. The ability to consent to a future marriage was set at age seven while actually entering marriage usually had to wait for a later age, usually ten or twelve at a minimum. Christians were supposed to marry one another and avoid marriage and even sex with Jews, Muslims, and heretics. A church council held in Nablus in Latin Syria in 1120 ruled that a man raping his Muslim slave should be castrated and the slave become public property. This council also imposed castration on male adulterers and rhinotomy (loss of the nose) on the wife, unless the husband forgave her. Castration, mutilation, and other harsh penalties reflect the fear of sexual pollution in a frontier society and the influences of Byzantine laws that favored graphic punishments. As Christendom expanded its sphere of influence in the twelfth century, the desire to maintain spiritual and physical purity ran up against the temptations to mix with others, often by force against slaves and captives. This century witnessed fresh emphases on emotionalism, the rise of the individual, the greater prominence of Mary's cult and the infant Jesus, and courtly romance and poetry. These newly prominent ideas provided the context in which men and women thought about the purpose and nature of marriage.

In November of 1215, the largest and most important church council of the Middle Ages met at the Lateran in Rome. Many rules emanating from this Fourth Lateran Council affected society for centuries, though teachings on transubstantiation or annual confession and communion required a long time to become accepted facts of daily life. This council encouraged public marriage by instituting *banns*, which were some form of announcement in a parish church that a couple intended to marry. This news made the community aware of an impending marriage and allowed time for anyone to object to it, on grounds ranging from bigamy and feigned consent to incest. This council also made marriage easier by reducing the degrees of prohibited marriage from seven to four, thus more narrowly defining incest as sex or marriage among one's closest kin. Now counting four ties in Germanic style from partner to partner, people sharing the same grandparents were still prohibited from marrying, but not those sharing the same great-grandparents. (The Romans counted kinship up and down the family tree, so a Germanic fourth degree was eight by that reckoning.) The reasons for this change have been debated and include the Church's desire to make marriages more stable by limiting specious claims for divorce. Also, the new rules made dispensations more acceptable and brought the theory more in line with the realities and especially aristocratic marriages, where the pool of acceptable spouses was simply too small under the old rules. By the thirteenth century, the church was making divorce harder and had stamped out clerical marriage if not concubinage. In the later part of this century and the beginning of the fourteenth century, theologians consolidated and increasingly refined canon law and the line between church and civil courts. Urban societies and communes, for example, increasingly regulated public prostitution and in some places established brothels as a simple way to tax the trade. Some cities also had rules on the size of dowries and inheritance rights of wives, daughters, and sons. Cities and states followed the Church's lead and imposed increasingly severe penalties on sodomy.

The Big Death of 1348 created a great age of inheritance and marriage among the survivors. Thinking about marriage reflected a world in which Chaucer's much married Wife of Bath was a demographic example of frequent widowhood and remarriage. The records of civil and church courts everywhere become more abundant and revealing about the nature of real marriage and its problems – the gap between theory and practice. Marriage proved to be more unstable than the law supposed, many poor people lived in informal unions, concubines and lovers were common, adultery was a staple of literature, and increased literacy fed a growing appetite for pornography.

Two later medieval writers supply different views on marriage and the family. The first, Jean Gerson (1363–1429), was a famous theologian who eventually became chancellor of the University of Paris. He wrote a large number of works, often in French in order to reach the laity, was a famous preacher, and his primary interest remained the business of saving souls. Gerson was not a proponent of marriage and he urged women (especially his own sisters) and men (especially his own brothers) to remain virgins and celibate. A broadly educated man in the spirit of the Italian humanists and the early Christian Fathers, Gerson urged women to remain unmarried because childbirth was dangerous, children were lots of trouble, and husbands often proved worthless! Worrying about children led women to being preoccupied with material possessions, and this could threaten their salvation. Lust was bad enough, but marital lust was worse and fed upon itself. Gerson concluded that it was better for women and men not to marry at all. He recognized that Christendom would survive even this advice because enough Christians would still persist in raising families.

Gerson's writings suggest that he learned a great deal from listening to confession, and observing young people in the complex societies of Paris and Bruges where he lived. As a writer of tracts on education, Gerson was very interested, perhaps unhealthily so, in the sexual lives of children, especially boys. Children were supposed to be pure, even angelic, but Gerson wanted them to be watched constantly, both to prevent masturbation and same sex contacts, but also to make sure that adults would not molest them. Gerson's ideal school was a ceaseless series of lessons. Boys were not allowed to speak French; they were supposed to avoid dirty songs, pets, idle chatter, and sharing beds. They should expect to be beaten when necessary but cared for in their physical and spiritual needs. His ideal school seems a dour place where every human contact raised the prospect of sin and pollution. As a theologian in the grim years of the aftermath of the Big Death and French defeats in the Hundred Years War, Gerson still maintained a deep belief in the power of prayer, which ameliorated his gloomy opinions about human nature. He recognized a strong emotional component to family life, understood the problems women faced in a patriarchal society, and wanted to protect children from themselves and adult predators. The children he observed were in a distinctive stage of life, fraught with spiritual and physical perils, and deserving of adult sympathy and attention. Gerson knew all about Socrates and did not think the ancient Greeks provided a wholesome model for Christian education.

Leon Battista Alberti (1404–1472) was an illegitimate child in a famous Florentine family who went on to become celebrated as the ideal Renaissance man, talented as an architect, playwright, author, artist, and social commentator. Thoroughly educated in the Greek and Roman classics, he tended to ignore the long period separating his own age, Florence of the Quattrocento, from the glories of the ancient Roman world. In other words, he was about as far from being a scholastic theologian as one could get – he was a celebrated layman.

Alberti's four books on the family, written in Italian in the 1430s, discussed paternal responsibility and conjugal love, marriage, the household and how its possessions should be managed, and the external relations of the household, mainly the friendships its members had with other people in society. Alberti seldom mentioned Christianity in his work, and he drew his inspiration from classical authors, mainly Xenophon and Aristotle who had discussed the household as an economic and familial unit. Alberti was never married, and his views on parents and marriage were as distant and theoretical as the average theologian – but Alberti was more likely to rely on Plato and Cicero than Augustine or Aquinas. For example, he observed that the ancients practiced divorce even though in his own time civil law and religious authorities regarded marriage as a sacrament.

Perhaps his most interesting claim as a social thinker derives from his astute observations on the economic bases of family life. Alberti defined the family as a big household, including children, the wife, and other members, both relatives and servants, all living under a common roof. Alberti understood that the pursuit of wealth was not contemptible because people needed money to maintain their families. He was proud of the Alberti family and its activities in honest trade in the Eastern Mediterranean. His family had been rich for a long time and thus able to pass wealth on down to the family generation after generation. Not all families had been this lucky; some grew wealthy because of hard work, and others became poor from laziness and above all wasting their resources. Hence, Alberti valued household management of resources as the key to the family's survival. He may have seen this in Xenophon, but he had certainly observed this social fact in the vicissitudes of contemporary Florentine families. Fortune played an unpredictable role in these ups and downs, but wise people could use discretion and judgment to keep their spirits free and their families safe. To have enough to support one's family was honorable and meant that one was not at the beck and call of others, like a slave. Alberti was a snob with little interest in the domestic arrangements of working people or the lives of peasants, whom he despised. Alberti liked the farm as a villa but not rural people; employees needed to be managed, like wives. He identified with the classical ruling elite and those families that ran Florence.

Among the men in that noble circle and nobles across Europe, friendship was an honorable emotional bond. Companionship within marriage, as his contemporary the Venetian Francesco Barbaro (1390–1454) had observed, also resembled perfect friendship and allowed men to view their wives as partners responsible for managing the economic life of the household in the same way that the husband ran the family business. A division of labor in the family put noble women in charge of the domestic sphere and this included the important task of raising children. Barbaro believed that children benefited from the high status of the mother, so everyone should marry in his own class, or higher. At the same time Alberti saw the family as a patriarchal institution, but one with emotional and financial aspects more complicated than most theologians recognized. Gerson would have noted the complete absence of prayer from Alberti's ideal family and would have worried about its salvation – a concern not central to Alberti's thinking.

Other major themes about the later medieval Christian family include a shift in naming patterns – gradually after 1200 more and more people had family names, and the pool of first names became smaller and emphasized the names of prominent male and female saints. These trends cannot be unrelated. The rise of the cults of the Infant Jesus, Mary, and eventually St. Joseph testify to a model of family life that emphasized the innocence of childhood, the duties of mothers, and even a tardy notice of paternal care in the guise of the elderly Joseph. The important story in secular society was the gradual weakening of paternal authority everywhere. This trend had started long before 1000 and would continue as fathers no longer exercised the power of unquestioned violence and absolute control of property in the family. The recognizable nuclear family of wife and husband and their children became coterminous with the household even as some grandparents or siblings remained under the same roof. These households were emotional as well as economic units. Especially after the Big Death, when the outside world seemed harsh, hostile, and depressing, the family was a place of refuge. Yet, it also remained for some a place of sorrow, as violence, incest, and other forms of abuse showed that not all households resembled the Holy Family.

OTHER SOCIAL THOUGHTS

Thinking about pagans, Jews and Muslims remained a way for Christian society to define itself. The Lateran Council of 1215 required Jews and Muslims to wear distinctive clothing, eventually in some places badges or specifically colored head clothing (as was also the case in Muslim Egypt). In 1249, Prussians who did not agree to be baptized were to be expelled. In 1268, Louis IX of France expelled foreign usurers – Cahorsins, Lombards, and Jews – because the crown believed that these people were damaging the economic welfare of its subjects. Benjamin Z. Kedar has argued that policies of expulsion, and the social and economic thought motivating them, are distinctive medieval legacies in Europe. These corporate expulsions, a species of ethnic cleansing, also rested on claims of defending social purity, however defined. Biblical examples of expulsion, most notably the fate of Hagar, served as models for imposing a type of punishment for complex motives in which economic gain may be a secondary factor. The rise of a profit economy had consequences for Jews as they were increasingly confined to unattractive economic activities, such as pawnbroking, and served as scapegoats for a society more and more preoccupied with avarice in its own behavior and seeking to blame this minority for the ills of the new economy.

R. I. Moore has argued that in the twelfth and thirteenth centuries Christian Europe became a persecuting society toward its Jews, lepers, Muslims, and heretics. Why this happened remains intensely debated, but surely any explanation must take into account all boundary makers: the official social thinkers and rule makers, as well as everyone else. The impulse to persecute, which has remained a durable feature of European culture (and others), does not have to fit in a crude model of either a "top down" or "bottom up" phenomenon. At times opinion leaders do shape popular attitudes, and at other times, they seem to follow widespread attitudes. Increased social mobility makes top and bottom distinctions less meaningful. For minorities, old ideas about religious and ethnic purity, color symbolism, and disease may simply have been waiting for institutional mechanisms to give force to deep impulses. The rapid pace of social and economic change after the year 1000 disconcerted some people, including the very minorities who had become the targets for majority's attacks.

The policy of expelling Jews reveals how some states made laws embodying new ideas about the place of Jews in the world and imposing real hardships on the Jews expelled. The kingdom of France is the best known case. The monarchy was torn between a desire to take property from the Jews because they were a royal resource available to be pillaged and to expel the Jews partly to relieve debtors and also to curry favor by punishing a despised minority. Often the debtors found that the king had assumed their debts, and so ordinary people discovered that the absence of Jews did not improve government or their treatment. The French monarchy persisted in a weary pattern of expelling Jews and then allowing them back in: out in 1182, back in 1198; the main expulsion of 1306 when perhaps 100,000 people had to leave the kingdom, even the aged, the sick, and the lepers. Allowed to return in 1315 after paying a big fine for the privilege, a small number of Jews remained in fourteenth-century France until the final expulsion happened in 1395. These Jews endured some massacres in 1320 and in the aftermath of the Big Death. England expelled its Jews in 1293 and most famously the kingdoms of Aragon and Castile in 1492. These events merit notice as examples of social thought because they reflect a growing sense in Western Christian society that Jews polluted their world by their mere presence, economic activities, or possible sexual contacts with the majority population. Jews retained protected status (long with Christians) in Muslim states and some made their way east into German and Slavic lands or, by the end of this period their safest haven, into the Ottoman Empire.

Jews who converted were not expelled because the Church taught that they had become full members of the community and should be accepted as such. Nonetheless, popular opinion held in some places that there were things about the Jews that could not be changed by baptism, that there was something physically unalterable about them. This view brings up the complex issues surrounding a European sense of identity or ethnicity. Beginning in the thirteenth century, Europeans became more aware of New Worlds surrounding them – an icy Arctic north filled with unfamiliar peoples like Lapps; a sub-Saharan Africa with peoples whose skins were called black and evoked a host of negative associations among Europeans. To the East, contacts with the Mongol state, beginning in Poland and Hungary in the 1220s, opened European eyes to complex and ancient societies in East Asia. Within European society, ethnic tensions had resulted in harsh stereotypes between near neighbors, such as the Germans and Poles, or the English and Scots, separated by language and culture if not creed. Big barriers that distinguished the blacks and whites or the Tartars and the Slavs challenged people, especially in the border regions, to think deeply about their sense of identity.

In Europe, Christendom became synonymous with those peoples who looked to Rome and increasingly justified harsh treatment of Greeks, Serbs, and others in the East who appeared as Others (not Roman Christians). A renewed slave trade in the thirteenth-century Mediterranean thrived on making distinctions that justified enslaving people who looked different or worshipped the wrong way. A hierarchy of color developed in the Mediterranean lands that privileged an intermediate skin tone called white and deprecated darker peoples as timid, melancholic, and worthy to be slaves. The old science of physiognomy, a venerable way of reading temperaments from aspects of physical appearance down to the smallest details of the eyes, buttressed European opinions that their colors and appearances were the best.

Probably the most ethnically complex part of Europe remained the Mediterranean. By the fifteenth century, thousands of sub-Saharan Africans were being imported into Portugal as agricultural laborers, and the newly formed kingdom of Spain contained peoples of every skin color. Even where no Africans existed, as in Germany, Poland, or Scandinavia, images of Africans or darker peoples occurred in art (one of the Three Magi or Kings) to school people in the lessons of what can only be called racism. These racist assumptions rested on a sophisticated body of thought that taught that there were divisions among humanity deriving from unalterable traits. These signs, like skin color, signaled qualities about people useful to potential mates and owners. Monogenesis theories of human origins, which the Church taught, insisted that all people descended from the common parents, Adam and Eve. In practice, most people in Europe believed that the human family consisted of unequal races and that their inferiors merited expulsion, enslavement, or worse.

Thinking about numbers also changed after 1000, not only because the needs of business rewarded those who understood them. Around 1200 marriage became increasingly historicized as thinkers like William of Auvergne thought about the Bible as well as new peoples like the Mongols. Christian Europeans became aware of what a small percentage they were of the world's population. Numerous Muslim, Mongol, and other peoples farther to the East became better known through the travels of merchants and missionaries. These numerous peoples disconcerted Europeans who worried that they would be overwhelmed. Arabic and Aristotelian biological thought raised the issues of why such foreign peoples were so numerous. William thought about the fertility of other peoples, and he even believed that more men were born than women, if only to staff the needs of the Church! He was no uncritical student of Aristotle; he rejected the ideas that women were simply inferior men and that infanticide was a legitimate way to control population.

By about 1300, some Europeans felt that high population levels suggested that their world was filling up with people – close to a sense of Malthusian limits. The biblical injunction to increase and multiply had not been repealed. Yet, signs ranging from delay of marriage to use of contraceptives suggest that people were trying to avoid having offspring. A greater preoccupation with numbers of people was common before the Big Death. Even Dante (1265–1327) wondered about his native Florence, and whether back around 1150 the older city was smaller, more virtuous, and indeed purer. Questioning his ancestor Cacciaguida, Dante imagined a world in which dowries were not so large and daughters not a burden to families. He knew that his Florence was bigger than it had been, but that did not mean it was better.

Another of Dante's concerns was the social climber who did not know his or her place. Sumptuary legislation first appeared in twelfth-century France and Italy and became more widespread in the next century in Iberia, and by the fifteenth century, such laws were common across Europe from Scotland to the East. Known to the ancient Romans, sumptuary laws sprang from two main impulses: a desire to suppress ostentatious display and luxury in funerals, entertainments, dress, and food, and a plan to make social rankings clear by limiting types of consumption to specific groups – nobles should dress like nobles and not other people. Such concerns about social order and consumption reflect spiritual and secular thinking about the vices of luxury and the need to limit it sometimes for the economic benefit of the larger society. Evidence on the enforcing of sumptuary laws is often hard to find. The rules embody social ideals that we want to know. After 1300, the typical sumptuary laws were increasingly secular, paying less attention to funeral and wedding expenses (excluding the size of dowries) and much more to dress codes, especially those concerning women.

Dress was supposed to reveal rank. The cleric Robert de Sorbon once took the noble Jean de Joinville to task for dressing better than his king Louis IX. Jean smartly retorted that at least he had inherited the right to such dress, while Sorbon had peasants for parents and by right should dress like them. In this way, the claims of merit, in the case of the highly educated and charitable Sorbon (his college in Paris the Sorbonne), did run up against the noble claims of inherited privilege. Some laws affected everyone; in England in 1336 the government tried to limit courses at meals to two, with little success. This type of law tried to restrain conspicuous consumption at a time of scarcity and war and was probably gender neutral, if we could be sure portions were fair. A suspicion of luxury for its own sake also sometimes embodied a theory of trade – that imported luxuries impoverished a society and caused dearth. True or not, even the Florentines had salaried officials whose job it was to spy out and fine women who violated the numerous rules on the types and cost of clothing they could wear in public. Such rules were also a means to raise money and Florentine women could buy exemptions and wear badges intended to spare them from being harassed by the *ufficiali delle donne*! Some rules regulated male dress but the pervasive concern in the laws was how women dressed – their appearance in public. Rank mattered, but even the rich were supposed to be cautious; Venice in 1333 simply limited women to wearing jewelry worth at most thirty ducats.

Women pushed back at these laws by developing a keener sense of fashion and pressuring their male relatives to allow exemptions and preserve the public rank of their female kin. Fourteenth-century society preferred to know at a glance who was a prostitute or a Muslim by dress. The upper classes wanted their social precedence recognized and protected. Some city governments may have seen the sumptuary laws as simply another way to raise revenue through fines and exemptions. Rules about rank received general assent. Sumptuary laws on how many dresses a woman might own at one time derive from more complicated motives among the men making the rules to sustain patriarchy. A greater sense of male and female fashion in the later Middle Ages enriched the purveyors of fashion and the arbiters of taste who helped to shape courtly life. As we will see in Chapter 6, the Big Death changed public attitudes about conspicuous consumption and waste. Before that calamity, justice seemed to demand that social climbers be kept in their places, at least when it came to how they should dress. A woman's fine clothing displayed her family's rank, but men paid many of the bills and did not want competition on the streets or the size of dowries to get out of hand.

The collective weight of medieval social and economic thought put moral sentiments at the heart of family life and the marketplace. Both institutions in theory benefited. Yet people were not always angels, and how they behaved remained complicated. Celibacy and poverty preoccupied theologians. Their professional concerns were no sure guides to ordinary people. In their daily lives, the laity needed guidance about children, money, and the fear of death. They wanted to know how to live comfortably in this world and still avoid Hell. Secular and religious groups depended on one another, and they knew it.

SELECT BIBLIOGRAPHY

Leon Battista Alberti, *I libri della famiglia*. Translated by Renée Neu Watkins. Columbia, 1969.

Peter Biller, *The Measure of Multitude: Population in Medieval Thought*. Oxford, 2000.

James A. Brundage, *Law, Sex, and Christian Society in Medieval Europe*. Chicago, 1987.

Samuel Cameron, *The Economics of Sin: Rational Choice or No Choice at All?* Cheltenham, 2002.

Steven A. Epstein, *Purity Lost: Transgressing Boundaries in the Eastern Mediterranean, 1000–1400.* Baltimore, 2007.

S. M. Ghazanfar, editor, *Medieval Islamic Economic Thought.* London, 2003.

William C. Jordan, *The French Monarchy and the Jews.* Philadelphia, 1989.

Benjamin Z. Kedar, "Expulsion as an Issue of World History," *Journal of World History* 7 (1996): 165–80.

Odd Langholm, *The Legacy of Scholasticism in Economic Thought.* Cambridge, 1998.

————, *Economics in the Medieval Schools,* Leiden, 1992.

Lester K. Little, *Religious Poverty and the Profit Economy in Medieval Europe.* Ithaca, 1978.

Brian Patrick McGuire, *Jean Gerson and the Last Medieval Reformation.* University Park, 2005.

R. I. Moore, *The Formation of a Persecuting Society.* 2nd ed. Maldon, MA, 2007.

John T. Noonan, Jr., *The Scholastic Analysis of Usury.* Cambridge, MA, 1957.

Susan Mosher Stuard, *Gilding the Market: Luxury and Fashion in Fourteenth-Century Italy.* Philadelphia, 2006.

Diana Wood, *Medieval Economic Thought.* Cambridge, 2002.

6

THE GREAT HUNGER AND THE BIG DEATH
The Calamitous Fourteenth Century

HE SURVIVING SOURCES FROM THE FOURTEENTH CENTURY permit a closer look at big questions and sustain at last a chronological approach to the central themes in the social and economic history of medieval Europe. Two major external shocks afflicted Europe: the Great Famine of 1315–1322 across most of northern Europe and the Big Death that swept through all of Europe and the Middle East beginning in 1346. Death rates from hunger and illness cost the North perhaps 5 percent of its population and the later plague took at least one-third of Europe's people within the first few years. These catastrophes had profound consequences that shaped Europe's development for centuries, and we will explore these aftereffects in detail. Yet, we must not fall into the logical trap of assuming that every big change after the plague resulted from it and the periodic new waves of disease that continued to kill staggering numbers of peoples into the fifteenth century and beyond.

The ever-increasing volume and types of sources also make generalizations more difficult. Contemporaries failed to understand the causes of these problems and often did not describe them. Wherever plague and famine can be studied, they have generated a great mass of contradictory accounts, often in isolated contexts that make it hard to see the big picture. Even so, some gaps in our understanding of these events still exist. New research on mass graves, dental DNA, and frozen corpses may yield fresh information that can easily overturn commonly held ideas and the textbook story. So much of what people think that they know about this century is wrong. Any summary runs the risk of continued error compounded by its passing out of date very quickly. The problems for historians posed by the calamities of the fourteenth century continue to test our ingenuity in asking the right questions and coming up with good arguments that do not simply recycle the known facts and stale debates of the past. Let us begin with bad weather in the North.

THE GREAT HUNGER

William C. Jordan has written a masterful account of this crisis, and his work provides a reliable picture of famine in northern Europe. He defines famine as a "catastrophic subsistence crisis," and this one lasted from 1315 to 1322 across a wide swath of northern Europe, stretching from Ireland across England, northern France, the Low Countries, southern Scandinavia, and northern Germany to the frontiers of Poland. Three big questions frame the analysis of this famine. First, why did it occur when it did? Second, why was the famine confined to the North and Mediterranean Europe spared? An important corollary to this question is: why was the greater market uniting north and south unable to transfer food surpluses from where they were abundant enough to where they were scarce? Third, how did the famine affect the societies enduring the troubles and what were the long-term consequences?

The first question raises the relatively simple matter of chronology – the famine began in 1315 because a rainy summer followed a cold and severe winter. Unfortunately for northern Europe, 1316 was an even worse year and too much summer rain flooding fields was the norm through 1320. Years of bad weather did not constitute a change in climate, and better weather returned in the 1320s. This bout of trouble remains inexplicable. During the cold winters, parts of the North and Baltic seas froze. Muddy roads and flooded streams compounded travel and transportation problems in the summers. Human follies, such as continued war, made things worse, but the main culprit was the weather. The big, open-field agricultural systems explored in Chapters 1 and 2 did not fare well when the land was under water. Mud made planting and harvesting nightmarish and sometimes impossible. Marginal and hilly lands suffered erosion and other problems like soil exhaustion that would take years to overcome.

Risk management and coping with the weather are constants in the farming life. The big question remains: how does a healthy society cope with these problems and for how long? Evidence from Norway, England, and northern France suggests reduced yields in the main wheat crop by 25–50 percent. As we will see, other crops suffered as did animals, especially cattle, but wheat is the best index of trouble because bread remained the "staff of life." The Malthusian argument, in its modern form, looks closely at the carrying capacity of the land, given available technology, the weather, and demographic trends – the birth and death rates. The debate about the severity of this famine begins with the relative health of northern European agriculture around 1315. Had population levels reached the point of Malthusian equilibrium, where maximum efficient farming in good weather could sustain the existing numbers but not any more people? Evidence suggests that from the 1280s, or a bit later, this economy ran into a demographic ceiling, and its numbers were no longer increasing. As we have seen, the burst of productivity in the earlier centuries, resulting from so much new land being put under the plow for the first time, was beginning to fade as lands were losing fertility. Crop rotation, periods of fallow, liming, and other techniques, derived from traditional knowledge of peasants and the book learning and study of stewards and farm managers, fought against the constant menaces of hail, crop and animal diseases, vermin, birds, and problems of storage. The basic story seems to be that agricultural yields from older fields were declining in the late thirteenth and early fourteenth centuries, and the key yield in wheat hovered around a yield/seed ratio of 3:1. This meant for every bushel of wheat sown (and spared by the birds and mice), three were eventually harvested – and, of course, one of these had to be set aside for seed, leaving, at best, two to eat. A 50 percent reduction meant hunger would set in very quickly and be compounded if peasants were forced to eat their seed that should have been saved for the next year's planting. We know very little about grain reserves, but the evidence of swift hunger suggests that northern Europe was living from harvest to harvest and had just enough reserves to get from one to another with perhaps a few months in reserve. If so, this suggests that 1315 would have been endured if the spring crop in 1316 was bountiful, but it was not. And there were other problems.

A disease of cattle, a murrain likely to have been *rinderpest*, later compounded by anthrax, led to big reductions in dairy herds and above all in the oxen necessary for plowing. People were, of course, also tempted to eat these animals, which suffered too from the cold winters and the lack of fodder as haymaking proved so difficult in the muddy fields and pastures. The weather was very hard on sheep wintered outside, and losses on English estates were commonly 25–50 percent and, in some cases, as high as 70 percent. Horses and pigs suffered from lack of fodder. The loss of oxen was catastrophic for open-field plowing and also for transportation. Pigs were omnivorous foragers and suffered the least. The herds of these adaptable creatures were gradually reduced as humans ate them.

Other crops, such as barley and oats, suffered too, and the bad weather brought on a series of poor vintages that reduced wine stocks in France and Germany. Salt, so necessary for diet, preservation, and activities, such as churning butter and making cheese, was harder to produce on the waterlogged coastal plains and mines in the interior. Salt prices perhaps doubled.

Real prices are difficult to fix in an era of inflation and currency debasements, but the price of wheat in northern France seems to have increased by 800 percent in the first three years of the famine. Prices were, however, quite volatile as surpluses moved from region to region. Market integration should have allowed the trading networks of fairs and their water and road connections to move food to areas where it was needed. High prices are supposed to signal traders that there was money to be made in shipping wheat to the north. Monarchs and city governments should have stepped in to secure food supplies. Their efforts to discourage hoarding and fix prices may have worsened the catastrophe by discouraging sellers. The Church, as the main dispenser of charity, was expected to use its accumulated resources to feed the poor, who were moving toward the cities in the first years of the hunger. Markets alone cannot solve the problem of famine. In fact, they can draw cash and grains quickly out of the hardest hit areas to benefit cities. High prices should have reduced consumption, but, at a certain point, the demand for food is inelastic, and malnutrition brings on other diseases like typhus that actually kill people. Simple starvation was not common. Many children, the aged, and the poor died during the famine because weakened people succumbed in increasing numbers to illness.

The weather patterns in northern Europe explain why crops failed and animals died. Transportation costs and difficulties help to explain why these problems remained confined to the north and why the Mediterranean lands were unable to export enough food to make any real difference. The ecology of the microclimates and microregions in the Mediterranean had always made trading food supplies necessary for human survival there. Silos and underground pits made storing grain more efficient in the drier south. Similar factors of high population levels and intensive agricultural efforts were already at work in the south. So, these regions too experienced a Malthusian equilibrium and could not relieve the misfortune of others. Venetian and Genoese merchants were already importing wheat from the northern shores of the Black Sea to Italy. Food shortages in Genoa in 1319, aggravated by civil war, were alleviated by importing grain from the eastern Mediterranean. These distances stretched to the limit late medieval systems of transport. The south's traditional granaries could not pick up any more slack. Egypt's reliable grain surpluses fed the Muslim world, and Sicilian and Puglian production was already intensive, and its stocks were relied upon by cities along the northern Mediterranean coasts. Rowed galleys, along with small round ships that were the workhorses of Mediterranean trade, were not suited to transport bulky items out of the placid southern sea into the strong waters of the Atlantic. Geographic boundaries, such as the Alps and Pyrenees, made land transportation of food stocks very difficult, and the rivers ran from north to south, just the wrong way for shipping grain to the north.

For all of these reasons, the trading networks of the south were not going to be able to make up such a huge, protracted shortfall in northern food supplies. The best they could do was to send some shipping up north to help transport grains from closer sources. For example, in 1317 the city government of Bruges spent money on importing grain, probably from southwestern France, the region around Bordeaux. Some Italian shipping may have helped facilitate these imports, which kept the death rates in Bruges lower than in nearby cities, such as Ypres and Tournai. In the Baltic, beyond the lands of the Teutonic Knights who made a considerable effort to feed their peasants, Polish agriculture was not yet in a position, in terms of roads, trading networks, and ports, to export food supplies to the hungry and populous west. At the margins, in places, such as central France or the easternmost German lands, local trading connections probably alleviated the worst effects of famine. But the core areas of hunger were simply too far away to help and were too isolated a global trading zone to be saved through trade. Studies of modern famines suggest that authoritarian regimes exacerbate famines as they use force and market controls that over time only make the hunger worse. Hence, most medieval governments, except perhaps for those that merchants controlled – rare enough in the north, were likely to make the situation worse.

The effects of the famine were mostly short-term effects because recovery in the 1320s was speedy. This fact suggests a surplus of people because so many died and yet economic and social life continued, as did wars and taxes. Wages have to be considered along with human deaths and the tendency for wages to be sticky, that is, to respond sluggishly to demographic changes. Because 85–90 percent of the population in the north remained rural and the initial problems were in agriculture, we should look for signs of mobility toward the urban areas, such as Flanders, and hence for regional and class variations. Volatility and shock characterize the general response, and a few local examples reveal how, like any crisis, this famine produced winners and losers. In Germany, ecclesiastical landlords with traditional saltworks and rights had windfall profits. Other religious houses had a series of disaster sales to sustain the consumption of the monks or nuns in the face of collapsing rents and yields in-kind from their lands. Many religious institutions, the canons of Canterbury are a good example, continued to attract pilgrims and gifts during the crisis. Here, the cathedral chapter remained able to spend resources to feed the local poor. Lay lordships had similar problems and opportunities, although their records are harder to find. Lords were in the best position to cope with the crisis because the rich had the most resources to sell or pawn until the weather improved.

Peasants bore the brunt of risk because they had little stored wealth to see themselves through a crisis. Grain prices are not a reliable index of their real cost of living. Peasant life offered many opportunities for income, but their lords and landowners would try to squeeze them for income and any customary rights they had to rents in-kind – suddenly worth a great deal more. From the 1280s, peasants had been more stressed, indebted, and taxed and hence were poorer. Famine led to some abandonment of land and even entire villages in Scotland and the Low Countries, although this was a constant process that the famine may have only accelerated. The smallest settlements on the most marginal lands were especially vulnerable to soil exhaustion and lordly demands. The volatile land market benefited anyone with cash and in some places, such as Denmark, free farmers had to sell lands and become tenants in order to survive. From Sweden to Germany and France, the most vulnerable rural folk, the casual laborers and landless, by 1317 at the latest, had exhausted the rural possibilities for "strange diets" and were hitting the road to the cities. In areas of mixed agriculture, such as East Anglia, Normandy, and Burgundy, a variety of local foods meant that people survived better. Still, the famine was a catastrophe for rural areas and on the well-studied wheat manors of the bishop of Winchester perhaps as much as 10–15 percent of the population died, mostly from illness. Balancing fragmentary figures from the hardest and most lightly hit areas suggests a general loss of about 5–10 percent, but these numbers are largely guesswork.

The greatest city in Europe, Paris, with perhaps 200,000 people at around 1300, experienced volatile prices, but the old rule seems to prevail – urban economies drew in food stocks from the countryside because the money was there to pay whatever price the markets set. The urban poor, including recent migrants from the countryside, had a hard time feeding themselves and were the ones most likely to succumb to illness. Many cities, such as Cambrai and Dortmund, sold annuities to raise money to use for charity and to buy grain. Other cities, such as Ghent and Würzburg, established hospices to take in the increasing numbers of sick and poor. Urban governments were in the best position to respond to the crisis because the merchants who ran these cities were practical men who were prepared to spend public and private funds to preserve the social and spiritual fabric. Monarchies were not able to do much except encourage grain imports, which was easier to urge than to accomplish. England tried price controls on livestock and ale with predictably negligible consequences – enforcement was too rudimentary and price controls during famine simply encourage hoarding and further scarcity. Hunger prevailed except in those cities that succeeded in attracting food. Lessons from modern famines suggest to Amartya Sen and other observers that free societies and markets cope best with food shortages. Starvation and epidemics are most common where markets are rigged or blocked by authoritarian or simply greedy powers. Not surprisingly, the famine was less consequential in the freer cities and also in those capitals, such as London and Paris, where the authority of monarchs could command certain supplies at the expense of rural areas.

Revolts of the Pastoureax in France and Aragon in 1320 and the savagely repressed Lepers Plot of 1321 reflect local and traditional problems about relations among the centers of power and the powerless in these societies. The shepherds and other rural people joining their revolt began in Normandy and the region around Paris but worked their way south, ostensibly on a crusade. Massacring Jews in Languedoc became their main activity before they dispersed or were crushed. Widespread bogus rumors about lepers using poison and witchcraft against society lead to bloody revenge against these diseased sufferers. Urban elites directed these reprisals that frequently led to murderous attacks on Jews as well. The famine may have exacerbated these revolts and affected their timing, but they occurred largely outside the core areas of hunger and probably reflect other problems.

Favorable weather everywhere in the north beginning in the 1320s allowed the survivors a better diet and ended the hunger. William C. Jordan has astutely suggested that the hungry children of the famine years suffered from long-term health consequences that made them more likely targets for the Big Death as adults in the late 1340s. In Flanders, where many children died, people may have suffered less from the plague later because betters diets and survival rates during the famine produced sturdy survivors. The spaces left by the dead were quickly filled, but there are no signs that the population was increasing. Instead, we continue to see stability at high levels, indicating an economy blocked or in a stalemate between productive capacities and consumption.

BETWEEN CATASTROPHES

A few macroeconomic events between the famine and plague merit notice because of their general effects on the European economy. The formal suppression of the military order of the Knights Templar in 1312, instigated for some time by Philip of France as a way to settle scores with this order and enrich his treasury, resulted in one of the largest transfers of wealth in the Middle Ages. The papacy insisted that Templar holdings across Europe, the results of centuries of pious donations, be transferred to another military order, the knights of St. John. These Hospitalers were now located on Rhodes and on the front lines of a continuing struggle against Muslim powers in the eastern Mediterranean. Many Templars were executed, some received pensions, and most of the order's wealth apparently went to the Hospitalers as intended, although this was a slow process, compounded in the north by problems resulting from the famine. While the Hospitaler order was responsible for some hospices and poor relief across Europe, its main focus remained warfare in the East. This expensive undertaking, now requiring a navy and fortifying Rhodes, meant that a steady stream of income from across Europe now drifted toward the East. A smaller but still significant transfer of wealth occurred when the Jews were finally expelled from France in 1322. The departing Jews were allowed to keep some of their wealth, but once again the monarchy, this time under Charles IV, had expropriated wealth from a harassed minority.

These policies to reorganize European resources for war took place in a context of ever-increasing warfare and organized violence in the general economy. The first phase of the Hundred Years War witnessed a bloody and expensive struggle between Edward III of England and the new Valois dynasty under Philip VI of France (1328–1350) about who had the right to rule France. The economic history of this struggle, as well as many other wars, foreign and civil, across Europe in these decades concerns not the military or political history of conflict but rather the effects war had on the economy – notably through taxation. War was becoming more capital intensive as armies increased in size; their equipment became more elaborate, and, above all, as mercenaries became an ever-growing part of everyone's military strength. Mercenary companies grew out of wars in France and Germany and, when unoccupied, these groups of men under famous captains found employment in Italy and elsewhere. Catalan mercenaries under Roger de Flor, falling into dispute with their Byzantine employers, eventually set themselves up as rulers of a duchy of Athens in 1310, and they would not be the last mercenaries to subvert states. Warfare, besides disrupting trade and frequently devastating wide areas of pillage, transferred wealth from taxpayers to the military and from creditors to debtors – national monarchies and any government that employed armies rather than compelling its own citizens to take up arms.

Economic and social questions concerning warfare appear before and after the Big Death, a tribute to the resilience of organized violence even in the face of hunger and disease. Economic historians have wondered about the costs and benefits of these wars. Was the galvanizing effect of warfare one of the driving forces behind the great medieval spurt of growth, or was the increasing violence in the early fourteenth century a sign of a stalemated economy now fighting harder for wealth? Without documented national budgets and expenditures, we are left with a great deal of speculation about whether war was a great waster of resources or the impetus behind a more rational use of resources and even technological and other innovations.

War affected national destinies – it certainly mattered that the long and frequently interrupted series of wars between England and France resulted in French victory and English defeat. But the process of war, and its occasional windfalls, such as the huge ransom paid for King Jean after the French lost their ruler at the battle of Poitiers in 1356, transferred prodigious sums of money from one society to another. Perhaps the most famous of these transfers, at least to bankers, concerned the collapse of the Florentine company belonging to the Peruzzi family in 1343. Along with the Bardi, these two great firms were private banks becoming increasingly rich by supplying the capital needed to sustain international trade, which for Florence meant wool and wool cloth. These firms traded in a wide variety of commodities and maintained branch offices and partners across Europe. Florentine merchants led by the Bardi, Peruzzi, and other family firms, controlled much of the Italian grain trade and above all had become in the 1320s increasingly involved in importing English wool to feed Florentine looms. The Florentine firms found it necessary to pay Edward III large sums for the right to export wool and to loan the crown money to finance war in France. The companies experienced a crisis in the early 1340s as the amounts Edward III owed and never would repay dwarfed the profits of the wool trade. In the collapse of 1343, the Bardi and the Peruzzi lost perhaps as much as one and a half million florins, real gold, and generations of accumulated profit consumed by war in the north. Florentine prosperity survived this crisis though the Bardi and the Peruzzi, and their investors, took a staggering beating – their losses amounted to five times the annual income of the Florentine commune according to John Najemy.

These widespread economic difficulties in the early decades of the fourteenth century indicate an economy and society at its Malthusian limits. Perhaps a better way to describe the situation is stalemate, or a Schumpeterian steady-state economy, with no clear way ahead except more of the same. Creative destruction and entrepreneurialism were no longer driving development. A great external shock would change that.

THE BIG DEATH

This topic demands a broad perspective because it affected nearly every corner of Europe. It is best to begin with the big picture (see Figure 6.1) in order to fathom the immense and unprecedented level of sudden mortality. Historians differ about every aspect of this plague, but there are a few general points of agreement. From 1346 to 1352, an epidemic disease swept across Europe in a great clockwise circle, beginning with Caffa in the Crimea in 1346 and ending up in Novgorod and Moscow in 1352. The epidemic spared no major area and killed about one-third of the population. For some reason, perhaps low population densities, the plague seems to have skipped over mountainous regions, such as the Alps and Pyrenees. Stephan R. Epstein found Sicily to be typical of the worst hit regions. Palermo declined by half its population down to 50,000, and, on the island as a whole, the losses came to 60 percent of the medieval height. The disease remained endemic and recurrent bouts of plague continued to kill many people for centuries – but never with the severity of the initial phase. The worst population crisis in Denmark occurred from 1380 to 1420, and its population was higher in 1300 than in 1801 – a tribute to the long-term consequences. The basic social and economic institutions, as well as all of the others, endured this calamity, and all observers have been struck by how this European society continued, which is a real tribute to human resilience. Nevertheless, many things changed, some quickly, and some too slowly for contemporaries to note at first.

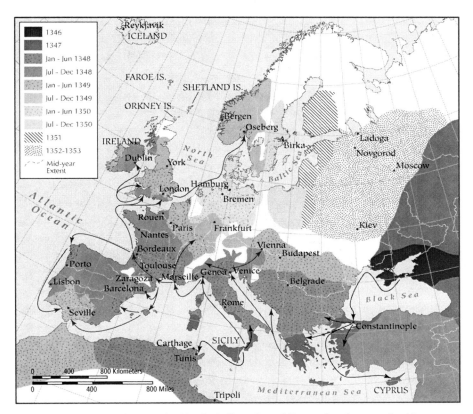

Figure 6.1. Big Death (map by Keith A. French and Darin Grauberger, the University of Kansas Cartographic Services).

Outside the broad areas of agreement, disputes among scholars appear at every turn. First, what was the killer, and does it matter what the precise epidemiological and medical details are? Second, why was the disease so lethal at first, and then change in its targets and severity? Third, what were the proverbial immediate or short-term, mid-term, and long-term consequences to the plague? We should cast our net widely here and look beyond traditional social and economic categories to include psychological, artistic, and even spiritual effects that profoundly shaped late medieval culture and subsequent European history beyond the end of this book.

Three logical errors tempt us to exaggerate or minimize the plague's significance. As noted before, we must be wary of assigning every change after the plague to the unprecedented high levels of mortality. Many consequences indeed flow from this shock. Some scholars have looked far forward to events, such as Columbus's voyage in 1492 or the Protestant Reformation in the early sixteenth century as long-term effects of the Big Death in the mid-fourteenth century and its aftershocks. The steps in these arguments are faulty, but they warn us not to minimize the effects of catastrophe. Second, just as some scholars see the deaths behind every change, others ponder the continuities and think that Europeans, staggered by plague, shrugged off the deaths and moved forward. Perhaps so many surplus people lived at the Malthusian limits that their deaths, by no means a healthy correction, did not disable society or the economy. After all, Europe did not sink into turmoil and a wholesale revolt against its institutions. The twentieth century witnessed in calamities, such as World War II, the Holocaust, and the great massacres in Cambodia in the 1970s, death rates that in places approached or in some cases exceeded the costs of the plague. Intense scrutiny of the survivors as individuals and collectively as societies has produced massive scholarship on new topics ranging from survivor's guilt and people's search for meaning in tragedy to posttraumatic stress syndrome in survivors, their descendants, and indeed entire cultures. These modern horrors prepare us to see more clearly, perhaps more perceptively than most intervening generations, what happened in the fourteenth century.

Third, the sources on the Big Death are uneven and imperfect. The absence of evidence should not be mistaken for evidence of absence. Not every city or region provides wills or price levels or chroniclers to illuminate the course of the disease. These gaps do not necessarily show that the plague skipped over some regions. The only reliable clue that Figure 6.1 gives on this problem is that the higher elevations in the Alps and Pyrenees seem to have been spared, but that simply may be because too few people lived there to sustain an epidemic. It is equally problematic to take good eyewitness evidence from one place and assume that it applies everywhere. The basic subject remains a demographic catastrophe. The Big Death is the first case study of massive death and its consequences. As in the hypothetical scenario of the neutron bomb, the epidemic took the people and left Europe's stock of physical capital untouched. Lands, buildings, treasure, libraries, most animals, down to the clothing of the deceased, all survived and often left traces in the records. Hence, this epidemic counts as one of the greatest periods of wealth transfer in human history, a great age of inheritance. The two-thirds of people that lived to inherit Europe's wealth must not be forgotten even in the midst of a legitimate and necessary focus on the dying.

WHAT WAS THE KILLER?

Samuel K. Cohn, Jr., has rightly urged a return to the expression "Big Death" as one phrase contemporary observers used to describe the plague or illness that struck them. The common term "Black Death" is a later usage, and its color symbolism is not helpful. The real problem, of course, is that the standard textbook story has been for nearly a century that this killer was bubonic plague, and most books still refer to the medieval disease as this sort of plague. Most people, if they have heard of the medieval plague, call it the Black Death and think it was bubonic plague. They believe a simple medical story that goes like this. Modern bubonic plague, a real bacterial disease that can still kill people not treated with antibiotics, exists today and is endemic in rodent populations, such as some prairie dogs along the Front Range of the Rocky Mountains in the western United States, for example. Every year a few people sicken, and some occasionally die. British doctors in India in the late nineteenth and early twentieth centuries closely examined outbreaks of this disease in India and others studied similar outbreaks in China. The bacterium causing bubonic plague (*Yersinia pestis*) was found by Alexander Yersin, and scientists clarified a very complicated story of how this disease of rodents, for our purposes rats, jumped from them to humans. The vector proved to be a flea, which bit the rats and absorbed the bacteria, became a host with a huge internal infection, and then transferred the killer with a bite to a human being. Inside a new host with no natural immunity, the plague ran its course and killed many victims. In some cases, the bacteria flourished in human lungs and could be coughed or sneezed out, but this was, in practice, a hard and uncommon way to communicate this illness as it has been observed by modern science. These scientists saw, in people with bubonic plague, large boils or swellings (which medieval people called *buboes*) in the groin areas or along the neck, in the obvious clusters of lymph nodes normally swelled and filled with pus and fluids when fighting infection. Historically minded doctors saw parallels to the medieval plague and assumed that the diseases were the same killer – bubonic plague.

Another old story apparently ratified this tale. Gabriele de Mussis was a lawyer in Piacenza who wrote an account of how the disease arrived in Europe before he died in 1356. His story began in Genoese Caffa in the Crimea, a city in 1346 besieged by a Tartar army of the Golden Horde. A terrible plague broke out in this force. In what some later historians described as the first known case of biological warfare, the Tartar commander catapulted the corpses of his men into Caffa, and soon the killer broke out there as well. The infection quickly spread and followed some Genoese refugee ships out of the Black Sea to Constantinople. Soon Venetian and Genoese ships brought the killer to Sicily, where we know it arrived in August of 1347 at Messina. De Mussis was sure that Genoese merchants brought the plague to Piacenza. Because he observed the course of the disease, it is worth noting that he knew from the beginning that many died, that it was highly contagious, and that he presumably saw the big buboes or swellings that marked the sick (who also vomited blood). Perhaps his legal training prepared de Mussis to view the epidemic as an instance of divine and just vengeance upon humanity.

The standard explanation ties together the rat and Caffa stories to uncover a distinct moment and place in 1346 where the plague entered Europe. Maps of the contagion follow sea routes first in the eastern Mediterranean to Syria and Egypt and then west to Sicily and beyond. Somehow the rats, most often identified as black Asiatic rats and their fleas presumed to be the bacterium's host and vector to humans, accompanied merchants and travelers aboard ship. A pulmonary or pneumonic form of plague may explain how travelers spread the disease so quickly, but the hosts must also have been present. How Tartar corpses brought plague to Caffa has never been explained because fleas alone blocked with *Yersinia pestis* (bubonic plague) would not sustain the illness – the host rats remained essential. The standard story has the virtues of clarity and drama. Historians have even imagined the black rat slipping down mooring ropes at night to infect a new port, or wagonloads of flea-infested cloth bringing the killer across roads to cities.

The problems with this account are simply that research over recent decades has cast real doubt over every stage of the story, rendering it increasingly incredible but hard not to repeat! Even now, this text has contributed to the litany of error by simply repeating it. Cohn's objections to the traditional story are worth considering. First, there is no evidence that the black or brown rat had anything to do with this plague. Archaeologists have now found evidence of black rats in Europe since antiquity. Most importantly, no contemporary account from Europe or the Middle East notes any great die-offs, or epizootics, of rats. This omission is telling because modern bubonic plague leaves in its wake masses of dead rats that do not escape notice. Second, humans have no natural immunity to bubonic plague. Hence, the patterns of the epidemic make no sense – why should subsequent outbreaks have been less lethal? Third, the medieval descriptions of the illness do not match modern accounts of bubonic plague. Contemporaries as early as Giovanni Boccaccio noted the buboes, but it was also common in many accounts to note black and blue spots or blisters, pustules about the size of lentils or freckles, that covered the sick. The general course of the illness was speedy and highly contagious, with victims usually dying in two or three days, if not sooner. Seasonality marked the illness, with June and July the most dangerous months in Mediterranean Europe, while the worst phase in the north lasted from September to November. Some observers noted an apparently healthy person in the morning who was dead by night. People saw that the disease spread quickly in households and among groups living in close proximity, such as monks and nuns. Some professions, such as clergymen, physicians, and gravediggers, were especially dangerous. The late fourteenth-century chronicler Jean Froissart claimed that the death rate was one-third, and down to the present, this guess commands respect. Finally, while the plague struck men and women equally, over subsequent outbreaks people saw it increasingly as a disease of the poor and one that affected children.

Modern bubonic plague does not resemble this illness – its death rates are never so high, lentil spots and coughing blood are not symptoms, children are not especially vulnerable, lots of dead rats appear – the list goes on. Efforts by modern researchers to identify graves of plague victims and isolate from their dental DNA or other remains some evidence of the killer have thus far proved inconclusive. It is possible that the current plague bacterium has evolved over the last seven centuries and no longer affects people the same way as it did then. Perhaps another type of disease – anthrax or a hemorrhagic fever like Ebola, have been suggested – accounts for the rapid spread and high levels of mortality. But if we put the rat and flea story aside, we are in a better position to explore the reasons why the killer, whatever it is, was so lethal.

WHY WAS THE PLAGUE SO LETHAL?

The high levels of mortality from this communicable disease must result from three possibilities. The killer was a new illness for which there was no natural immunity, and so there was no treatment, cure, or prevention. Also, we must look at how medieval contemporaries, before the germ theory of human illness, understood this plague and what could be done about it.

The idea that the plague was an illness new to Europe draws strength from the disease pool theory explained by William H. McNeill. The well-known epidemic catastrophe of measles, smallpox, and other illnesses that killed millions of Indians in the Western Hemisphere in the decades and centuries after the Columbian contact serves as the model for how disease pools explain the evolution of diseases in a world of biodiversity. Before jet travel and modern ideas of a boundaryless world where people, goods, and ideas can travel so quickly, the planet was divided into fairly discrete zones of human populations. For simplicity, we'll consider sub-Saharan Africa, Europe, and East Asia as three such pools where humans and the illnesses had evolved together for millennia and reached a kind of equilibrium. The disease pool theory suggests, on analogy with the New World devastation and modern experiences, such as the influenza epidemic of 1918, that diseases are much more lethal when they travel from one population pool to another (and indeed from one species to another), where they find people with no natural immunity or recent experience with the killer. Whatever caused the Big Death, it arrived in Caffa in 1346, probably came from the Asian disease pool, and was brought west by the Tartars.

There are two problems with this explanation. First, the Mongols had arrived as far west as Poland and Hungary by the 1230s, and Asia and Europe had been in continuous contact via the Silk Road and travelers like the Polos of Venice, as well as Tartar armies of the Golden Horde, for decades. The disease pool theory usually explains a more sudden onset of illness than this century delay. Second, we know a lot less about the evolution and symbiosis of human disease than we think. For example, some scholars believed that the Malthusian crisis and a malnourished European population before the plague accounted for the high levels of death as a mixture of a new disease and a killer. But if people had no natural immunity to bubonic plague, for example, their levels of nutrition would not affect the death rate from that illness – although other killers like cholera and typhus could account for some of the toll. Yet, we must recall that the Big Death gradually became more associated with the poor and children, and there may be clues here about the true nature of the illness.

Second, it makes sense that the Big Death was so devastating because contemporaries had nothing to treat any bacterial or viral illness. Figure 6.2 displays, with a few refinements, the prevailing medical system of the medieval world – the ancient medical tradition inherited from Galen and others and refined by Muslim, Christian, and Jewish physicians in subsequent centuries. Nature fell into convenient groups of four elements, four seasons, four humors, four temperaments, and even four directions. The key to Galen's system for explaining human health was the four humors – the precious bodily fluids that needed to

		♀ Women, Colder and Moister		
		North		
		Water		
Coldness		Winter		Moisture
		Phlegm		
		Phlegmatic		
	Earth	Element	Air	
West	Autumn	Season	Spring	East
	Black Bile	Humor	Blood	
	Melancholic	Temperament	Sanguine	
		Fire		
		Summer		
Dryness		Yellow Bile		Heat
		Choleric		
		South		
		♂ Men, Hotter and Drier		

bacterium = *Yersinia pestis*
rat =   *Rattus rattus* (grey)
          Rattus norvegicus (brown)
Flea = *Xenopsylla cheopis*

Figure 6.2. Humoral System of Galen (adapted from Danielle Jacquart and Claude Thomasset, *Sexualité et savoir medical au Moyen Age*, Paris, 1985, p. 68).

be in the right balance in a healthy person. Yellow bile, black bile, phlegm, and blood existed in the human body and when in excess or short supply, symptoms appeared that a trained doctor could associate with the right fluid. So, for example, too much black bile (whatever it was) made a person dark, dry, cold, and melancholic – sad. These clues do not describe plague victims – who were hot, feverish, and often coughing up blood. These victims were too sanguine, flushed, often a sign of cheerfulness but not in the dying. Most people died so quickly that physicians, also dying in high numbers, could do little for their patients anyway. But if they had time to treat the illness, besides prescribing various flowers, such as posies, and herbs intended to repress sanguinity, they would have tried to remove blood from the victims by bleeding, hoping then to correct the proper balance of humors in the body. No one believes that this treatment, phlebotomy, helped those suffering from the mysterious killer.

Although physicians hence could do nothing to treat the plague, their advice over the long run may have helped to prevent more serious outbreaks and, in part, explain why the illness became less lethal in the following decades. Doctors and others encouraged better sanitation and efforts to limit contagion. This may have helped. Quarantines were instituted, beginning with Mantua and Milan in 1374 and Ragusa in 1377. The precocious board of health in the duchy of Milan in 1424 marks a long-term but significant benchmark in the history of public health. This group could close borders and order the quick removal of corpses and quarantine among other measures to stop an outbreak of plague. Flight was a common response in Christian Europe at the first plague and was not as marked in later ones. The frame of Boccaccio's *Decameron*, whose introduction contains the famous description of the disease's course in Florence, is precisely the tales told by a group who have fled the city to escape death. Some later physicians advised fleeing at the first sign of plague, and this response would always be more practical for the wealthy and those who could afford a doctor's advice.

Finally, in our search for reasons why the plague was so bad, we should look briefly at how authoritative voices in Europe and the Middle East explained the cause of the killer. Embedded in those explanations were possible human responses that might help to limit or end the Big Death. A report from the medical faculty at the University of Paris, from the first raging of the plague there in October of 1348, inevitably understood the illness in the context of available conceptual frameworks. Received truths, not research or study, would shape these opinions. The major observation the physicians made concerned a terrible astrological conjunction back in 1345 that poisoned the air with a miasma that killed. Weather patterns inevitably spread poisoned air. Other observers pointed to the stars and planets as exercising an unhealthy influence on the Earth. The working assumption behind this science, a body of knowledge making predictions and testable assumptions, is that eventually the heavenly patterns would shift and alter the malign horoscope of Europe. This point of view counseled patience and making the sick comfortable. Other people looked for different causes for the poisoned air – perhaps an earthquake somewhere opened a vent of dangerous fumes causing illness, or a volcano belched bad air. These were not unreasonable views because dangerous gases indeed occurred in some places and made people sick or killed them. The universality of this killer suggested that the winds had spread the poison everywhere, and there was nothing people could do about the weather or its consequences, except pray.

Ordinary people did not all accept the educated opinions of professors and astrologers as sufficient explanations for the crisis of large numbers of deaths. The extreme stress of seeing so much suffering and death prompted, in some places, a search for scapegoats. No student of medieval society will be surprised to learn that the main victims were Jews, lepers, and the poor. Popular rumors held that the Jews were poisoning the water. First apparently in Toulon in southern France around April 14, 1348, waves of killings extended south to Barcelona where there were large massacres in May, and then in the autumn in the German lands and the Rhineland – 2,000 Jews were killed in Strasbourg alone. Terrible massacres occurred in Nuremburg, Vienna, Frankfurt, Basel, and many other cities. In most places, it was the urban and rural social elites who incited the mobs that killed the Jews. Very few people stopped to observe that their victims were dying of plague in large numbers. Popular hysteria does not pause for such rational analysis. While communities of lepers suffered terribly from illness as well as murder and the poor died and were suspected of causing death, the real onus fell upon the Jews, for whom the long-term consequences were catastrophic.

From the earliest stages of these massacres, Pope Clement VI (1342–1352) condemned them. (This pope survived the first onslaught of plague in Avignon, according to observers, by taking good medical advice to remain between two constant fires in a superheated room to avert the poisons in the air.) As early as July 5, he promised to protect the Jews, and later he ordered the clergy across Europe to take any steps necessary to stop the killing. On September 26, 1348, the pope issued a long letter explaining, among other things, that the Jews could not be the cause of the plague, because they were also dying and it was raging in many places (he may have had England in mind, for example) where there were no Jews. Believers expected the head of the Western Church to explain the greatest calamity in human memory. Clement VI struck a constant theme that God was punishing people with this disease for their sins, and the best human response was repentance. It is important to understand the great coherence and traditional weight behind this authoritative conclusion by the pope. God was the author of the plans for this world that began in Paradise and would end at the Apocalypse. His judgments were occasionally severe but always just. People were sinful and the weight of these sins provoked God's wrath. It was time for people to say they were sorry and mend their ways. Then the disease might stop – a killer that was simultaneously taking even larger numbers of priests, monks, and nuns. We will look later at the efforts people made to use prayer to abate the plague.

A useful point of comparison here is the religious response to the plague in the Muslim world, only a tiny part of Europe in 1348, but one well known to Christian Europe. The same death rates prevailed in the Middle East – great Cairo lost perhaps 200,000 of its 600,000 people, with similar percentages across North Africa and into the Middle East. In general, religious leaders made three following points that commanded wide if not universal assent. A Muslim should not flee or enter a plague-stricken land. Calm acceptance of Allah's will was the proper response because the plague was a mercy and a martyrdom from God for a Muslim and a just punishment to the infidel. Hence, the plague's Muslim victims went to Paradise. Finally, most Muslim scholars denied contagion because they believed that God was the ultimate cause of the disease. But some observers, such as Ibn Khaldun (1332–1406), a survivor in Egypt, believed in the miasma theory with the twist that the air had been poisoned because the world was overpopulated! Ibn Khatimah, active in Almeria in Muslim Spain, rejected the theory of contagion on religious grounds, but he clearly knew that the plague spread from person to person, and he even noted, among many other ideas, that flea-ridden clothing was dangerous. Still, God's choice of method to afflict this person and not that one was not as important as the basic message. All was in God's hands, and the dead were assured a pleasant afterlife and He (God) expected the living to control their fears. These authoritative explanations for the killer help us to understand why no Jews, Christians, lepers, or poor people were massacred anywhere in Muslim lands. Even in Castile and Aragon, where large numbers of Muslims lived, their Christian neighbors did not kill them and confined their hostility to traditional Jewish scapegoats.

The plague was so lethal because people everywhere could do nothing about it except pray, blame, and kill fellow sufferers, or vainly try to flee. Physicians could relieve the mass of blood the hearts of the sick could not control by removing some of it, but this cured no one. Over time, medical advice on improving hygiene may have prevented some illnesses that contributed to the death rates.

MAJOR CONSEQUENCES OF THE BIG DEATH

Much of the rest of this book concerns the consequences of plague, especially because local outbreaks continued, with severe widespread outbreaks in the early 1360s, around 1400, and beyond, to name only a few. While no later plague killed as many as the first, for about a century after 1348, Europe's population was not increasing. Hence, the demographic and economic consequences of continued mortality will merit close analysis, as well as social and market responses to the new facts of life. In Chapters 7, 8, and 9, we will take up technology and consumerism, war and social unrest, and signs of recovery in the fifteenth century as enduring adjustments European societies made to the great external shock of plague. In order to establish the proper context for examining these matters, it is best to consider some pervasive attitudinal shifts.

The survivors experienced psychological stresses that must have affected their attitudes toward death. Giovanni Boccaccio was eloquent in describing the circumstances of Florence in 1348, where he witnessed the breakdown of burial customs and even family life as he saw it. Whether or not relatives were as quick to abandon sick kin as Boccaccio thought is not certain, but he thought a streak of self-preservation marked the survivors. He believed that misery prompted people to ignore laws and ordinary social customs and that they tried to survive by panicky flight or self-quarantine as Florence filled with stench and corpses. This experience of the Grim Reaper helped to canonize a vivid Death that stalked the land, striking victims as with invisible arrows that killed them. As Death became a more immediate neighbor across Europe, the sense of death prompted in the living a love of life that held fast in a macabre context of new tomb styles that vivified rot, bones, and death. Individual responses to a pervasive PTSD (posttraumatic stress disorder) of course varied as survivors escaped guilt and bad memories though prayer, massacring scapegoats, increased consumption of wine and beer, flurries of marriages and subsequent births, and other traditional human remedies to horrors. An early saint like Sebastian, martyred by a firing squad of archers, became associated with the plague, which seemed to strike victims like an invisible arrow. St. Roch (Rocco in Italy), a native of Montpellier (1295–1327), had acquired a reputation as a healer in the early fourteenth century and became a more intense object of devotion after the Big Death. Paintings and statues of Roch showed him displaying a sore on his thigh that evoked the plague buboes (see Figure 6.3). The Virgin Mary everywhere was invoked as a protector against disease. All of these images focused prayers and piety on spiritual beings who could avert plague's arrows and the illness.

David Herlihy pointed out that the catastrophe of plague challenged traditional social and spiritual authorities to explain what was happening. The fates of some lepers and Jews suggest that official answers were not immediately satisfactory to all, though the durability of European society indicates that there was not a complete loss of confidence. Bad horoscopes and dangerous volcanoes might cease to afflict the world, but the illness continued to baffle physicians and did not lead to a revolution in disease theories. This world remained a sinful place and for those Christians who accepted the Church's teaching the path to repentance remained open. Widespread processions of flagellants sought God's forgiveness through self-whipping and prayers. Thousands joined such pilgrimages first in Italy in 1348, and then spreading in waves north through southern Germany and Bohemia into Hungary and Poland. Often the processions had rules and leaders, with joiners often marching for thirty-three-and-a-half days to imitate the life of Christ in years. By the summer of 1349, the processions heading west across German lands had reached Flanders and northern France but were beginning to run into some local hostility, perhaps because of their huge numbers. Although Pope Clement condemned the practice as excessive and stimulating hostility toward Jews as the pilgrims approached Avignon in 1349, flagellation's appeal remained pervasive. Flagellants also suffered from plague and may have helped spread the illness. Some people might have wondered about the proportionality between the sins of humanity and the increasing numbers of dead children, worthy priests and nuns, and others innocent and guilty. But if so, they remained largely quiet.

CONSEQUENCES FOR THE CHURCH

Because the papacy presided over a Church that commanded nearly universal obedience across most of Europe, it was the institution most challenged by the plague, partly because so many of its own staff died, and also because people turned to it for solace. Good evidence from across Europe indicates that the death rates among the regular parish clergy exceeded 50 percent, with

Figure 6.3. St. Roch (Art Resource AR 333782).

similar terrible tolls in many monasteries and convents. Finding new priests became a major task of the upper clergy at a time when the next generation of priests at universities was also dying in high numbers. The solutions among the survivors were to found new colleges at existing universities, to establish new ones, like Prague in 1348, and to push young men through holy orders quickly in order to replenish the ranks of the clergy. Ordinary people saw their priests administer the last rites and attempt to preserve regular burial customs and die in large numbers for these efforts. Although the new clergy may not have been as educated or as diligent as many of their predecessors, the fact remains that the Church endured this crisis with no new international waves of heresy or even much criticism. In England, John Wycliffe's later criticisms of the Church focused on the defects of its leaders, not the basic religious truth of Christianity. The papacy in Avignon had good intentions and it helped stop the massacre of Jews, though it could do little to control expressions of popular lay piety like the flagellants. The main problem for the Church remained how successful it would be in reassuring people with its message that sin was at the root of the plague.

PSYCHOLOGICAL IMPLICATIONS

Possible shifts in attitudes among the survivors are a good way to move from social to economic consequences, because the mood of these people determined how Europe would come through the crisis. The notarial cartularies of Genoa, the great record of contracts and daily life, show signs of haste and confusion in January and February of 1348 as people rushed to dictate wills. A similar crisis began in Bologna in late June, and July was terrible. Wherever wills or records of mortality exist across Europe, it is often possible to find the exact week when people started to die in large numbers, usually in advance of the news that calamity was approaching. We have already seen signs of mass hysteria in massacres of scapegoats and flagellation in Christian Europe. Studies of survivors of contemporary mass killings and death suggest that the survivors feel guilty for remaining among the living and that many suffer from a collective depression. On top of these responses, we must remember the continued outbreaks of plague and expect to see more limited horizons about planning for the future. Art historians have concluded that these survivors sponsored visual arts characterized by piety, melancholy, and death – images of Death in the *danse macabre*. Boccaccio's *Decameron*, two-thirds of the stories spiced with sexual intrigue, and Geoffrey Chaucer's later *Canterbury Tales*, suggest that the search for diversion went beyond the morbid.

Benjamin Z. Kedar looked closely at the well-documented merchant class in Venice and Genoa for signs of a general response to catastrophe. He assumed, as most observers still do (a point examined in more detail in Chapters 7, 8, and 9), that for at least the next century Europe experienced a depression not limited to the usual economic definition of decline and then no growth. For the moment, we are concerned with social and psychological responses. His general finding is that merchants became more insecure and short term in their thinking. Their habits of naming children and even ships retreated into a safe, augurative set of names invoking spiritual protection against perils from powerful saints, such as Antony, Bartholomew, Rock, and, above all, Mary. A patient attention to the context in which merchants used words revealed a growing aversion to risk after the plague. Once associated with opportunity, risk now meant uncertainty and trouble. Adversity now ruled the day and favorable outcomes seemed harder to find. Hence, life rewarded prudent, cautious, and circumspect people. Fortune, which traditionally favored the bold, now seemed especially capricious, and disasters struck well-prepared merchants and ruined all their plans. The consequences of these collective changes in mood went beyond naming patterns and tastes in diversions and beverages. Kedar posits a collective loss of nerve and a contraction to a world of more limited, less open horizons in every direction. The Portuguese had stumbled across the Canary Islands in the 1320s, but their progress down the coast of Africa in search of gold stopped after the plague and did not resume for decades. In the aftermath of plague, northern contacts with the settlements on Greenland became more tenuous and soon after 1400 stopped entirely, the Greenlanders themselves disappeared from the historical record. A fledgling Italian mercantile and missionary presence in China also lapsed after the plague as contacts and trade across the Silk Road became increasingly rare for Europeans. Even the memories of these intrepid travelers faded, and, in the early twentieth century, great surprise greeted the find of a few fourteenth-century Latin tombstones in China.

The plague interrupted a wave of travel and discovery and made Europe more insular for at least fifty years. Short-term secure profits and voyages lasting weeks or months rather than years seemed safer options in an insecure world of epidemic disease and high mortality. Investing in shares of public debt for lower but steady returns seemed to be more prudent than risky long-term investments overseas that no partner might live to see. At this point, mood becomes relevant to exploring the economic consequences. People make market decisions, and their moods affect buying and selling. Sometime in the 1370s, probably in Genoa, merchants and notaries began to write standard insurance contracts for ships and their cargoes (soon including slaves – the first lives insured). This was certainly an innovative and successful response to the problems of insecurity and a need to share risks. Insurance spread almost as quickly as plague, and it is hard to pin down its exact origins, but the impulse to insure things makes perfect sense. A rational calculus survived the plague.

ECONOMIC CONSEQUENCES

No neat line separates economic and social consequences. Context remains important because some numbers changed after the plague, and along with psychological states, this affected peoples' decisions and choices – our subject. We postpone technology and consumerism, revolts and war, as well as eventual long-term recovery for Chapters 7, 8 and 9.

Economics, sometimes dismissed as the dismal science because of its Malthusian roots in demography and death, can also be counted on to find the silver lining in any cloud – even for the Big Death. Economic historians are used to thinking about immediate, mid-term, and long-term consequences of shocks to a market system. In our Europe, the short-term effects should appear immediately or certainly within the first five years, the mid-term consequences take us to the 1390s or the terrible general plague around 1400, and the long-term vistas go deep into the fifteenth century and in some matters beyond. Keynes famously observed that in the long term we are all dead, and so we should not expect to find contemporaries looking too far into the future. They, however, left records that enable us to look beyond the appropriately narrower concerns of the survivors.

Because the high levels of mortality were pervasive across Europe, the silver lining was that an immediate consequence of the Big Death was a great age of inheritance. Pestilence did not destroy Europe's wealth, now in fewer hands, so per capita wealth skyrocketed except for the heirs of the destitute. A few opposite trends trimmed the increase of wealth. In general, the price of land and urban rents declined. Some lands, of course, were so marginally productive that they dropped out of farming, and this would limit the general decrease in land prices and caused desertion of entire villages. Good lands held value better and some specialized types of properties like vineyards, orchards, and olive groves to name a few, maintained their value the best. On Sicily, regions began to specialize in wheat, sugar, and silk to make the best use of land. The stock of urban housing everywhere suddenly became far too large for the survivors and so rents plummeted, especially after continued outbreaks stymied demographic recovery. Institutions that depended on landed endowments for income suffered immediately, but the Church did benefit from a burst of legacies from the many who died, and who had believed that gifts to the Church pleased God.

Other prices present a more confusing picture, and again the typical benchmark is wheat. If the plague arrived before the spring planting or the summer harvest, dislocations in rural areas could also create short-term food shortages, but if the harvest was in and then the people died, prices would quickly fall. So we would expect to see prices of wheat and food, in general, to be mixed over the short run, but with a gradual general downward trend because there were fewer mouths to feed. Wheat prices did not immediately decline because people favored it over other grains, such as rye and spelt, and also, as we will see, it was expensive to harvest. By the 1370s, wheat prices were generally lower in northern Europe, with southern areas following the trend by the 1390s. Because the plague did not kill farm animals, this food remained in abundant supply, and we see a fairly quick decline in meat prices – hence more consumption and better nutrition. Wool also remained in abundant supply – all of those sheep survived, as did the clothing of the deceased – although some of this would be burned because it was thought to be dangerous. Still, the price of wool and woolens declined fairly quickly. Yet, we would expect to see cotton and silk hold up better, especially because increases in disposable inherited wealth made fabric substitution a reasonable response. In brief, there was a lot of short-term chaos, but as markets settled down over the midterm, rents, land, and most food prices declined, but a switch-up market kept some prices stable – wine is a good example here. Another immediate consequence for the survivors was a better diet, and we presume increased fertility for the women – whose hopes must have been repeatedly dashed as the plague became increasingly a killer of children. High death rates depressed general life expectancies in the midterm to less than 20. If one survived childhood and pestilence, a longer life was still possible.

One difficulty in collecting data on wages and prices is of course inflation, an inevitable result of a larger per capita wealth chasing some goods in short supply. Governments continued to debase the coinage to stretch their supplies of money – for example, in Flanders prices rose by 96 percent from 1350 to 1374, but gold coinage was debased by 83 percent and silver by 69 percent, flattening price increases considerably. Wages were likely to keep pace with inflation because daily and piece-rate salaries made workers very sensitive to their purchasing power. Local troubles mattered a great deal, and as we will see, wars affected how some economies thrived and others stalled in the years after the plague.

The price of labor, wages, directly concerned the great mass of people who inherited little but found their hands in short supply. This fact affected urban and rural workers, and inaugurated the much debated "Golden Age of Labor," the longest and most significant rise in wages in premodern European history. Significantly, slaves also increased rapidly in price and became prestigious fixtures in wealthy households. But for ordinary farmers and craftsmen and women wages mattered and they were certainly increasing – according to the complaints of their employers doubling or tripling in the immediate aftermath of the plague. Bargaining in a free market for labor had significantly and quickly changed. Surviving employers, from landowners to masters in guilds, would not simply accept these wage increases and not surprisingly they attempted to use political power to control wages and even prices. The best documented example is the kingdom of England. In 1349, Edward III issued an ordinance attempting to fix all salaries and wages to the rates prevailing in 1346. He also tried to compel people to take up work by telling healthy beggars that they had to work or go to prison. The famous Statute of Labourers passed by parliament in 1351 admitted that the ordinance had been ineffective but still tried to turn the clock back for the entire kingdom by putting wages back to what they were five years before, requiring employers and employees to take oaths to observe the new rules, establishing commissions to enforce the stature and set fines and other punishments for law breakers. Rigorous enforcement yielded significant fines – a sign that employers tried to cheat in competing for workers. Still, all signs point to a more moderate increase in wages in England than elsewhere, and prices for handicraft products were also controlled.

The French monarchy also responded to the increases in wages by issuing a Grand Ordinance in February of 1351, again after the immediate shock had faded. King Jean was concerned about wages, prices, and beggars. The new rules recognized a fair increase of wages as being one-third higher than before the plague. Vinedressers were specifically limited to this raise, a sign that they were in short supply, and that the demand for wine remained buoyant. Masters were prohibited from luring away employees from other masters. This very specific ordinance set winter wages for builders at twenty-six pennies a day for masters and sixteen pennies for their assistants; in summer the wages rose to thirty-two pennies and twenty, respectively. Actual accounts from the hospice of St. Jacques in Paris reveal much higher wages for masons, about seventy-two pennies for masters and thirty pennies a day for their assistants – about triple the previous rate. In France, the enforcement mechanisms do not seem as effective as in England. But in France the government seems even more aware that any attempt to control wages must rest on a similar effort to limit price increases, especially of bread, wine, beer, fish, meat, poultry, eggs, and cheese. Interestingly, land prices and rents remained beyond the ambitions of any government to regulate.

In 1349 Pedro IV of Aragon issued an ordinance for Catalonia, including his main city Barcelona, that noted some workers as asking for wages that were four or five times higher than before the plague. Here a commission was charged with setting just wages that were backed up by threats of corporal punishment. All of Aragon received more elaborate rules in 1350, as in England attempting to put wages back to what they had been before the plague, with some adjustments allowed for daily and piece-rate wages to increase. Enforcement mechanisms here shared fines equally between the accuser, the king, and the local authority, a good way to stimulate informing. One new wrinkle in Aragon invoked a kind of force majeure rule and canceled all previous work rules in the trades. No one was allowed to hire more than twelve workers, except as harvesters – a loophole for the big landowners. Yet, the king abolished all these rules in 1352 because of abuses by rural employers for whom no rules was probably a favor. The kingdom of Castile also tried to control prices and wages in 1351 and was still tinkering with the rules as late as 1369. Here there was a real effort to abolish beggary, and the law required everyone to work, except the elderly, the sick, and those younger than twelve. Violators were whipped on the first offense – an accuser and two witnesses were sufficient to convict. Workers and employers faced stiff fines for breaking rules on wages. General hostility to the idle suggests that hunger and market incentives were no longer sufficient to compel everyone to work or at least as many as employers needed – hence, the use of force to affect bargaining over the terms of employment.

In Florence one trade tried to respond the realities of a postplague market. In 1349, the wool cloth guild imposed specific production quotas on all its member masters with an upper limit of 220 cloths. This effort to limit production must be a typical corporate guild response – share the market in a period of lower demand. Yet, by the late 1360s, Florentine wool cloth production had nearly tripled, a sign that the old rule was ineffective or had been abandoned. Wool was in abundant supply, and people could afford new clothes. These manufacturers were not the last to believe that they could produce themselves out of a slump in demand. Venice and other Mediterranean ports faced a different problem – a need for rowers in the labor-intensive galleys. Here the focus was on ways to increase the labor pool by putting more boys at an oar, reducing crew sizes, and luring fugitives back to the city. All this took place in the context of smaller fleets everywhere.

European societies by the 1350s were midway through a calamitous fourteenth century that had already witnessed famine, disease, and wars started and yet to come. Local responses and eventual signs of recovery require a closer look. The resilience of society and the economy continue to impress observers. The daily rhythms of farming, learning trades, and raising families continued amid great uncertainties. Yet, at first glance, we must conclude that social and economic institutions survived the catastrophes but would not remain unchanged. Technology is a good subject to investigate, before and after the plagues, for its development occurred in the context of growth and crisis.

SELECT BIBLIOGRAPHY

Ole J. Benedictow, *The Black Death 1346–1353: The Complete History*. Woodbridge, 2004.

Jean-Noël Biraben, *Les homes et la peste en France et dans les pays européens et méditerranéens*. Paris, 1976.

Ann G. Carmichael, "Plague Legislation in the Italian Renaissance," *Bulletin of the History of Medicine* 57 (1983): 508–25.

Samuel K. Cohn, Jr., "The Black Death and the Burning of the Jews," *Past and Present* 196 (2007): 3–36.

———. *The Black Death Transformed: Disease and Culture in Early Renaissance Europe*. New York, 2002.

Michael W. Dols, *The Black Death in the Middle East*. Princeton, 1977.

Stephan R. Epstein, *An Island for Itself: Economic Development and Social Change in Late Medieval Sicily*. Cambridge, 1992.

David Herlihy, *The Black Death and the Transformation of the West*. Cambridge, MA, 1997.

Rosemary Horrox, *The Black Death*. Manchester, 1994.

Danielle Jacquart and Claude Thomasset, *Sexuality and Medicine in the Middle Ages*. Translated by Matthew Adamson. Princeton, 1988.

William Chester Jordan, *The Great Famine: Northern Europe in the Early Fourteenth Century*. Princeton, 1996.

Benjamin Z. Kedar, *Merchants in Crisis: Genoese and Venetian Men of Affairs and the Fourteenth-Century Depression*. New Haven, 1976.

William H. McNeill, *Plagues and Peoples*. Garden City NY, 1977.

John M. Najemy, *A History of Florence 1200–1575*. Malden, MA, 2006.

David Nicholas, *The Metamorphosis of a Medieval City: Ghent in the Age of the Arteveldes 1302–1390*. Lincoln NE, 1987.

7

TECHNOLOGY AND CONSUMERISM

ECHNOLOGY GIVES US THE OPPORTUNITY TO REVISIT ECONOMIC and social themes first appearing before the Big Death and then altered by it. Consumerism also began before the plague, and survivors had more money to drive tastes and trends in the markets. Important links connect these themes, and we will begin with technology. This text is not a history of technology – many fine surveys already exist. Technical details on how certain machines worked need not distract us from the big picture, which remains the pace of technological change and how these developments affected people.

The pace and scope of modern technology keeps many of us from understanding a world in which tradition remained strong and the pace of change imperceptible. Technology allows people to manipulate the material world. Why should they want to do that? People need to eat, wear clothing, and be protected from bad weather – the minimal comforts of life. Technology is fundamentally a search for comfort through using tools to provide more food, better clothing, buildings, and whatever else consumers want. Institutions may also foster this search for comfort – wage labor and apprenticeship are examples of how to organize work more efficiently. Histories of technology usually focus on the things people use to make more and better things. So, to rephrase the first question – what incentives do people have to make better things? In a market economy today, we presume that the common incentive is money. Beyond their own personal comfort, inventors have the incentive of wealth – make a better mousetrap, and the world will beat a path to your door. This model also embodies an assumption about progress – all things being equal, our tools, and hence our comfort, should be constantly improving as people devise better ways of making themselves richer and us more comfortable.

This neat picture does not conform to the realities of the technological scene in Europe from 1000 to 1500. Let us note the problems. Not everyone believed that increased comfort was the purpose of life. St. Francis of Assisi and many others sought out hardship, physical suffering, and simple food and clothing in a search for spiritual purity. A society valuing these impulses might look askance at those preoccupied with human comfort. With a few rare exceptions, the common theme in medieval technology will be the accomplishments of nameless tinkerers making small improvements in existing ways of doing things. The modern concept of the genius inventor bringing a new technology to market did not exist in our period of study, or today. Yet, we must assume that some incentives encouraged men and women to tinker or else nothing would have changed in how people manipulated their environment. Current debates about technology often involve the idea of intellectual property – that inventors have a property right in the new methods they discover. At the very end of our period of study, we will see signs of the first patents and a legal recognition that a temporary monopoly was a privilege some have a right to enjoy. Even this idea is far from modern ideas about music – which it never occurred to anyone in our period of study that someone might own or have as property.

If intellectual property remained in the future, medieval people certainly understood profit, a venerable incentive. Trademarks as guarantees of quality signaled consumers and were proxies for best technologies and practices. Yet, artisans also understood that new technologies cost money to implement and sometimes failed. Profit motives and risks in adopting new technologies influenced the cycle of "creative destruction." New shops and firms, with better tools and techniques, replaced older and less-efficient ones, just as more canny merchants outworked their competitors. The surviving records are not very good on technology in general, let alone on the personal motives of those trying new techniques. Contemporary witnesses were slow to note or praise new techniques, and often we must depend on crude illustrations of looms or mills to mark the changes. Great surviving monuments, such as medieval cathedrals, were built over long periods of time usually by anonymous planners and builders who seldom left behind any records at all describing how they did things. Old tools do not survive well, and because most medieval ones were made of wood, archaeologists have found few examples to analyze. For all of these reasons, the history of late medieval technology in Europe must be assembled from scraps and hints. The subject has received far less attention than theology, and medieval people might have approved of this balance. How people worked to make their material lives better remains an important issue for understanding how the Europe of 1500 was poised to become such a major force in the world, certainly more than it had been in 1000.

A few general points will help introduce technology. First, everyone consumes, even if it is only locusts and honey. So we can assume that if people are hungry, they want more to eat or if people are cold, they want warmer clothing. If they cannot see well and eyeglasses are available, they will want them, at a good price. People manipulating the material world will want and need more than their own muscles to accomplish tasks. Nearly all medieval energy was natural or renewable – human strength and that of horse and oxen, water, wind, and even solar power. People overwhelmingly used wood for fuel and its derivative charcoal, and just a little coal. New and more efficient supplies of energy comprise a great deal of the history of medieval technology. A second issue harkens back to themes that have appeared in other chapters, and it concerns the benefits of more advanced neighbors. As we will see, behind many medieval technological innovations will be some sort of claim that the idea originated in China, India, or the Muslim world. Rather than inventing the idea of invention, medieval Europeans may have been the first of the great free riders benefiting from borrowing the best practices of others. If so, we can certainly credit their open horizons and lack of prejudice as they were eager to see and adopt better ways of doing things. This is an important issue because of the later question of the "Great Divergence" – the parting of the ways among Europe, China, and India, as rough examples, in their levels of technology and hence material comfort and prosperity. Clearly, there are many logical leaps to explore here, but we need to consider the connections between technology and economic development – a mix of sustained comfort and prosperity. One obvious reason to do this is that an important area of technology concerned self-defense or offense, the means of war. Better tools to manipulate the battlefield certainly affected the comfort of warriors as well as the societies that paid for and won or lost these struggles.

STYLES OF TECHNOLOGY

Agriculture remained by far the most important economic sector and the main employer as most people manipulated the environment for food. Technological advances before and after 1000 have already been explored. The later Middle

Ages witnessed a more widespread use of the heavy plow with an iron plow-share, better harnesses, and other techniques. No startling advances occurred between, say, 1200 and 1500 because, as yet, there was no substitute for human and animal muscle in the hard work of farming.

Cloth production was probably the second main employer – casual weaving in many rural areas and specialized manufacturing in the urbanized parts of Europe. Wool and flax for linen were present in Europe since antiquity, and cotton and silk were drifting to the West, especially after 1200. This economic and social history cannot treat the technologies of every industry. Moving wool, from the backs of sheep to the backs of women and men, remains a story central to the later medieval economy and technology. The many trades associated with steps in this process will enable us to look the broader issues surrounding technology.

John H. Munro and others have closely examined each stage of this process, and this work provides a fine entry into the technologies associated with man-ufacturing textiles. English wool, for example, arrived at the carders in great sacks of typically about 364 pounds, containing the fleeces of as many as 260 sheep. This wool clip, mostly from ewes, needed to be unpacked and carded and combed for the spinners to make thread. Weaving of course was an ancient art. The transverse yarn or weft was woven at right angles to the foundational warp fibers – in the classic upright loom, the cloth produced would be limited roughly to the average height of the weaver. A linen warp with a woolen or later a cotton weft yielded fustians. Other combinations (mixing animal and vegetable fibers) and patterns of cloth were possible.

All of this had been known for millennia. We must focus on what was new. First, the wool itself, typically from short-stapled (fiber) sheep traditional in Europe began to face competition in the late thirteenth and fourteenth centuries from long-stapled finer wool (stronger yarn or thread) from the Merino sheep bred in Castile. Knives or better shears were used to take the wool from the live sheep, keeping them as a renewable resource. More iron and some steel would make these processes more efficient, but nothing much new here in our period. Combing and carding were necessary to disentangle and align the fibers in preparation for spinning. Finer carding tools, probably borrowed from cotton production in Muslim Sicily and Spain, made it possible to use short wool fibers better. Drawing out the fibers by hand, spinning, using a traditional distaff, with a spindle and whorl was ancient technology. The important innovation here was the spinning wheel (Figure 7.1), which first appeared in the late twelfth

Figure 7.1. Spinning Wheel (from Robert Friedel, *A Culture of Improvement.* Cambridge, MA, 2007, p. 74).

and early thirteenth century, used a mechanized spindle and whorl to pull out thread or yarn on a bobbin. The spinner still turned the wheel, but the process was faster and probably tripled productivity over hand spinning. There was a small quality problem because the thread produced was not as uniformly strong and hence warps might break. Spinning wheels were known centuries before in India and China, were copied in Muslim lands, were seen there (Spain and Sicily were obvious points of contact), and then spread across Europe. In the fifteenth century, a better spinning wheel appeared in Europe, doubling productivity by using a mechanically driven flyer and bobbin to twist the yarn into thread. A gender division of labor developed as women predominated in spinning while men worked at the more obscure task of making the wheels from wood.

The early medieval upright loom prevailed in weaving until sometime in the eleventh century, when the main medieval advance occurred, the first signs of people using their hands and feet to weave at the horizontal treadle loom (Figure 7.2). The introduction and gradual elaboration of this device was central

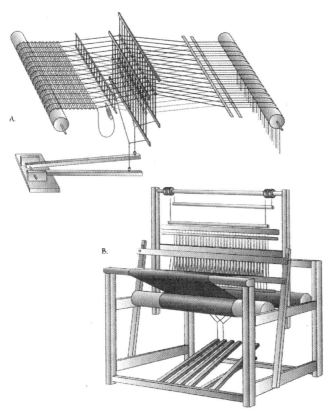

Figure 7.2. Horizontal Loom (from Robert Friedel, *A Culture of Improvement.* Cambridge, MA, 2007, p. 76).

to medieval technology, and we know very little about it – no looms or manuals survive, and even contemporary pictures are rare. Scholars presume that this loom was also "borrowed" from the Muslims, who in turn may have learned about the machine farther East. To see a horizontal treadle loom would open the mind of a curious person to grasp the improvements it offered. No one imagines that an actual loom ever traveled anywhere (although weavers might have), but the idea of such a loom, once explained to a carpenter, made sense. Hands and feet together, and eventually two weavers working as a team on a broadcloth, significantly increased the productivity of weaving, again tripling productivity. A seated weaver could use his (or sometimes her) feet to operate a treadle for opening the passages for the shuttle carrying the weft through the alternating warp and still operated by hand. The vertical loom had used a stick called a heddle to keep the warp apart. The horizontal loom could also wind the finished cloth, often to lengths of thirty yards or more, so it was no longer limited by the height of the vertical loom. The horizontal loom also produced a tighter weave. A broadloom increased the width of the cloth beyond the arm span of a single weaver as two weavers now managed the shuttle. Using good data from late medieval Flanders, where weaving technology was as sophisticated as the main rival weaving centers in northern Italy, Munro has calculated that two weavers used eighty-four pounds of wool to make a broadcloth measuring 32 by $2\frac{3}{4}$ yards in twelve days. This means that a typical team of weavers, working 240 days a year, could turn out ten broadcloths – a rate of productivity as good as any until the big technological advances of the eighteenth century. A fifteenth-century loom was an expensive piece of machinery, owned by a master weaver. Who manufactured these looms and how entrepreneurs supplied them to weavers remain unclear.

Once the cloth was woven, fullers used special clay (fuller's earth), grease, and urine (making soap) to treat cloth in vats in order to mat the fibers and prepare the cloth for dyers, if the yarn had not already been dyed (in the wool). Originally, fullers used their feet for this work, but fulling mills, introduced in Italy in the tenth century and later in the north, made their task more efficient. Again, master fullers were the ones with enough capital to own and operate mills whose technology we examine below. After the fulled cloth was dried and its nap sheared, dyers went to work, using traditional colors, such as madder for red, or indigo for blue. The most important innovation here concerned the widespread use of alum as a fixative or mordant for dyes to make the colors fast. This chemical was found in large quantities at Phocaea in Asia Minor, and by the end of the thirteenth century, Genoese merchants were shipping it to northern cloth centers, such as Bruges.

The important innovations, the spinning wheel, horizontal treadle loom, and fulling mill all appeared before the plague and helped to clothe the increasing number of people in the years of demographic growth. Lighter and cheaper woolens clothed urban and rural people, replacing coarser homespuns. These technologies, along with a specialized division of labor, including expert shearers and dyers in cities relied on the guild system of master employers and wage-earning journeymen and women and apprentices. After the plague, it became increasingly common in parts of Europe to literally farm out parts of the process through a putting out system that brought raw wool to country workers outside the guild rules who could more cheaply card or spin wool yarn. The best cloths with the tightest and most intricate weaves still required an expensive treadle loom that was not found in rural areas. Wool cloth also became an important item of commerce inside and outside of Europe. The medieval centuries witnessed the patient efforts of generations of nameless tinkerers who improved and socialized textile manufacture. First they heard about, made, and improved machines, such as spinning wheels and looms. Over time, social forms like the guild system of education sustained these improvements and institutionalized the process of passing best practices down from one generation to the next. Robert Friedel has called this process a "culture of improvement," a sustaining belief that things could be made better and hence in the terms used here increase the comfort and happiness of people. More examples may help us understand how Europeans became so open and willing to adapt technological improvements without (as yet) strong beliefs in progress or intellectual property rights.

ENERGY

The textile business at every stage required human muscle power and manual skills. Improvements in technology made people more productive, but they still had to work hard at every step in the process from shearing sheep to dyeing cloth. Where might humans look for help? Later medieval Europe was "Green." The sun met nearly all of its energy needs, providing food for human and animal muscle, wood to burn, and even the wind for mills. Gravity created waterpower. Horses and oxen sustained medieval agriculture and later provided the general measure of energy use – horsepower – the energy needed to raise 75 kilograms one meter in one second. Alas for the horse and oxen, over time their individual effort only amounted to about one-quarter horsepower. People were even weaker, and it took seven to nine of them to accomplish as much work as a single horse. We need to keep in mind that animals could be put to work turning a shaft or axle so they could turn millstones or pull carts and wheeled plows. Hence, the ratio of working animals to people is a reliable index of available energy, but unfortunately, medieval people counted animals less often than themselves.

Animals required food and care, and they died. Nature provided other sources of energy that we need to consider. Everywhere people burned wood for all of the obvious needs, and charcoal burners provided a lighter fuel that burned more intensely. Charcoal burners across Europe's forests provided a fuel that suited urban dwellers. The great story is the retreat of Europe's forests before the plague and afterward some lands in the west went back to forest and scrub as a diminished population needed less fuel. Coal too burns and where it appears close to the surface, around Liège and Newcastle, for example, people knew as far back as the eleventh century that it might substitute for wood. The problem was a stronger version of the one wood too posed – coal was heavy, and its transport was expensive as even waterways could take the coal only so far. It is surprising that coal contributed so little to Europe's energy needs before 1500, until we remember that surface coal was not common and that transport costs were the limiting step.

All around medieval people, water and air moved. Harnessing this energy was the obvious and cheapest way to augment human strength. Great sailing ships, the round ships and cogs usually with two masts, took advantage of the wind to move cargoes and peoples across the seas. By about 1300, these vessels had reached a technological maturity. The typical cog, carrying 200 tons with a crew of about twenty men, was a very efficient and complex machine. In the Mediterranean, these round ships competed with the traditional galley, with its one great lateen (triangular) sail and large crews. Sails, made from heavy cotton canvas, were costly new products. The galleys had smaller cargoes, perhaps fifty tons, but were speedy, and muscle power substituted for light and variable winds. After the plague, trade by ship diminished so there was initially some extra capacity as disease spared machines but not people. Still, these wooden vessels, without metal-sheathed hulls, would not last for long and would need to be replaced. Advances in cogs produced vessels with a shallower draft and flat bottom – faster, cheaper vessels efficiently manned by small crews. Lots of varieties in wind-powered ships testify to human ingenuity in solving the problems of bulk carriers of items, such as grain, wool, and timber. The great galley around 1400, with twenty-four benches each holding three rowers on both sides of the vessel, required 144 rowers, let alone the captain, pilot, cook, marines, and others. Galleys would be fewer and more expensive after the plague. Through 1500, free men, not slaves, continued to row European fleets.

On land, water and wind also augmented human energy. We will save windmills for later and look first at the water mill, the most common means of capturing natural energy. Mills too were ancient technology; the Romans knew nearly everything about them. The great survey of England, the *Domesday Book*,

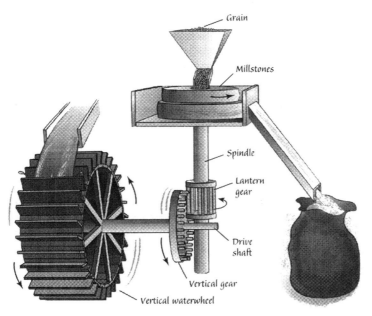

Figure 7.3. Grist Mill (from Robert Friedel, *A Culture of Improvement.* Cambridge, MA, 2007, p. 36).

indicates that about 6,000 mills were there in the eleventh century. The primary task of mills was to grind wheat or other hard grains into flour. Wheat stored for long periods as kernels and was easier to transport, while fresh flour was an advantage in baking. Of course, very old technologies concerning various forms of hand mills, querns, existed since the Stone Age, but using water power to turn millstones saved people a dull and tiring task, freeing them for other activities. A mill turned stones too heavy for humans, and finding and chiseling suitable stone for mills was a skilled art. The basic gristmill (Figure 7.3) embodied many subtle parts and required considerable ingenuity in locating it in the best place. This mill has an overshot wheel, so called because the water comes over the wheel from above. The big idea here is to take advantage of gravity and gear ratios to increase the power from the wheel. Modern calculations suggest that such mills were, in effect, engines operating at between forty and sixty horsepower. Nature provided few ideal spots along rivers, so channels were often dug to divert water to a mill sited where a good drop suited an overshot wheel. Running water dropping from a height was the best way to run a mill. While the drive shaft might directly turn the stones, a better use of the energy required that the shaft's direction be changed to a spindle by using gears – this too is old technology. The spindle turned the horizontal stones that ground grain into flour. Medieval ingenuity placed floating mills on rapidly running waters, such as the Garonne near Toulouse, which in the twelfth century had about sixty mills in operation along an artificial dam, the famous Bazacle. Floating mills used undershot current to operate the wheels, which worked best around bridges where the waters were channeled and faster. Medieval people knew how to use dams and artificial channels to increase available hydropower. As early as the eleventh century, in some ideal spots in northern Europe, tidal mills took advantage of the seas to draw out needed energy.

Mill technology required capital, but there was money to be made in milling. Lords claiming rights over rivers could also increase their incomes by granting privileges to millers to construct mills. Lords also commonly required tenants to use their mills and extracted payments, often a tenth of the flour, for this service. In some places, hand mills became illegal, a presumed sign that peasants resented the mill owners. In cities, the division of labor complicated the social relations among consumers purchasing loaves, master bakers within guilds, and the millers who supplied the flour – sometimes bakers controlled this step as well. In southern Europe, which had less running water and sluggish tides in the Mediterranean, animals still did much of the work of grinding wheat and rye. Also in the south, an old technology, the edge-runner mill, relied on a simple vertical stone to turn and smash olives to produce their oil so important as food and for lighting. Ordinary turning millstones were also available for other important tasks, such as sharpening blades, polishing, and flattening metals, to name a few. The plague seems to have had no effect on this technology and social relations, except perhaps making it possible to abandon old and inefficient mills, improving the quality of capital stock.

The first medieval windmills, appearing in the late twelfth century (a notice from Yorkshire in 1185), were post mills. The problem with wind power was that even in areas of strong winds, such as the flat plains of northern Europe along the North Sea, the direction is variable enough to make a fixed windmill impractical. People, by using watercourses and sluices, could move water's direction, but the wind had to be used as it came. The idea behind the post mill was to have the entire device placed on a post as a pivot that could be turned in the right direction so that the mill's typically four sails could use wind power to turn a shaft. Wind mills were an ideal way to harness natural power in flat areas where waterpower could do little. Because of the timing and location of the first windmills, they were a genuine European innovation, even though other civilizations used them. Ships with sails were a common sight on the North Sea, as were strong winds and sluggish streams. The idea of putting a sail to use as a vane to turn a shaft was brilliant and seemed obvious enough after someone thought of it. Turning the mill was admittedly a clumsy solution that limited the size and power of the mill.

By the late fifteenth century, probably somewhere in Holland, this problem was solved by the turret mill. A large fixed tower of brick or more rarely stone had at its top a simple revolving turret that moved more easily the shaft with the sails. This idea made more substantial mills possible and seems to respond well to the problems the Dutch faced in finding the energy to move water off their lands. Also, because they imported much of their wood and charcoal, any other energy source was a clear bonus. Two points merit notice before we return to the more common water mill. First, these applications of wind technology in Europe were spontaneous and indigenous responses to opportunity. Second, wind mills were still expensive to start, and the post mill and then turret mill appeared generations before and after the Big Death. Hence, they both suggest a more complicated path to new technologies than a simple approach to the supply of labor or assuming that capital smoothly substitutes for labor.

Perhaps the most important innovation in water mills concerned a minor but crucial alteration to the horizontal shaft, turning it into a cam shaft with tappets (Figure 7.4). The stubs on the shaft turned the rotary motion of the shaft into a vertical reciprocal strike that could move hammers to pound anything that needed to be pounded. Regular force and rapidity of the hammer strikes far exceeded human efforts and improved productivity in many endeavors. Once again, cam shafts appeared in parts of Europe as early as the eleventh century, while they had existed in China long before that. Opinions differ about whether this is another example of technological borrowing or independent discovery. Once an imaginative person sees a camshaft, reproducing the technology and applying it are not difficult tasks. Even hearing about such a device might be enough to prompt experiments. Medieval Europeans were using gears to shift the direction of the turning shaft, and the tappet itself looks like a single tooth of a gear, which in turn took advantage of the swinging weight of the hammerhead to pound away. Leaving aside the fruitless debate over priority of invention, we should focus on the important point of how quickly people in Europe applied this new technology in milling to other endeavors. These applications include sawing wood, beating wool cloth for the fullers or rag

Figure 7.4. Tappet Camshaft (from Robert Friedel, *A Culture of Improvement*. Cambridge, MA, 2007, p. 44).

mashes for paper manufacturers, or beating iron blooms or operating bellows for the smiths. In Muslim Valencia, pulp mills were turning linen rags into paper by the twelfth century. As we have seen, fulling mills in Italy were even older. Ores with high levels of iron were common especially in parts of northern Europe, and we will explore the application of new technology to the old problems of the Iron Age – how to make tools more durable than stone and wood or even copper and bronze.

IRON

Iron ore was common in much of Europe. If only people could figure out how to smelt it, make the iron less brittle, and keep its edges sharp, this metal made tools and weapons stronger than any others. Local experiments with different qualities of ore and methods for purifying it produced a useful mix of competitive practices across Europe. For example, people discovered that local ores rich in manganese made better steel, and ones with phosphorus had a lower melting point. Medieval miners understood the results and not the chemistry, but generations of local lore taught about subtle differences in ores. Ancient technology continued to produce iron blooms – the product of ore slag heated in pits with alternating levels of wood or charcoal. The resulting bloom was mostly iron, but many impurities remained in the bars or rods, which could be reheated and beaten to produce wrought iron at about 1550°C. This work was rural, close to supplies of ore, often in swampy areas (hence the phrase: "bog iron") and also depended on charcoal from speedily denuded hillsides. At this stage, iron became useful for essential items in the early medieval economy, such as plowshares, sickles, nails, horseshoes, and, of course, weapons and chain mail. The most advanced techniques for producing blades involved beating exceptionally thin strips of iron and them welding them together with additional forging to produce a handmade steel blade. Steel remained an expensive rarity often imported into Europe from Muslim lands and through them even from India. Medieval European smiths were content to forge a thin steel edge to an iron blade by repeated beating of the edge over a charcoal fire in order to literally pound a tiny percentage of carbon into the iron to produce an edge of steel.

Thus far, every stage of this process had been known for centuries, in some cases millennia, since the dawn of the Iron Age, and required hard human labor from making charcoal to wielding a hammer. Once again, transport costs made moving ores impractical, and they were often smelted where found. Iron bars and rods were valuable enough to ship to nearby urban areas for further work. (Milan is a good case study of a city known for its ironworks from the eleventh century, and it figures in every stage of the militarizing of iron from chain mail and swords to guns over the next five hundred years and beyond.) Once again, the problem is how to apply naturally occurring sources of energy to the stages of iron manufacture in order to increase productivity. Raising the temperature inside a pit required the construction of a stone or brick furnace to transform ore into iron bloom. Supplying more oxygen to the fire required bellows, operated by hand and another ancient tool. A camshaft could supply the regular strikes required to operate bellows as well as hammers, so synergies were in widespread use by 1300 between the mill, the pit furnace, and forged iron. Every good iron tool made working wood easier, and this meant better spinning wheels, looms, oars, ships, and gears for mills. Yet, iron's real value rested in its application to farming and war. Everything we know suggests that this was the best possible incentive to produce higher-quality iron in larger amounts, because demand can summon forth supplies.

The great medieval change in smelting iron came with the use of the blast furnace – the earliest known example found in Sweden and dating from about 1350. Sweden had abundant high-quality supplies of ore and plenty of wood for charcoal, so the location is not surprising. The idea behind a blast furnace is to raise the making of a bloom out of a pit into a constructed stone or brick furnace that used mill-powered bellows to force more oxygen into the furnace. The greater supply of oxygen raised the temperature inside the furnace, making it easier to remove impurities (slag) and increase the percentage of carbon in the iron. By making a molten iron with as much as 4 percent carbon in it, the iron remained liquid at even lower temperatures, making it possible to bring the molten iron out of the furnace and channel it into sand or clay pits in order to cast it. At first, these cast blobs were simply called "pigs," hence cast or pig iron. The blast furnace turned out much higher quantities of less brittle iron that could for the first time be cast in shapes other than simple rods or bars. Some of the drudgery was removed from the smiths who could spend more time making better tools rather than monotonously beating impurities out of bog iron.

This important step in making iron first appeared right during the Big Death in Sweden, a tribute to the resilience of the human spirit in the face of catastrophe, and must result from some tinkering before the plague. So, once again, there is no neat cause and effect between demographic loss and rising wages and substituting capital for labor in new technologies. Another problem complicates this story. Casting iron from blast furnaces had been known in China for perhaps as long as two thousand years before it appeared in Sweden and soon other places in western Europe. Travelers from the west, beginning with the Polos of Venice in the late thirteenth century, must have seen blast furnaces there, or in Persia where they also existed by this time. Because we cannot connect any dots between Sweden and Persia, and because no surviving traveler or missionary account mentions the blast furnace, this appears to be another case of independent innovation at the extreme ends of Eurasia. By 1400, blast furnaces also appeared around Styria in the Alps and Liège, other places where mills, ore, and, in Flanders, coal came together in the right areas to minimize transport costs and foster innovation. Better iron made traditional means of producing steel more effective, but no new technical means gave Europeans any big advantage in this area.

Their weapons are another story. Substituting steel for wood conferred obvious advantages. For example, the crossbow, which appeared in the eleventh century, allowed a bowman to use his entire upper body strength to pull the bowstring to propel a bolt. Holding the bow upright on the ground, the bowman, using a foot on the bow and a hook on his belt, was slower than a traditional archer with a longbow. But the crossbow, soon enhanced with sinew and horn, had a far greater range and force than traditional arrows and was an ideal weapon to use behind fortifications and onboard ships. Beginning about 1370, Europeans began to make crossbows from steel, and this innovation further increased its tension and hence range. A crank added to the tension in the bowstring. More complex technologies in offensive weapons, such as bows, inevitably fostered a switch from older chain mail to more-resistant plate armor. This typical spiral of offensive and defensive weaponry of course stimulated the market for more and better steel.

By far the biggest military consumer of quality iron or steel was the chain mail hauberk. This basic item of defensive armor protected the torso and upper arms. Thousands of riveted rings, each attached to four others, made its wearer safer on horseback or on foot. The rings, usually made from drawn wire or sometimes punched from sheets, were laboriously put together into a durable and expensive product, good booty often serving generations of warriors. Bigger steel helmets also cost money but made their wearers more effective in battle. Plate steel armor began to appear in the late thirteenth century and became more common later when more powerful crossbows and eventually gunpowder appeared on the battlefield. Many industrial needs drove advances in metalworking, but the warriors remained demanding and well-informed consumers of the best weaponry.

CRYSTAL AND GLASS

A brief word on this industry seems appropriate here as a transition to the traditional big three of late medieval technology – clocks, gunpowder, and the printing press. These technologies once again raise important questions about technological diffusion across Asia. Yet, to some degree, which is difficult to quantify, extending the working life of the literate by helping the farsighted to be able to focus on nearer objects seems to be a real blessing to readers. Generations of students and teachers, as well as all other types of close workers, have been grateful for the invention of eyeglass or spectacles. There is no need to apologize for the use of "invention" here as in this case the alias anonymous tinkerer who discovered the right way to use lenses to correct vision accomplished something unique in human history. Amazingly, we hardly know where or when this happened. Written evidence from a sermon in 1305 in Italy is the first official notice of eyeglasses, said to be a recent invention of the last twenty years – so the usual textbook date is 1285. The sermon was given in Florence but mosaic and crystal workers were more numerous and skilled in Pisa or Venice so one of these places, usually the latter, receives the credit. The inventor is unknown, although the English friar Roger Bacon had observed back in the 1260s that a convex lens increased the size of a letter.

Another important trick or two was necessary to make eyeglasses, and once again the innovations seem simple and obvious, once one has been told them! First, Venetians had been making fine glass out of good white sand (as pure silicon dioxide as possible) and ashes (some alkali, oxides, or carbonates of sodium or potassium – classic soda ash and potash). In 1291, the city moved the master glassmakers and their furnaces to Murano, where Venetian craftsmen and women made all sorts of glass and eventually mirrors that became important objects of Venetian commerce in the later Middle Ages. The problem is that even the best Venetian glass was not yet clear or transparent enough to work as a lens for correcting vision – this advance would not occur until the fifteenth century. Hence, early eyeglasses required naturally occurring rock crystals that lapidaries cut and shape into first hemispheres and then convex lenses to correct vision. Fine rock crystal can be found and mined, and was put to many uses from jewelry to mosaics, especially in colored forms. Glass was cheaper and already substituted for crystal in many uses, hence the assumption that some glassmaker was the real inventor. This person must have also been the one to see that a pair of lenses worked best, and they were more productive when worn as a pair by the viewer, rather than being placed right upon the writing or whatever object one needed to see. Simplistic monocausal explanations abound for how inventions decisively affect subsequent events. The revival of classical learning in the fourteenth and fifteenth centuries, one facet of the Renaissance, did not depend on eyeglasses to begin or to sustain it.

One important feature of the glass industry concerns the way Venice used its trading networks to dominate commerce in the Mediterranean and parts of northern Europe. In the early Middle Ages, Syria produced the best glass, known for its transparency and thinness. Glassblowing had been invented in this region and products from Damascus and elsewhere were known from Germany to China. Venetian merchants knew a good product when they saw one, and Venetian glassblowers improved observed techniques. By the late thirteenth century, their galleys were bringing back as ballast high-quality Syrian alkali for the glassworks on Murano. By the mid-fourteenth century, Venetian merchants were exporting high-quality glassware and mirror glass back to Syria and Egypt, part of a process by which these merchants were able to compete successfully and ruin Middle Eastern industries in paper, glass, and cotton. Glass, like later books or cotton, was an ideal product for the galley trade and a good way for Venetian labor to add value to products as opposed to simply rowing commodities and finished goods across the Mediterranean.

CLOCKS

This mechanical device enabled people to tell the precise time by using for energy the force of gravity applied to weights. This simple statement begs a few questions, not the least of which is: why was it important to know the time? Ancient systems of reckoning time left medieval Europe with an odd legacy from a base twelve system going back to the Babylonians – twelve hours for the day and twelve for the night, and each hour broken into sixty minutes, and each of them into sixty seconds – the last two subtleties for a long time impossible to measure and hence inconsequential. The obvious problem is that by convention the daytime and nighttime hours varied in length according to the season – very short daytime hours in Scottish winter, for example. This feature of reckoning time would have to be abandoned. Ancient and early medieval societies had ways to measure time – all with their strengths and weaknesses. Sundials were imprecise, hard to set accurately, and did not work at night or on cloudy days. Water clocks using a regular drip for countable beats were complex, large, and hence impossible to move, and could freeze. Alfonso X of Castile (1221–1284) had a clock using mercury to solve that problem, but this made the machine (it had an astrolabe on its face) even more a luxury one-off item. Many variations in the composition of tallow and beeswax for candles, and their size and expense, counted against a regular use of marked candles to measure the time at night. Sandglasses were only as reliable as the person remembering to turn them and were really only useful for short measures of time.

Given all of these technical difficulties, it might seem that there were ample incentives for a better way to measure time – provided there was some reason for knowing it. Several groups of medieval people appear to have particular reasons for knowing the exact time. Monks and nuns in monasteries needed to keep track of the canonical hours that regulated the seven daily prayer services over a twenty-four-hour period from before dawn to after sunset. The first mechanical clocks were probably bell-ringing devices used in monasteries to summon people to services. They first appeared in the mid-to-late thirteenth century somewhere in northwestern Europe and quickly spread. Even before the invention of the clock, medieval merchants in cities, such as Genoa, had been dating commercial contracts down to the canonical hour of the day, from lauds to prime, terce, sext, nones, vespers, and compline. This precision, predating the clock and hence relying on church bells regulated by sundials, candles, or dead reckoning, helped busy people to remember where they were when a contract was struck. Keeping appointments made business more efficient. Masters and their workers also relied on an idea of the working day regulated by church bells. Because, during the thirteenth century, wage labor was, as we have seen, becoming an increasingly important part of urban and even rural economies, the length of the working day was a public issue about which all parties wanted precise agreement. There is no reason to assume that these practical needs for reckoning time represent a secularizing of the spiritual canonical hours or indeed the rise of Western rationalizing of time as money. Instead, the ubiquitous ringing of church bells helped working people and merchants order their days, just as the call of the muezzin to prayer marked the day in Muslim lands. The first great public clocks, which used a dial to indicate the hour, began to appear across Europe shortly after 1300, and so sight as well as sound helped to mark the hours of the day.

The mechanical clock depends on a series of clever solutions once again conceived by the now familiar anonymous craftspeople. Weights solved the energy problem, but the power had to be transmitted by a gear train to a mechanism using oscillating motion. Some way had to be found to block and release the power train according to a regular pattern – this technical problem alone required hours of equal length. The first solution was the escapement, the verge, and foliot (Figure 7.5), regarded by many as the most ingenious and important medieval inventions. The crown wheel, a gear, turned the verge, a modified camshaft that had small pallets. Hence, the verge could turn one way or the other, the length of time regulated by the *foliot*, the crossbar that swung back and forth in a way the clockmakers thought a crazy (folie) motion. Weights on the foliots determined the length of the interval or beat and hence the pace of the dial or bells attached to the entire mechanism. The first clocks were large instruments permanently mounted and not precise enough to measure seconds. Other devices attached to the basic mechanism rang bells announcing the hours. These are the standard municipal clocks appearing on towers on city halls and attached to churches across Europe.

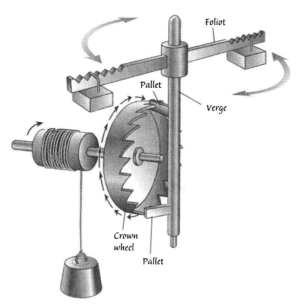

Figure 7.5. Verge and Foliot (from Robert Friedel, *A Culture of Improvement*. Cambridge, MA, 2007, p. 104).

Another major technological innovation took place in the mid-fifteenth century, when a coiled spring substituted for the large and awkward system of weights. The use of a spring required advances in brass and steel metallurgy and a device to solve the problem of regular force – which decreases as a spring unwinds. A cone-like tapering piece of metal, the *fusee*, placed between the spring and the clockwork, used the changing circumference of the fusee to make constant the force of the unwinding spring. This innovation made smaller, portable clocks possible, first appearing over the course of the fifteenth century, and early in the next century, the (large) watch. Making time measurement miniaturized and hence portable and more private made it possible for the wealthy to keep time in their houses, but not quite yet on their persons. Clock making, a new trade, combined many skills into high-value products that astonished the world. Once again this innovation straddles the Big Death, and there is no reason to see demographic change or even wages driving this development. Efficient use of time seems to be the major impetus, as well as the need to keep appointments, to pay regular wages, and to pray.

GUNPOWDER

In Chapter 8, we will look more closely at war as a driving force behind social and economic changes, just as these matters affected how and when people resorted to violence to solve disputes about trade and values, among other things. Much of medieval technology, from building more impregnable castles to better armor and faster ships, developed from war, which in turn cost so much money. Synergies among the various innovations always existed. In Ragusa in the late fourteenth and fifteenth centuries, the same people maintained clocks and made crossbows – because they understood springs. A brief word on gunpowder is relevant here because its use is part of the constellation of changes before and after the Big Death that help us to see the connections between labor shortages, cross-cultural borrowings, and technological innovation.

Gunpowder is an explosive chemical mixture, hence a source of energy, consisting of about two-thirds saltpeter (sodium or potassium nitrate [niter] – found barnyards or in nature – known to the Muslims as Chinese snow), one-sixth carbon (made from charcoal), and one-sixth sulfur (mined). The Chinese first used gunpowder before the millennium and had weaponized it to shoot projectiles and make small bombs. In the 1260s, Roger Bacon knew the composition of gunpowder and speculated about its potential uses. Since the Mongols had opened up war and trading connections to Poland and Hungary by the 1220s and missionaries and merchants were visiting China from the 1240s and 1250s, this Eastern invention traveled west quickly. The composition of gunpowder was no secret, although saltpeter was hard to find in Europe. What struck all observers were its possibilities for weapons, as the Chinese had already demonstrated. Relevant for our purposes here, however, is the very slow appearance of new weapons based on gunpowder. The first primitive cannons or bombards appeared in the early fourteenth century, better siege cannons in the late fourteenth and fifteenth centuries. This period also saw the first hand-held weapons – the culverin (a mortar) and the harquebus, the ancestor of the more familiar musket. Gunpowder itself was also improved in the fourteenth century by a process known in English as corning by which the ingredients were first made into a paste, then into small balls that exploded with more force. Obviously advances in metallurgy mattered as the first wooden cannons became the great copper and bronze instruments of the fifteenth century, some smaller versions placed on wheels (certainly during the Hussite wars in Bohemia in 1427) and others aboard ships. Artillery in the fifteenth century revolutionized siege and naval warfare. Only in the sixteenth century did hand-held weapons change the balance of force on the battlefield that the pike men had ruled for so long. Some of these matters will appear in more detail in Chapter 8; however, for the moment, two issues matter – borrowing and factor substitution. Tinkering with chemicals did not lead Europeans to gunpowder; they acquired the technology complete and slowly refined it. Weapons powered by gunpowder slowly became more prominent after the Big Death, but once again the pace of change seems far too slow to simply reflect the substitution of capital for the labor-intensive and larger armies before the plague.

PRINT

Moveable type, the last of the innovations considered here, shares some features with the other innovations; yet, it provides more clarity and a good way to summarize what we have learned about late medieval technology. In the workshop of Johann Gutenberg of Mainz, originally a silversmith, a small group collaborated on learning how to cast letters in the right soft metal. Eventually hitting upon a mix of lead, tin, and antimony, they set frames of type that could print many copies of the same page – and eventually a book – the famous Gutenberg bible appearing in 1455. Woodblock printing had been known in China for centuries and had appeared in Europe in the late fourteenth century. Copper plates in the next century made it possible to print finer pictures, playing cards, posters, and even pamphlets. What Gutenberg and his colleagues provided in moveable type was a vast improvement over block printing because of the speed by which longer works could be turned out in multiple copies. Moveable type, a printing press, and rag paper, cheaper by far than printing on vellum (calfskin) or parchment (sheepskin), came together to bring about the greatest transformation in the technology of the word since the invention of writing.

There is no better testimony to the significance of printing than the amazing speed by which it spread across Europe. By 1500, 236 towns had printers and they had printed perhaps as many as twenty million incunabula (books printed before 1500). This was an impressive number in a society with perhaps seventy million people, only a small minority of whom could read vernacular languages, let alone the Latin and Greek in which most books still appeared. Books became cheaper, more standardized, and single rare copies of manuscripts soon found wider audiences. Books and pamphlets about technology helped to spread news about advances more generally than even the old and reliable handwritten manuals and word of mouth had accomplished. Printing helped to "fix" knowledge so that the accomplishments of the Renaissance humanists in editing and collating the best manuscripts would be preserved and again made available to wider audiences. A few printers could easily do in a day what would take many scribes far longer to copy by hand. Provided that the type had been proofread properly, the printed work could avoid the errors and slips that caused even the best handwritten texts to diverge. What surprise can it be that the Latin Bible was the first printed book? What book was it more important to have in a reliable copy? And how long would the demand for vernacular bibles be resisted? – the last a question for the next century.

The substitution of a modest amount of capital in the form of type and a press seems to make printing the best example of a post-plague labor-saving technology. Even the century between the Big Death and Gutenberg's bible can be explained away by the need for metallurgy to develop so that moveable type could be mass-produced from a steel die originally cut by hand. An alphabet with a small number of letters made printing more efficient than it could ever be in languages like the ones in East Asia relying on thousands of characters – at least before mass-produced type was possible.

This brief survey of medieval technology has stressed the ways that a culture of knowledge, valuing improvement, changed the material world so that more people were comfortable in it. Openness to new ideas and tools existed in trades organized in guilds whose masters valued the secrecy and mysteries of their crafts. Stephan R. Epstein has stressed that guilds were not obstacles to technological innovation, because even when they tried to stifle new techniques, they failed. Apprenticeship embodied hands on training, experience-based knowledge hard to transmit even in the best handwritten and copied manuals. All trades followed this method of vocational learning that rewarded patient tinkering with methods across a wide variety of crafts. Trained workers, the journeymen and women of later medieval Europe, migrated freely across regions and helped to spread knowledge of best practices, thereby reducing information costs. When skilled silk workers left Lucca for new locations in the early fourteenth century, it proved to be a bonanza for competitors. The Venetian state tried to keep glassmakers and their methods secret by isolating them on Murano, and this policy worked at least to the extent of maintaining a lead in this industry. Ambitious rulers like Edward III of England understood that technical knowledge was best preserved and transmitted in the minds of people. (What we call "human capital" is a new phrase but not an original concept.) So he recruited Flemish weavers when he wanted to build a competitive industry in fourteenth-century England. Later medieval cities were magnets for skilled artisans who often traveled long distances and usually found a warm welcome. The guild efforts to preserve trade secrets foundered on this worker mobility.

Venice also had the first patent law in Europe, which in 1447 granted inventors a ten-year monopoly for "ingenious devices." The idea of a patent came from the simple idea of granting a monopoly, a privilege in the market, to an individual. In practice, it is hard to prove in this period that patents played any role in speeding the pace of technological innovation. Florence in 1421 granted a patent for a new type of ship to the architect Filippo Brunelleschi, on the theory that he then did not have to hide his invention, and therefore all of Florence would benefit, and he could profit from it. This patent expired and the ship was never built, useful reminders that not all new ideas have a practical effect in the world. The bishop of Würzburg in 1479 granted the first book privilege, in this case a monopoly for printing breviaries in his German diocese. Venice was also precocious in printing and the book trade – another manufactured item easy to ship. In 1486, the city granted the first author's copyright to Marco Sabellico for his history of Venice as a business matter that incidentally recognized in spirit the idea of intellectual property. By the end of the fifteenth century, the king of France was granting privileges to printers to cover every work they published, to reward their hard work, and also the living authors. As for all authors in the manuscript age, the dead had no copyrights. Printing was a relatively capital-intensive industry because type and presses cost money. Even in this case, entry barriers were not high; the rapid spread of presses proves this. Patents may have been more useful as signals that someone had a good idea or book than they were immediate cash benefits to their holders.

Brunelleschi applied new ideas about building to the construction of the great dome on the cathedral of Florence (1420–1436 – interrupted by financial and other woes). He conceived of a way to build a dome of bricks with minimal scaffolding just as the clock makers were devising smaller and marvelous objects for keeping time. The diminished numbers of people after the plague were increasing the pace of technological innovation in a broader context of a general economic depression (stagnant growth) for a century after the Big Death. Because we have seen that so much of this innovation in a variety of fields began well before the plague, more than labor shortages must contribute to the admittedly faster pace of change in the fourteenth and fifteenth centuries. Better mills put to new uses, such as beating rag pulp for paper or bog iron into steel, demonstrate how the anonymous tinkerers were taking more of the same technology to the verge of proto-industrialization. In Chapter 9, we will consider why this movement seems to flag in the fifteenth century and not result in a technological and economic takeoff. Already it seems clear that substituting capital for labor had only partly solved the energy shortages the late medieval economy was experiencing. Adam Smith later claimed that apprenticeship interfered with a free market in labor and this may have been a bottleneck holding up innovation. If too many bright people never received vocational training because of nepotism and entry barriers, long-term innovation would suffer. Yet, in this postplague golden age of labor, opportunities abounded and the road always beckoned.

Most observers have been struck by how open Europeans were to new technologies, either those originated in West Asia or the many important ideas that passed from East Asia to the West. These are large comparisons. A closer look at the most urbanized and technologically proficient areas of Europe and China, for example, has prompted a big debate about the "great divergence" – when and how did their levels of productivity, technical abilities (engineering), and the standard of living begin to diverge? Or, when did Europe stop borrowing ideas from its neighbors and instead begin to dominate them with better guns, ships, and all the rest? Again these are large issues for the last chapter, but this look at technology has suggested a few clues. First, after about 1350 and the Big Death, Europeans did not need any more big ideas from outsiders, or at least they seemed satisfied with the ones they came up with themselves. So perhaps their initial openness had hardened into a sense of cultural and spiritual superiority to the so-called outer races. Some historians have concluded that Christianity was the difference causing the divergence – that this religion fostered compassion – hence labor-saving technologies, positive attitudes toward work, hence guilds and wage labor. Even the clock and the pipe organ have been placed in evidence as innovative machines deriving from religious needs for accurate time and loud music. The impulse to explain openness has been so strong that even religion has to be subdivided – arguments explaining the lack of technological progress in Byzantium and even the world of Islam have resorted to simplistic ideas about the lack of music or bells serving as disincentives. These problems have encouraged some scholars to abandon altogether the idea of invention and progress as too value-laden to explain the slow growth of improvement and comfort. In the sixteenth century, people across the world facing European guns and steel would not have questioned superior tools in war or anything else; they wanted them as quickly as possible.

The best exemplar of and antidote to the cult of progress may be Leonardo da Vinci (1452–1519). Starting life as the illegitimate son of a notary in Vinci in Tuscany, by his death in France, Leonardo was famous for his painting and many ingenious designs for ceremonies and mechanical devices. Thousands of drawings in notebooks are a testament to his incredible imagination in perceiving devices far ahead of his time. In fact, Leonardo was far from the neglected genius; patronage supported his many endeavors and some of his designs found immediate practical application. Many of Leonardo's musings concerned machines for water (the dry Mediterranean) and war. Leonardo's society was not prepared to completely embrace all of his ideas and put them into effect; in this sense he was ahead of his time. Yet, his genius did not languish, and it found some practical uses and rewards. Leonardo's not-so-secret handwriting (mirror-reversed and from right to left) was probably devised to protect his numerous ideas, which he never patented. Curiosity more than material gain was the motive behind Leonardo's musings about the world and how it worked. But he was constantly thinking about how things might be better, more efficient, more comfortable, and even pleasing to the eye.

FASHION AND CONSUMERISM

More integrated markets and disposable per capita wealth after the repeated outbreaks of plague also fueled a preexisting trend that some scholars have labeled as the rise of fashion and consumerism. Fashion is the demand for what is the current taste in food, clothing, or whatever is under review. Style is the particular spice or cut of sleeve that is "in style" at the moment. Fashion is routinized stylishness and also became a way of displaying status and wealth, whether at the princely courts or cities. "Conspicuous consumption" refers to cultural practices that use material things as markers for social status and even self-worth. Consumerism is an ethos that sanctions the acquiring of material objects or services for their own sake, from a stylish haircut to an ornate belt, clock, or fur cloak. Figure 7.6 illustrates a decision tree in which consumers choose among utilities – useful objects or services. People value types of comfort and pleasure differently according to their values and needs. These preferences were not always neatly separated. A bundle of preferences, like a new belt,

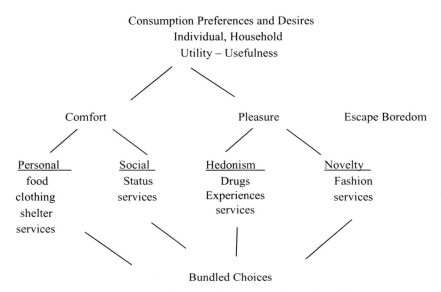

Figure 7.6. Consumption Preferences Ideas (adapted from Jan de Vries, *The Industrious Revolution*. Cambridge, 2008, pp. 20–25).

might combine personal taste, social status, and fashion needs. Household members made choices under a patriarchal regime that allocated resources for consumption among goods and services. Within households, domestic labor added value to inputs, such as food and even dirty clothing.

Much in the Western religions deprecated materialism and praised those like Francis of Assisi and Angela of Foligno who made public renunciations of wealth and especially clothing – one of the most traditional and reliable markers of status. Before the advent of modern advertising, consumerism had to rely on brand names and news of new fashions to spread as merchants brought new wares or artists incorporated the latest styles in their works, or printed illustrations made it easier to learn the latest trends. Travelers on the roads to Canterbury or Rome also brought news of fashion, as did mobile mercenaries with money and new weapons.

At the beginning of our period, say 1000, most of Europe seemed changeless in its fashions – for the moment we will concentrate on clothing. Women wore long tunics and men short ones – some wore pants, and those who could afford it warmed themselves in woolen or fur skin cloaks in winter. From the end of antiquity to about the twelfth century, dress remained stable, as then did fashion. Beginning in the twelfth century, fashion begins to appear – men's tunics became longer. In the mid-fourteenth century, men's tunics became much shorter, with an emphasis on the legs and hose. For women, dresses appeared and became more ornate, and for both sexes, from the late thirteenth century, a widespread use of buttons made tighter-fitting clothing possible. For Fernand Braudel, these changes marked the tentative beginnings of fashion, which remained hesitant and regional until the first great wave of international fashion, the Spanish custom of formal black attire becoming so prevalent in the sixteenth century. Even for Braudel, the real history of fashion did not begin until mass production and advertising after 1700. Other scholars have located the rise of consumerism in every century from the fifteenth to the twentieth.

More recently Susan Mosher Stuard has persuasively argued for the earlier beginnings of fashion in the thirteenth century and sees the next century as the real spread of fashion across Europe. Stuard argues that many important innovations in style occurred first in Italy and then followed the trading routes Venetian, Florentine, and other merchants developed in every direction. This view of fashion sees urban life as the engine behind stylistic changes that become fashion. Other scholars have also emphasized the role of courts, particularly the French Valois kings in Paris, as the arbiters of fashion. There is no reason not to meld the two approaches and see these courts, in London, Paris, Prague, and Budapest, and of course the popes in Avignon, attracting the latest fashions from Florence and Venice, but also sending back signals to astute merchants about what styles of cloth or jewelry would find eager customers. In fact, what was really new in the fourteenth century was a widespread and demand-driven taste for luxuries and comfort. No new technologies account for the increased role of fashion in displaying wealth, although, of course, some made possible new possessions, such as clocks and later mirrors and printed books.

Most of the evidence for fashion concerns clothing and comes from a variety of sources, mainly art and sumptuary legislation. The beautiful Arnolfini wedding portrait by Jan van Eyck (1434) (Figure 7.7) shows the richly and fashionably dressed expatriate couple in the latest styles known in Antwerp. This city's sea connections via Hanseatic and Italian merchants covered nearly all of Europe. The wedding couple came from prosperous but not noble or fabulously rich families and represented how any wealthy urban pair might dress, anywhere in urban Europe. They did not yet have the use of full-length mirrors, so one of the benefits of the portrait, besides serving as a bit of luxurious

Figure 7.7. Arnolfini Wedding (Art Resource AR 31694).

consumption, was that it revealed, through the latest techniques of perspective and lighting, how the couple and their stylish dog actually, if ideally, appeared.

The painting also embodies certain trends we can quickly note. Fashion was gendered in many ways. Men and women were supposed to dress differently and societies punished cross-dressers severely, as Jeanne d'Arc learned when she was burned at the stake for this and other "heresies" at nearby Rouen in 1431. The luxuries of fashion in clothing depended on using much fine cloth for display, from elaborate headdresses to set in sleeves. Men, controlling the money, tended to lead in fashion, and elites were preoccupied with how their appearance displayed status. They also regulated in Italy and elsewhere through sumptuary legislation how women appeared, down to how many dresses they could receive as wedding presents and how much jewelry they could wear. It is important to view the Arnolfini couple as contemporaries would have seen them in a patriarchal society where men made the laws to restrain consumption. Wealthy women could evade the law by pressuring their male relatives to change the rules, weakly enforce them, or grant exemptions. Finally, the elaborate candelabra and mirror are recent consumer items, costly and expensive ways to illuminate the room at night and see one's finery.

Fashion is usually and accurately presented as a trickle-down story. Nobles at courts and merchant oligarchs in Italy set a style of consumption that became more generalized among the classes that could afford them. The great mass of people could not dress as the Arnolfinis, though a few touches were possible. The entire point to fashion was to dress and do other things beyond the requirements of mere subsistence. Although these trends began before the plague, more wealth generalized them. This is what fashion has in common with technology – the ways they spread by diffusion and imitation. Also, small changes in style, in effect tinkering, help to feed the impetus behind fashion as well as technological innovation. Many products illustrate this important theme. Silk manufacture was increasing across Europe, and the rich had more access to these products. Wealthy consumers in England and Portugal could still see and desire genuine Chinese silks of rare and exquisite colors and designs, brought all the way across Asia at vast expense and trouble via the fabled Silk Road. If these items were rarer after the Big Death, so much the better for those merchants still in the business, and so much the stronger the incentives Portuguese sailors and merchants had to find the East for themselves.

On a more common level is the story of sweetness, sugar, beginning in our period but with a long sequel in the New World. Sugar started as a precious spice and drug available in small quantities from the Muslim East. Sugar plantations and manufacturing on Cyprus in the fourteenth century made the product more available, as did increased trade and continued production in Muslim Granada. Our interest here is in sugar as fashion, how the new style of sweetness in cooking created its own dynamic between consumers and producers, leading to ever-increasing efforts, including the use of mills to pound cane for syrup, to meet a swelling demand. A new style of jeweled belt with lots of gold or silver, perhaps first seen on the Tartars in the thirteenth century, became fashionable and in high demand among wealthy men and then women across Europe in the fourteenth century. The bullion famine developing across Europe from the late fourteenth century in part was caused by the increased use of silver and gold in costly fashion items, such as belts and, above all, tablewares.

Finally, along with fashion there was shopping for luxuries and necessities, the practical searches for comfort. All of the abstract discussion of the rise of the market should remind us to look at real markets where people could see, touch, smell, and even taste new products and begin to desire them. Fairs, like the ones in Champagne down to local occasional markets, served as places where on tables in stalls merchants displayed the latest fashions in their wares and how they themselves dressed and wore their hair. Regular shops certainly existed in thirteenth-century cities, either in the form of specially built permanent places open (without glass) for the public to see, or enclosed, private places for the elites. What observers witnessed in a cobbler's shop was not a selection of shoes – this was far in the future – but a working shoemaker making a product to fit specifically measured feet. One shopped for shoes or shirts by watching cobblers or tailors at work, not by trying on finished goods. People shopped for cloth by its patterns and weave, bread by its weight and taste.

In town squares, the one in front of the church of San Marco in Venice is a famous early example, jewelers and goldsmiths set up in wooden stalls and displayed a selection of goods available for immediate sale. Luxury has always depended on the impulse purchase of something immediately pleasing to the gaze. Goldsmiths, perhaps for reasons of security, tended to favor setting up more regular shops on bridges, from the Petit Pont in Paris to the still functioning Ponte Vecchio in Florence. Aside from fairs and market stalls, the first regular shops for luxuries included enamel workers, famous in Paris also from the thirteenth century, silversmiths, and, of course, those drapers selling the finest cloth. By the end of our period of study, a few paintings and murals provide incidental evidence of how some shops appeared. Figure 7.8 is one of a series of frescoes in a castle near Aosta in Italy – this one shows a woman shopper's gaze at an apothecary or spice shop. Her shopper's gaze imagined how powders in jars could make life more comfortable or less boring.

Figure 7.8. Apothecary Shop (Art Resource ART 352557).

By 1500, demographic catastrophe and technological changes taking centuries in some cases to bear fruit had produced a consumer culture fed by a hunger for the latest fashions, a taste for luxuries down to beer and wine for the most humble, and a desire for creature comforts and services in an uncertain world. Yet, all of this comfort was at risk, not just through disease, but also from that other omnipresent horseman of the apocalypse – war.

SELECT BIBLIOGRAPHY

Eliyahu Ashtor, *Levant Trade in the Later Middle Ages*. Princeton, 1983.

Fernand Braudel, *The Structures of Everyday Life: Civilization and Capitalism 15th–18th Century*. Translated by Siân Reynolds. New York, 1981.

Carlo M. Cipolla, *Before the Industrial Revolution: European Society and Economy 1000–1700*. New York, 1993.

Jan de Vries, *The Industrious Revolution: Consumer Behavior and the Household Economy, 1650 to the Present*. Cambridge, 2008.

Stephan R. Epstein, "Property Rights to Technical Knowledge in Premodern Europe, 1300–1800," *AEA Papers and Proceedings* (2004): 382–87.

————, "Craft Guilds, Apprenticeship, and Technological Change in Preindustrial Europe," *Journal of Economic History* 58 (1998):684–713.

John France, *Western Warfare in the Age of the Crusades 1000–1300*. Ithaca, 1999.

Robert Friedel, *A Culture of Improvement: Technology and the Western Millennium*. Cambridge, MA, 2007.

Frances Gies and Joseph Gies, *Cathedral, Forge, and Waterwheel: Technology and Invention in the Middle Ages*. New York, 1994.

David S. Landes, *Revolution in Time: Clocks and the Making of the Modern World*. Cambridge, MA, 2000.

Pamela O. Long, *Technology and Society in the Medieval Centuries: Byzantium, Islam, and the West, 500–1300*. Washington DC, 2003.

————, *Openness, Secrecy, Authorship: Technical Arts and the Culture of Knowledge from Antiquity to the Renaissance*. Baltimore, 2001.

————, *Technology, Society, and Culture in Late Medieval and Renaissance Europe, 1300–1600*. Washington DC, 2000.

Joel Mokyr, *The Lever of Riches: Technological Creativity and Economic Progress*. New York, 1990.

John H. Munro, "Textile Technology," *Dictionary of the Middle Ages* 11 (1988): 693–711.

Kenneth Pomeranz, *The Great Divergence: China, Europe, and the Making of the Modern World Economy*. Princeton, 2000.

Susan Mosher Stuard, *Gilding the Market: Luxury and Fashion in Fourteenth-Century Italy*. Philadelphia, 2006.

Richard W. Unger, *The Ship in the Medieval Economy 600–1600*. London, 1980.

Evelyn Welch, *Shopping in the Renaissance*. New Haven, 2005.

Lynn White, Jr., "Technology," *Dictionary of the Middle Ages* 11 (1988): 650–64.

8

WAR AND SOCIAL UNREST

AR AND SOCIAL UNREST, OR STATE-SPONSORED AND PRIVATE violence, are perfect topics for social and economic history. In fact, they are nearly inseparable because successful rebellion soon becomes official conflict, and revolts can often derive from, cause, or prevent wars. Besides looking for the causes of war and revolt, it is also useful to ask: why is there not war or rebellion? Stability can sometimes conceal suppressed or thwarted social tensions, or be an illusion of successful propaganda. Social unrest has not often been viewed as a promoter of economic development. But the analysis of the costs and benefits of warfare has played an important role in our understanding of late medieval society, its political economy, and economic development. The backdrop for this chapter and the next remains the Big Death and the possibility of an economic depression of the Renaissance extending to the late fifteenth century. We will consider war first and then revolts, but before doing so, we must look at the place of violence in social and economic history and thought.

This book cannot become a history of violence, although some have always viewed late medieval Europe as a particularly violent place. Violence, the actual use and not just the threat of force, spreads across a continuum of analysis from entertainment and crime to holy war. Social values appear in how medieval people amused and defended themselves. Here we must briefly note some pseudo-violent aspects of culture – a noble zest for recreation through the mock but dangerous activities of the tournament, a widespread taste for hunting, which was sometimes nothing more than practice of martial skills against animals. Fighting and wrestling were sometimes ritualized into stylish neighborhood struggles, such as the famous *pugni* of late medieval Venice. These Wars of the Fists, neighborhood battles originally for control of a piazza and then bridges, were a way to foster noble patronage of working people and their champions who did the actual fighting and entertained an audience of fans. Whether public, such as jousting and these fights, or more private, such as the chase of a deer, among the amusements of medieval people was certainly some simulated or real violence with some blood and even the occasional fatality. Cultural norms sanctioned these events even if the Church or some other official body occasionally tried to rein in excessive or violently threatening behaviors. Crime of course was often violent and just as savagely punished, in public. Violence against the self was a mortal sin and a complex social phenomenon, recently analyzed by class, gender, and region. Suicide, committed by the murderer always captured and considered a sin, serves as a reminder that medieval violence was also often a violation, a pollution. Killing oneself was not natural, hence a sin. It was also out of order, a twisting of norms, and a private revolt.

Terrorism existed as a type of violence, either private or official, that singled out some particular victims, often minorities, in order to affect the behavior of the wider group of actual targets. Violence, for instance, against lepers or Jews might have been a way at striking at more powerful but ostensibly untouchable kings. Savage reprisals against rebels count as terrorism here, as does piracy – either private, or in some cases state-sanctioned piracy, by the thin veneer of official corsairs. The victims of piracy were pillaged and terrorized. Piracy sits in the middle of violent acts, between public displays and wars – civil, plain war, and the crusades or jihads, types of spiritually meritorious violence in defense of one's faith. When, for example, the pope summoned Christians to a holy war, few doubted the spiritual power's claim to sanction violence in defense of Christendom, or some papal policy confused with it. The Ottoman advances into southeastern Europe attracted Muslim volunteers from across their world interested in expanding the frontiers of Islam. The Teutonic Knights, an order of the Church, forged a fiscal-military state along the Baltic coast, buttressed by a holy war ethos, which expanded unchecked until the great battle of Tannenberg in 1410.

Many Christian and Muslim thinkers wrote learned works on themes, such as the just war and the right to self-defense. To single out just one but perhaps the most famous book, Marsilius of Padua (c. 1275–1280—1342) finished *The Defender of the Peace* in 1324. This scholastic theologian closely followed Aristotle's analysis that free people had a right to self-defense because it was natural for them to avoid slavery. Hence authorities, he usually means the prince – a legitimate ruler – have the power to repress revolts, wage war, and sustain the military necessary for these tasks. Social order derives from this simple premise. In his view, the prince should decide who fights and who prays, so that no personnel shortages affect these essential tasks. The military might stop in peacetime, but the prince could never rest. On good biblical grounds Marsilius understood that it was necessary to render tribute (taxes) to the governments ordained by God to defend their people from enslavement. There were times when it was in fact necessary for everyone in emergencies to join the military in defending society. Marsilius thought that a priest should not call for arms to be raised against anyone, especially a Christian. This is an oblique but challenging opinion about the justice of holy war. In his view, divine law did not coerce people in this world, so only the prince had the power, the right to violence, over heretics, infidels, and enemies of the people. Many relevant themes appear in his book; let us note two. Violence in the next world, the vivid and tormenting penalties written about by Dante and others, awaited those who merited physical punishment, and among these were the cruel, the unjustly violent. Second, Marsilius took from Aristotle a theme not irrelevant to his own culture – the antithesis of freedom and slavery. The right to self-defense presumed that slavery, however legitimate or natural it might be, rested upon violence to keep the slave in his or her place. Justified violence against a slave was no crime, but self-defense of the free.

From an economic perspective, violence destroys, redistributes, and generates wealth. The wantonly destructive aspects of medieval war are a testimony to contemporary understanding of the fact that money was the sinews of war. To destroy an opponent's ability to defend by wasting physical assets and even people was common sense. War distributed wealth from losers to victors, from pillage to ransom and indemnities. Beyond these obvious costs and benefits is a more complex idea that war moves wealth into more productive hands and activities. Through taxes or other means, states got the money to build faster ships or better catapults or stronger castles. These activities employed useful people and encouraged technological innovation and were preferable to the waste and self-indulgences of peacetime luxuries. One need not agree with this view to see how it can lead to a thesis that war is an investment and can in fact generate new wealth.

The right to self-defense resulted in actual protection of a society's ability to generate wealth. This was clear in the simplest terms as a strong heroic king protected his farmers and naval powers kept the sea lanes open for peaceful, lucrative trade. Both farmers and merchants supported through taxes the militaries ostensibly guaranteeing this result – what economists call a protection rent – a public benefit with private, profitable consequences for those enjoying it. A protection rent is like an insurance policy whose premium, taxes for defense, paid dividends to the public. The very unequal benefits of protection might be consumed, literally eaten or drunk, or invested in even stronger armies and stouter ships. What should interest us is the efficiency of the process of utilizing violence – the ability of any government to provide the security necessary for a productive economy and society. Governments will inevitably vary in this capability, and hence we need as well to consider that the integrity of state power matters – does it have the financial and physical wherewithal to accomplish its purpose?

THE CRUSADES

A brief look at the phenomenon of holy war is necessary to place it in the context of overall social and economic development, and to see it as a type of warfare influencing other forms of organized violence. From 1095 and the papal summoning of the first crusade, Western Christians established Latin states in the East, which lasted to their fall in 1291. Subsequent campaigns against the Poles, Russians, and Prussians along the Baltic coast, the Muslims in Iberia, "heretics" in Languedoc, and the Ottoman Turks in southeastern Europe, were also holy wars and in some cases continued on past the end of this book. At first kings and lords financed their contingents' passage to the East by mobilizing their own resources and taking on debts, as did communes, such as Pisa and Genoa, providing naval support. Gradually, as we have seen, monarchies and communes became strong enough in terms of taxing authority to finance these expeditions. Crusades were not trade wars, and the earliest signs of commercial revival in the Mediterranean and northern seas preceded these endeavors. Religious warfare at times disrupted regular commerce, which could be seen as aiding the enemy.

We know too little about the budgets of early crusaders to draw firm conclusions about how these armed pilgrimages and new states and even colonies in the East affected the pace of European change as they consumed and channeled resources. Only a small percentage of eligible warriors ever took the cross and ventured to the frontiers of western Christendom to fight. At times, the demand on Italian and French naval resources although intense, was brief. What we can see is that the strong desire to conduct successful crusades (and defenses against them) encouraged the development of a fiscal-military state – a governmental bureaucracy and ethos based on the fact that money is indeed the sinews of war. This new type of state could be a strong centralizing monarchy under an effective king, such as Edward I of England, or a city republic, such as Florence. A fiscal-military state required early centralization and needed to rely on a civic administration to collect taxes. Crusading overseas was supposed to limit or sus-pend war at home and in theory make western Europe a less violent place and Prussia and Syria more so. Crusaders often arranged truces and treaties upon departure, and even the temporary absence of violent men must have left some peace in their wake. But from the thirteenth century on, crusading increasingly took place in Europe itself, first against Cathar heretics in Languedoc and papal enemies and, in the next century, against the Turks in the Aegean and Balkans and the Slavs along the Baltic. The idea that the crusades fostered economic development in Europe by siphoning off the most destructive Europeans must be discarded, as should the idea that these wars were somehow intended to promote the eastern trade. The crusades did, however, force potential warriors to conceive of a hierarchy of violence and choose the wars they could afford to fight.

The fiscal-military state required a bureaucracy or even a private system of collecting taxes that limited venality. Charity alone could never cover the costs of a holy war. If taxpayers perceived that their funds were looted or squandered on things far from the purpose of defending Christendom, the state would not be able to wage war of any kind. The raising up and sacrificing of financiers skilled in securing funds, too much occasionally sticking to their own fingers, is a commonplace of war finance. In Chapter 9, we will examine the career of Jacques Coeur, for a time the richest man in Europe, as an example of this phenomenon. After the Big Death, the tools of the European fiscal-military state were increasingly turned on other states in Europe – either in aggressive dynastic struggles, such as the Hundred Years War between England and France, or bitter trade wars between rivals, such as Barcelona, Genoa, and Venice in the Mediterranean. Before examining these, let us consider one feature of the crusading movement that endured – planning for war.

Norman Housley has raised some interesting points about what he called "costing the crusade," the effort to plan in advance for a budget to accomplish war aims – usually the recovery of Jerusalem by devious means. In the early fourteenth century, the Venetian Marino Sanuto, writing a plan for a crusade, understood the real expenses of naval campaigns and his strategies for war in the East depended on credible figures to support his ideas. Sanuto knew that a fully equipped galley and crew cost 850 florins a month, so even a small flotilla of ten ships for a year would consume 100,000 florins, a vast sum. The old dream of an invasion of Egypt, still seen as the best way to extort the Holy Land from the most powerful Muslim ruler in the region, would demand far larger sums, as Louis IX of France had learned in the previous century. Sanuto calculated that a serious invasion of Egypt lasting three years would require fifteen thousand infantry and bowmen, nine hundred cavalry men at arms, all to be transported and paid at a cost of about 2.1 million florins. Actually conquering Egypt would take a larger force, more time, and cost more than twice as much. Soon we will have some comparisons to put these sums in context, but they were fabulous amounts of money beyond the dreams of even the most efficient fiscal-military state. In this case, the existence of realistic plans may have discouraged war; for no such invasion of Egypt ever happened. In 1365 King Peter of Cyprus launched a raid on Alexandria, sacked the city, but immediately abandoned it. His own costs were very high, and he disrupted valuable Italian trading links there. A later dispute between his successor and the Genoese resulted in an invasion of Cyprus in 1373 and the imposing of a harsh peace the next year. The numbers are instructive. Genoa scraped together a fleet of thirty-six galleys and other ships to take an army of fourteen thousand men there. In order to finance this endeavor, the commune treated the invasion as an investment, and most of the money came from people hoping for a profit. And in this case, war proved very lucrative indeed. The Genoese demanded 40,000 florins a year forever to cover public expenses and the staggering sum of 2,012,400 florins over the next ten years to pay the investors. Eventually Genoa acquired the port of Famagusta as well. This episode showed that Sanuto's plans were indeed reasonable, and that even small wars cost a great deal, but could sometimes pay for themselves, at least for the victors.

After the Big Death, a knight and squire cost about ten florins a month, about double the rate before and no surprise in an era of rising wages and diminished numbers of people. Smaller expeditions were the rule, and good figures survive, for example, the effort by Burgundy to send a contingent of 229 men east on the French and Hungarian crusade that ended in defeat at Nicopolis on the lower Danube in 1396. The great French chivalric hero Jean Le Meingre, called Boucicault, managed seventy mounted knights at his own expense, but most there fought on tax money. Marching an army into Turkish controlled Balkan territories required planning because the men needed to be provisioned and paid. Gone were the days when men set off with all of the money they had and hoped for the best, as in the early crusades. Now the business was so expensive that the provisioners and paymasters were more likely to grow rich in war than the men actually fighting – although as we will see some certainly did, and some died trying.

THE HUNDRED YEARS WAR

Periods of furious conflict and long truces punctuated this long war beginning at the start of the fourteenth century and concluding in the early 1450s. Great English victories at Crécy (1346), Poitiers (1356), and Agincourt (1415) all occurred in France, where the war was fought, and where much of the country-side and especially the peasantry paid the price for raiding during conflicts and the wanderings of unemployed mercenaries during truces. English longbows and dismounted men at arms often devastated the flower of French chivalry still on horse and wearing increasingly ineffective and expensive armor. The story of the war is not the issue here. Even its most dramatic figures, Edward the Black Prince of Wales, the victor at Poitiers who captured the King of France, or Jeanne d'Arc, the Pucelle, the maid who lifted the siege of Orleans in 1429 and saved France, needed to pay troops and must have wondered about the costs of war. The English famously burned Jeanne as a heretic in 1431, partly for saying that God favored the French cause, but also for stubbornly dressing like a man to play her role in the army. In theory, rulers fought the war to determine who the rightful king of France was. By the end of the conflict, the English had lost everything worth having on the continent. Charles VII of France (1422–1461) had probably become the most powerful and richest monarch in Europe, with the first standing professional army to prove it. The war forged France into the first great fiscal-military state; the country that had finally mobilized its larger population and resources to defeat the even better organized, led, and financially efficient English monarchy. The war broke out briefly before the Big Death, and it fostered technological innovation, especially in artillery. In 1453 the French besieged Chantilly, and cannon fire killed the famous English commander, John Talbot Earl of Shrewsbury. Among the French spoils was John's magnificent Book of Hours, a soldier's prayer book, a mix of St. George and devotional prayers for safety and victory.

The wars had many social and economic ramifications in England, France, and Burgundy. To note one small detail, the treaty of Brétigny (1360), among other items, set King Jean's total ransom at the colossal sum of 3,000,000 gold crowns, about £500,000, or five times the annual regular income of the King of England. (At about three silver English shillings to the florin from 1350 to 1400, this ransom was worth well over three million florins – even more than Edward III's defaults had cost his Florentine bankers!) A glittering prize like this ransom, only the largest in a war of many ransoms, has made this struggle a good test for fathoming the costs and benefits of war. And yet even the ransom is deceptive. Like many, it was never fully paid – Jean was still in captivity in England when he died in 1364. Quarrels about the rest of the payments troubled English–French relations for decades. In order to fund the initial payment in 1356, the French government had to levy a stiff hearth tax, taille, of six francs on urban and two francs on rural households, as well as a heavy new sales tax of twelve pennies in the livre (5%). The king's absence, and these new taxes, certainly played a role in the great urban and rural revolt, the famous Jacquerie in 1358, as did state efforts to regulate prices and wages in the aftermath of the Big Death. We will look more closely at revolts below, but even this glimpse of the ransom suggests the need for a big context in drawing up the balance sheet of warfare.

Regular government expenses were so low, matching the modest ambitions of medieval rulers, that warfare had an immediate and large effect, often causing political and related fiscal problems. K. B. McFarlane made a rough but still useful estimate of all English taxes raised between 1336 and 1453. Direct taxes, mainly the poll tax and clerical and lay subsidies voted by parliament and the clergy, amounted to £3.25 million. Indirect taxes (with levies on wool accounting for at least 80 percent) amounted to another £5 million, so the total was £8.25 million, or around 50 million florins, a sum that would boggle anyone. These expenditures came in fits and starts, so the outlays were not continuous and cannot be costed-out at a steady 400,000 florins a year. Even this sum does not seem unreasonable for a kingdom still containing a few million people after the Big Death, especially in light of what the much smaller number of Florentines had to pay when necessary.

The issue is: what did the English get for these taxes, this premium, or pro-tection rent? McFarlane stressed these points. Unknown but considerable sums were recycled back to the Church in the form of buildings and endowments from some successful warriors. Surely this was nothing like what they paid in subsidies, but it was something. The taxes on movables and the poll tax fell largely on the English peasantry, but most of this money ended up in the pockets of the lordly class and the professional warriors who did much of the fighting.

Foreigners paid much of the export duties on wool (McFarlane guessed about half) because demand for English wool remained very high on the continent throughout the war. Hence, consumers of wool cloth across Europe ended up paying around a quarter of entire English expenses. Perhaps the higher prices for wool, and the fact that producers still ended up paying something for the right to export, made this trade less profitable than it might have been. So, the opportunity cost might be high here, even if it looked as though foreigners were paying for the war. For if in fact all of those millions of pounds had been cycled back into the hands of English producers, the resulting benefits to the English economy would have been considerable.

England cheated its creditors, inflated the international price of wool, and fought the war on French soil with all of the costs that entailed. In a rough generalization, the English paid for a big part of their expenses before the plague by foreign borrowing, first from Lucca and Siena and then Florence. Defaults made this harder after the 1340s and forced the crown to rely more on taxes, more likely to produce domestic grievances, as we will see. Taxes always raised important issues of equity and efficiency. The lay subsidies, for example, fell largely on the value of crops and livestock and cost less to those lords living mainly off money rents. A poll tax by head did not vary by the ability to pay and was easy to resent. Church estates, taxed heavily in the first phase of the war from the 1290s, paid on their entire income, one-half demanded in 1294 alone. Taxes on clerical incomes forced the clergy, monks, and nuns to squeeze their own tenants, reduce consumption, and alienate capital. Since the 1290s, the crown had been relying on wool taxes to finance a substantial part of the fighting. By heavily taxing wool and cloth hardly at all, the state was distorting the economy in ways that had partly unintended consequences for economic development in England. Raising the price of wool overseas pushed down prices to producers in England, hurting their incomes. The favorable taxing of cloth was an intended benefit to a growing wool cloth industry in England and a boon to the wages of weavers. So the war was in effect subsidizing the growth of the English cloth industry, at the expense of England's nominal allies in Flanders. For long stretches, England profitably ruled and taxed large parts of France. Some English nobles and professional soldiers did well out of this war, as did those entrepreneurs who supplied arrows, bows, food, shipping, and all of the rest of the supplies that the armies needed. The irony of course is that the English lost the war. Most observers see the war as a disaster for France, yet it emerged prosperous, victorious, and united.

Michael Postan looked at these facts and saw the balance as in the red because this long war ended up debilitating the English economy. He considered opportunity costs from the point of view of a labor historian. Tens of thousands of ordinary English and Welsh men, many serving as archers and sailors, were diverted from other pursuits, farming and fishing, that would have increased the kingdom's wealth more surely. The warrior class, the men at arms, contributed a large percentage of its numbers in service overseas, and Postan saw this too as a loss for the kingdom. Hence, Postan and others have emphasized the opportunity costs of war – the lost and more profitable endeavors that manpower might have undertaken during peacetime. Besides their time, these noblemen often had large expenses in equipping themselves that are not counted in the regular costs of the war. During peacetime they contributed to the daily government of society and paid some attention to their estates, and so even here opportunity costs mattered. Postan basically did not buy the efficiency argument based on military expenditure alone, because he also factored in the human time and lives he considered largely wasted in these military endeavors. Some men made new fortunes but others lost, without a net gain.

Ransoms cut both ways, and while the English took some profitable prisoners, they also, especially in the fifteenth century, had to pay up as well. It was the French countryside that was routinely pillaged. No one can measure these costs, but Postan argued that it was not the flower of English chivalry that was stealing French cattle and geese. In theory superiors were supposed to receive one-third of booty, but the actual pillagers, the ordinary soldiers, had the right to two-thirds. It is reasonable to presume that more stuck to their fingers. There were costs as well as benefits to temporarily ruling parts of France, yet even Paris had to be garrisoned and administered out of regular revenues. Even those nobles receiving French fiefs and titles had to invest time and effort in these matters. Finally, Postan was struck by the marked decline in English wool exports in the late fourteenth and especially in the fifteenth century. (In fact, Edward Miller later noted a 24 percent decline in wool exports as early as the first heavy taxes of the 1290s.) Royal policies favored increased production of local cloth but still aggregate exports were declining. This result is not a surprise in a depopulated world where other wool exporters, notably Castile, were becoming increasingly important. Postan's point was that although foreigners were paying wool taxes, which did indeed contribute mightily to English revenues, English wool dealers were paying as well, and more importantly were losing market share because of war-inflated prices. And, in the end, England had little to show for these expenses. It lost everything in France and had nothing to show for centuries of conflict except perhaps for some stylish tombs and a few rich war profiteers who had slipped into the diminished ranks of the noble class.

Another way of exploring this problem of the costs and benefits of war is to look more closely at money itself and specifically the theme of debasement, already considered as a way to raise funds for war. Part of the florin's triumph as a physical international currency as well as a measure of value was the triumph of gold from the early fourteenth century forward. Hungarian and then increasing African supplies in the early fifteenth century became more abundant in Europe. The chronicler Giovanni Villani wrote that Florence had enough gold to mint 350,000 coins a year. From the 1330s, gold coinage also became more important in the northern monarchies as Italian money became more available. The story before the plague is the rise of gold, and its accompanying theme is the debasement of the silver currency as a source of profit, as a literal means to make money. Not every government resorted to this expedient – the silver currency remained sterling in England and good in Naples, not bad in Barcelona and Aragon, but it was frequently terrible in France. Especially after 1346, the French monarchy reduced the silver content of the currency to the point where by 1355 the coins were only 20 percent silver – an example of black (tarnished) money that did not look or feel like silver. The French crown returned to a strong money policy and in 1360 the coinage was again 96 percent silver and remained close to that figure as late as 1413. Troubles after defeat at Agincourt resulted in a coinage that by June of 1422 was only 3 percent silver. This was good for the king and peasants, bad for landlords and others living on fixed, customary rents and incomes suddenly devalued.

Nicholas Oresme (c. 1320–1382) was a well-educated Norman French theologian who became a bishop. He translated Aristotle's *Politics*, *Ethics*, and *Economics* from Latin into French. He wrote a book around 1355 in French, and put it into Latin in 1358 in the version that became the famous *De Moneta*, *On Money*, a theological work that was also the first scholarly book written in medieval Europe on economics. In particular, he wrote a detailed attack on the French monarchy's policies of using currency debasement as a way to finance war. Oresme repackaged Aristotle's thought to tell the history of money – why it was invented and what it is. This is a pagan story, not a biblical one, and a challenge to a theologian who nevertheless found plenty of moral issues to engage his attention.

Money, coins in gold, silver, and debased billon (he knew no copper coins) was a tool necessary for commerce. (Oresme was not interested in barter.) Money had to be suitable, and by this Oresme meant that it had to be fixed by weight and name. Reputation was everything to money, which had to stand for something reliable in the marketplace. The labeling of money, its brand name, should be a measure of quality that made exchange more efficient. Hence, for Oresme, the key point became: who owned the money, all of the coins in circulation? His answer: everyone – money was a common good. The job of the prince was to issue sound, reliable money. Oresme presumed that there was a natural ratio, the market price, between gold and silver, and the prince should not presume to change this because the money did not belong to him. On the same line of reasoning, Oresme also objected to gabelles, in particular the French crown's monopoly of salt and its artificially high price. He viewed salt as something necessary to life, and like money it did not belong to the prince, hence the state monopoly was immoral.

Returning to his theme of money, Oresme observed that it was fine to change money – he notes the necessary and common expedient of cutting a silver penny in half to make halfpences necessary for small purchases. But to change the weight of the money by reducing the silver in it while retaining the same name, in other words debasing it, was cheating, fraud, and an evil act. The crown's income from debasing the coinage was an ill-gotten gain, a sin. Oresme knew that especially in the 1350s in a period of plague and military disaster, it was human nature to look for money wherever it might be found. Just as usury was wrong because money was sterile (the old scholastic argument) it was just as wrong for money to generate all by itself a profit for the crown, which was in reality the biggest usurer in France!

Oresme had a few more important points to make about money. He thought that debasement was even worse than usury because people did not want their money debased. Nevertheless, just as public brothels existed (and were tolerated and in some places were state monopolies) in order to prevent even worse sins – even usury was sometimes allowed. Exchange, he must mean credit, was also necessary, and it too prevented worse sins, perhaps theft. But to Oresme debasement was even worse because there was no legitimate reason for it. Does this mean he did not care at all about the royal budget or ransoming King Jean? Not at all. He knew well what had been happening in France. He also understood two fundamental facts about the way society worked. First, he believed that people would simply take their good money to where it was worth more, in other words, that bad money drove out the good, and so there would be less good money in the kingdom. He was certainly right about this. Second, Oresme did not think any emergency justified debasement. There were always better ways to raise money, and he recommended borrowing. We have seen that his views triumphed – the crown relied on taxes to pay the ransom and by 1360 restored strong money of high silver content that remained stable for fifty years. So this book mattered. It no doubt reflected a broad consensus about the meaning of money and the pitfalls of tyranny when it came to manipulating the reliable and just outcomes of the marketplace. *De moneta* is also the foundational work of political economy.

VENICE

Venice was a self-governing aristocratic republic with vast naval expenses in the thirteenth and fourteenth centuries as it waged a bitter series of commercial wars with its main rival, Genoa. Venice was on the front lines against the Turks in the eastern Mediterranean. By the fifteenth century, the Ottoman Turks had become the main Eastern challenge, while at the same time Venice had also put together a large state in northern Italy that required other expenses, mainly its famous series of mercenary captains. How Venice paid for these wars is largely the story of the Monte Vecchio, the Loan Office established some time before 1262 and at work until 1482 when the state reorganized the public debt. The usual expedient was the forced loan, which was levied on the rich, in theory, by the ability to pay. People paid these forced loans because their survival depended on it but also because they received something in return, by law a steady annual 5 percent. In practice, these loans became a perpetual debt, though from time to time the state redeemed some shares when it had the spare cash. This theory of taxation rested on the assumption that the government paid interest on taxes, which made paying them more tolerable. In theory, these taxes were also a protection rent, as the wealthy were the most likely to be thriving by trade and ancillary businesses that depended on a strong navy. But the protection rent did not suffice to motivate taxpayers – they also wanted a fee.

   The state paid interest regularly from 1262 to 1380, even during the Big Death and the Third Genoese War from 1350 to 1354. Renewed conflict amazingly and quickly followed the first bout of plague and was a tribute to the intractability of war as a social and political fact of life. Economic benefits from

Table 8.1. *Venetian Monte Shares 1380–1474 (data from Gino Luzzatto,* Il debito pubblico della repubblica di Venezia. *Milan, 1963, pp. 271–272).*

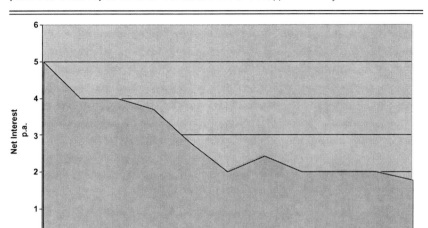

the Black Sea trade were still a good opportunity. Shares in the Venetian public debt were traded, usually between 75 and par (100) in this period, and they became a proverbial widows and orphans safe investment as a big part of the total shares became tied up in trusts. The real crisis developed during the fourth war with Genoa, the War of Chioggia (1378–1381), when a large Genoese naval expedition attacked Venice. Facing actual conquest, Venice raised huge amounts of money from forced loans, about one-quarter of real property wealth. Expenses were so high that interest payments had to be suspended for the first time in September of 1379 and then were reduced to 4 percent in 1383. It was also necessary to tax the shares. This fiscal crisis caused the share price in the Monte to drop to 18 by 1381 (see Table 8.1). In theory, the interest payment was 3 percent for those shareowners not paying the tax (estimo) on their investments. The real uncertainty in the market, once the Venetians defeated Genoa, was when and how the state would be able to use its ordinary revenues, largely gabelles and customs duties, to resume paying interest on shares. This factor was driving down the share price. The 1380 interest was paid in 1389 and in fact the state was never able to catch up in these payments and the problems became worse. By the late 1470s, the interest payments were about twenty years behind and the shares were trading at around 10. In the early fifteenth century, share process rose or fell according to how merchants valued the market in these de facto bonds. Share prices increased during plagues, as around 1400, when secure investments seemed prudent. Unsuccessful wars with the Turks from the 1450s depressed share prices.

These shares as investments are not our concern here. Their nominal or par value still determined the dividend, when it was paid. More wars like the ones with Milan and the Ottoman Empire in the fifteenth century required more forced loans, often amounting to as much as 1 percent of wealth per month. Around 1425, this assessment, probably quite political, and low, yielded about 40,000 ducats, implying that the Venetians were worth four million ducats, too little to be credible and a sign that these loans were not as severe as they seemed at face value. These loans stopped during peacetime so they were in effect war taxes. By the mid-fifteenth century, there was also a secondary market in *paghe*, the interest or dividends on shares, which now could also be sold as a speculative endeavor by sellers needing cash now and buyers who saw the chance to make money on the eventual payments and reorder their investment portfolios.

Venice's experience shows how a generally efficient and usually victorious system of war finance allowed the state to experience and survive periods of real threat and sudden demand for cash without enduring tax or other revolts. Collecting taxes could be a real problem so the system treated them like an investment paying dividends, something the Venetian wealthy understood. Some of this money went into the famous Venetian Arsenal, Europe's first great factory, where it paid the wages of thousands of men building galleys and in allied trades. These salaries enabled Venetian working families to pay gabelles on salt and other commodities that supported the interest payments the payers of forced loans demanded. This virtuous and patriotic cycle of wealth permitted Venice to survive challenges that crushed less fiscally creative or simply unlucky states. It also fed a growing arms industry in Venice itself and in other specialized towns, such as Milan, famous for armor and weapons, and Brescia, a leader in handguns. In Venice's case, the peasants on the islands conquered or threatened by the Turks, or those on the Italian mainland often overrun and pillaged by someone else's mercenaries, continued to bear much of war's real and damaging costs.

SOCIAL UNREST

Wars fed social revolts, which were often another expression of violence in society. Social unrest concerns that part of the spectrum of violence where grievances moved people to oppose with force the status quo. Hence, these revolts were often examples of organized violence, but they began as private and illegal activities. Medieval society provides a constant drumbeat of civil strife in the cities and countryside from the twelfth century to the end of our period of study. When we examine the factors that motivated people to revolt we can again use the plagues as a benchmark for determining how this crisis affected the overall trends in social unrest. Exploring the motives is always difficult because nearly all major revolts failed and the victors controlled the sources that tell the history of revolts. Hence, it is hard to get down to the level of hearing what rebels actually wanted, and seldom did they gain power for long enough to implement their plans.

Standard typologies of revolts usually emphasize the search for leaders, and economic or political motives, to the extent that these can be disentangled at all. There were very few grain revolts or risings of the hungry and poor. Desperate people on this level may have turned more frequently to crime or flight. Social unrest might take the form of "cultural resistance" – an array of acts from sabotage, disrespect, ostensible laziness, and other ways of striking back that ordinarily did not rely on physical attacks or provoke violent retaliation. Tax revolts did occur, and, of course, to resent taxes to this point, one had to have something to lose to taxation. Revolts by wage earners against their employers were rare because guild solidarity usually kept employers united and their workers did not have the reserves to be unemployed for long. The discontented were more likely to be fired, migrate, or both. Still, workers did sometimes rebel, but usually against political institutions often controlled by their employers.

Two interpretive frameworks will help us navigate through the bewildering array and number of revolts across Europe. Whenever it is possible to hear the voices of protest, they seem to be asking for political rights, to be included in decisions about taxes, in a word, for liberty. Sometimes colonial subjects, such as the Greek speakers on Venetian Crete, rebelled, unsuccessfully, to assert their rights against the occupiers. Jews, everywhere denied basic liberties, did not take to violence to challenge their status and instead used other methods. Sometimes this desire for liberty took the form of heterodox religious beliefs, such as the Cathars in Languedoc. Yet, their act of rebellion against the organized Church was not as violent by any definition as the crusade summoned against them. Those who felt they did not have any liberty, or enough of it, usually meant political or economic rights and knew enough to reject slavery or the circumstances of the most downtrodden serfs. Rebels also knew that lords, masters in the guilds, and others claimed to possess political rights that were defined in such a way as to exclude most people. Much medieval social unrest concerns the issue of inclusion – who was a member of a political community enjoying certain rights? The struggles for liberty considered here became violent because these rights had practical consequences that mattered. Obtaining or yielding these rights were not easily negotiated. Instead, the airing of grievances became tumultuous and threatening enough to prompt someone to resort to violence.

Any analysis of social unrest must examine the three classic cases from the postplague scene – the Jacquerie in the Paris basin in 1358, the revolt of the urban wool workers (Ciompi) in Florence in 1378, and the Peasants Revolt in England in 1381. Yet, this standard story obscures a lot of previous unrest and neglects many parts of Europe where unrest did or did not occur. And once again, stability can easily embody its own kind of repression so we must occasionally ask: why is there not revolt?

Samuel K. Cohn, Jr., has collected a big sample of revolts from 1200 to 1425 that covers the Low Countries, France, and Italy, with a little from England. We will be able to test his findings against some information available about unrest in Iberia, the German lands, and Eastern Europe. Some revolts, such as the Sicilian Vespers of 1282, a national uprising against French occupiers, were well known across Europe. Relying mainly on notices in contemporary chronicles, Cohn found 1,112 separate revolts. Those revolts (covering a wide range of activities) that can be securely dated yielded this chronology: 470 between 1200 and 1348 (2.73 a year) and 621 from 1348 to 1425 (8.06 a year). There was a lull in revolts during the first bout of plague, but they appeared everywhere from about 1355. In general, it is not always easy to distinguish urban from rural revolts, but some trends are apparent. Peasant revolts were more common after the plague of 1348, typically in the most prosperous regions, such as southeastern England, rural Flanders, and northern Italy. In fact, there were hardly any popular revolts at all in England before 1381. (Disgruntled nobles waging civil wars were another matter.) The big waves of revolts in Tuscany from 1401 to 1404, led by the prosperous mountain folk, are evidence for the causes behind these revolts, which Cohn sees as centered on politics and above all taxes. Peasants did not typically rebel against their feudal lords or place common rights or rents at the center of their grievances. (In this sense, the English rising of 1381 may be partly atypical and should not be the only model considered.)

Cohn sees a similar pattern in urban revolts in that artisans did not directly fight their employers or the guild system per se but instead usually attacked the state; however, they perceived it and their own exclusion as voiceless citizens. In this sense, as we will see, the Ciompi revolt in Florence is interesting because a central demand of the rebels was for their own guilds, not for the abolishing of a guild-based republic. Cohn found very few grain riots (the ones women were most likely to join). Urban governments' abilities to respond to starvation were impressive. The common theme is also that economic protest was really about politics, and above all about liberty. Cohn found plenty of artisan and peasant leaders, as well as occasional nobles who found a reason to put themselves at the head of an insurrection. Many revolts were successful in the sense that those voicing grievances were addressed rather than simply massacred. So revolts were not rare, or even that risky, because medieval people, artisans and peasants, were pugnacious and not risk-averse. In Italy, townspeople did not form alliances with peasants, while in the north they sometimes did – though in the case of Paris in 1358 the bourgeoisie soon abandoned their rural allies.

Before looking at some specific revolts to test these generalizations, we should consider more closely the meaning of liberty. In the parts of Europe where slavery existed it affected the meaning of liberty. Elsewhere, the very word "slave" still conjured up a horror to be avoided. The many women and men working as domestic servants remained subordinate to their masters and could be beaten – a crime when inflicted on a free person. Liberty became a profound desire for rights and equality. Finding their voice was the concern of those with something to lose. Hence miserable persons, the poor, did not revolt, and the old model of rebels being those with frustrated rising expectations fits this emphasis on liberty. Ideology was not the exclusive preserve of the aristocracy, scholastic theologians, or urban elites devising rules for communes and guilds. Yet, we will need to question the demands by rebels to see how the principle of liberty was expressed in very specific economic and social terms. Also, we need to be precise about the actual course revolts and their repression took, so that we can gauge the levels of violence.

Political economy does not expect a sharp break between political and economic thought. Consider a revolt that becomes a touchstone of Cohn's book. In Viterbo on September 5, 1367, a member of the cardinal of Carcassone's retinue was washing a pretty little dog in the fountain of the artisan neighborhood of Scarlano. A woman fetching water shouted at him, presumably because she objected to this fouling and waste of good water. This episode sparked a revolt resulting in a massacre of churchmen. Long-seated tensions in the Papal State about the role of the clergy and their privileges came to a head with this graphic imagery of a dog wash. The fury unleashed was not an abstract defense of pure water, or apparently about liberty at all.

Ideas about freedom and liberty certainly existed before the plague and for most people concerned the exact circumstances of serfdom. For example, around Laon, where serfdom followed the mother's status, rural agitation in 1289–1290 had resulted in serfdom virtually disappearing by about 1300. Economic factors yielded this outcome because peasants were able to acquire formal manumission of their servile status by paying their lords. These peasants had the right to make choices about what to do with their extra income, which might be consumed or invested in more land or animals. They did not invariably choose to buy their own freedom, and this is the value of a close attention to local trends because in and around Laon they did. Yet, in 1338 (beginning of warfare) there was a big tax revolt, which was suppressed. The state and local taxpayers negotiated a settlement about how the taille was to be levied. Sometimes disputes ended peacefully, more or less.

The *Jacquerie* of 1358 occurred during the captivity of the French King Jean, prompting the royal government to raise taxes for the ransom and giving the discontented people in Paris and the Seine valley an opportunity to take power. The *prévot* of the merchants in Paris, Etienne Marcel, led his social group to rebel but he also mobilized the support of urban workers, whom he urged to arm themselves. Paris, the largest city in Europe, was showing signs of becoming a self-governing commune in the face of the royal power vacuum. The key event was the assault on the royal palace on February 28, 1358, when thousands of artisans enabled Marcel and their employers to seize control of the city by force. Meanwhile, in the neighboring countryside, rural artisans and peasants were sacking chateaux and burning records concerning their rents and other exactions. Outside Paris the motto of the rebels was, "Let all happen as it will and may everyone be masters" – certainly an ideological program with a strong measure of liberty and equality. The word "master" evoked both the employer and landlord and was a sign that urban elites had as much to fear from the majority as did the nobles. In the spring of 1358, the Parisians began to send out expeditions to destroy fortresses and manor houses. For a moment, it seemed that the peasantry and urban classes might join forces against the inept military aristocracy leading France to defeat after defeat against England.

For complex reasons, these urban and rural revolts failed to make any permanent changes in France. During the late spring and early summer of 1358, the merchants and employers in Paris, the true *bourgeoisie*, deserted the rural rebels probably because they had little in common, especially about the meaning of liberty. The mounted French warriors might not have done very well against Welsh bowmen, but they were more than a match for weavers and farmers. In the countryside, violence and massacres ended the rural revolts. A judicious mix of terror and mercy silenced the people, and there is a great mass of evidence on this process in the form of petitions for forgiveness, which the crown often granted to minor troublemakers. In Paris, Marcel was assassinated at the end of July for reasons not connected to the urban revolt. By the end of the year, the government under Jean's son the Dauphin Charles was back in control of Paris and the rural areas had been pacified as well. The crown resumed the efforts to raise money for the ransom and also to restore a sound currency.

This revolt was a "perfect storm." The context of plague, weak agricultural prices, government efforts to control wages and prices and raise taxes, military defeat, and a king in prison across the Channel came together to motivate many people to resist by force. Rebels opposed efforts they perceived as intended to keep them in their places as docile workers, peasants, and taxpayers. Rising expectations were dangerous to anyone who thwarted them. The noble class and its employees had just enough prestige and military skills to survive, but only after dividing their rural and urban opponents. The mix of factors is complex: the defeats and costs of war, epidemic disease and its consequences, popular discontent and a desire for liberty, economic depression and stresses, taxes, disputes among elites, and social cleavages among nobles and various levels of urban and rural society.

In the summer of 1378, the Florentine commune was at war over territorial borders with the pope, under interdict, and suffering from disruptions in its vital trade in wool and wool cloth. Only those masters in the main guilds had a voice in city government, and they constituted a tiny minority of Florentine men. The employers in the *Lana* (wool) and *Calimala* (cloth) guilds controlled their trades, and weaving was organized by middlemen who managed the various stages of production through a putting-out system. Thousands of wool workers in Florence, engaged in the various labor-intensive stages of cloth production described in Chapter 7, were suffering from unemployment. To make a long story as concise as possible, in July of 1378, the common artisans, the *Ciompi*, took control of the governmental palace, ejected the city council and its leader, and installed one of their own, Michele di Lando, a wool carder, as standard-bearer of justice. This truly popular regime immediately created three new guilds, the dyers, shirtmakers, and one for the Ciompi, which enabled thousands of new people to become eligible for political office. The new government had a complex political and economic program. It suspended interest payments on the public debt, created a civic militia, halved the salt tax, tried to reduce the price of grain, and most importantly attempted to impose production quotas on the big employers in the wool guilds. This policy was intended to put people back to work. The new regime also planned to use 2,000 gold florins to buy up black silver coins used to pay workers, in order to drive down the price of gold and take steps toward establishing a better silver currency. How much any of these policies actually changed things matters, but so too does their collective weight as a political program with astute economic goals.

The bloodless coup in July did not mean that this new broad-based communal regime would continue to exist without having some means of exerting violence. The commune largely fought its wars with mercenaries funded by borrowing, creating a funded debt, such as Venice, whose interest payments were met from consumption taxes and monopoly prices on salt – a familiar fiscal regime. The Ciompi understood that the papacy would continue to fight Florence, that mercenaries still cost money, and that employers would not accept their loss of power without a struggle. Their program existed and involved a practical increase of liberty for many through acquiring a voice in politics via guilds. The Ciompi also had a plan to use this political power to change some fundamental features of the Florentine fiscal-military state. The radical phase of the Ciompi revolt ended in late August of 1378 when the employers simply bribed Michele di Lando to lead the forces of repression to eliminate the most radical voices and the guild for the wool workers. The other two guilds continued to exist, and their members abandoned the struggle. For a few years, the balance of power tipped in Florence in favor of a broader mass of employers in lesser guilds. Yet, by 1382 the elites in the major guilds were back in charge of the commune, and the other two new guilds were thrown out of government.

The Peasants Revolt in England is partly a misnomer because the rebellion had urban and rural participants and covered much but not every part of the kingdom. The context is a familiar one – continued outbreaks of plague during the long phase of a mid-term stagnant economy. Yet, the survivors were richer in per capita terms, and the crown knew this. The spark that ignited the revolt was the effort to raise a stiff head tax to pay for the wars in France, which had been going on now on and off for nearly fifty years with no end in sight. The initial violence took the form of murdering tax collectors, and this treason, a capital crime, motivated the original rebels in Kent to find supporters. A large mob of rural people from the southeast of England found leaders in Wat Tyler and a "renegade" priest John Ball. What the rebels wanted unfortunately depends on the accounts of hostile witnesses, but the common demands seem to be abolition of the poll tax and all vestiges of serfdom, and a fixed and equitable land tax that fell on all landowners rich and poor. Ball's preaching, at least as it has survived in hostile accounts, had a strong dose of social equality. Ball made a vivid case that the landowners, the gentlemen as they called themselves, were no better than anyone else, in his words, no greater masters than the common folk. The motto of the rebels was the famous line – "When Adam delved and Eve span, who then was the gentleman?" A gender division of labor had men digging and women spinning, after Eden, when they needed to work in order to eat. Peasants and artisans understood how necessity constrained liberty. Also, this monogenesis theory of human origins was a demand for social equality, for liberty, and the details were in the specifics about fair taxes and relics of serfdom.

One unusual feature of this revolt is the urban component, where discontented artisans took the opportunity of disorder to make their resentments known. In Canterbury, they settled local scores and attacked wealthy employers. In the northern towns of York, Beverley, and Scarborough, the artisans from a variety of crafts had ill-defined but serious grievances against the oligarchies that ran their towns and markets. Violence was high in some places, and among groups attacked were the Dominicans and in Cambridge the colleges which many viewed as oppressive landlords. The major city was of course London and thousands of peasants converged on the capital. Urban wage earners, journeymen and journeywomen, and apprentices were sympathetic to the rural rebels in that they too felt voiceless and were excluded from the political life of London. The dramatic moment of the revolt occurred at the edge of London at Blackheath on June 13, when the peasants presented their demands to their king Richard II, a young man of fifteen. By this time, the rebels had come up with a list of eight high officials they regarded as traitors, including the eminent Simon Sudbury, archbishop of Canterbury, chancellor of England. The crowd took matters into their own hands and the next day found and killed the chancellor as well as Robert Hales, head of the Hospitaler Order in England and treasurer of the kingdom. Richard II met with the rebels again at Smithfield on June 15, when the story is that the mayor of London killed Wat Tyler. The young king then managed to bring the rebels to his side by some vague promises of charters and liberties that he in fact would not keep.

The death of Tyler led to an immediate round of reprisals against leaders and urban troublemakers. An unknown but large number of people, certainly in the hundreds, were rounded up and executed. The great mass of protestors drifted home, thinking that they had won something, only to find that the crown and its royal justices would systematically look for and fine and punish malcontents and other disturbers of the peace. This great paroxysm of rage against the establishment caught the government unprepared and in disarray. The problem for the rebels was that peasants and wage laborers had no institutional means for exercising political power except through killing and destruction. The city government of London, the merchants and craft leaders in the guilds, the official Church, the landlords, and those who could fight all eventually rallied to the crown. The peasants had their own leaders and a sustaining ideology that had specific demands about taxes, land, and personal liberties, and even the names of particular traitors. Among some rebels there was also a trace of a heresy in England called Lollardy that viewed with suspicion the wealth and power of the official Church. The elites reneged on their promises, and the rebels were in no position to judge whether their apparent concessions were credible. Peasants in England had no de jure power, and even their postplague de facto advantages were under attack.

But the Peasants Revolt defies simple labels. In the aftermath of 1381, the powers that be remained vigilant for signs of unrest. The most irksome aspects of serfdom, demeaning dues and lack of personal liberty on basic things such as marriage and residence, were fading because of constant pressures to make landowning pay in the changed economy after the plague. Landlords and others wanted stiff enforcement of the labor ordinances and were suspicious of any group, even religious confraternities that might serve as a vehicle for future rebellions. The absence of organized revolt for a long time does not mean that the grievances had all disappeared. Peasants and workers lacked institutions that protected their liberties. The violence of the revolts probably encouraged fearful generations to ferret out and silence potential troublemakers, but also to make sure that rising expectations had some positive outlet. But it would be a long time before elites conceded to any claims for social equality.

The period from the disturbances in the aftermath of the first plagues to the great revolts of the early sixteenth century, the big rural revolt in Hungary in 1514, and the Peasants War in Germany in 1525, was not free of disorders. Cities and the countryside experienced a bewildering array of developments that seem to vary by lord and village, by town and neighborhood. At the risk of imposing an artificial order on these developments, let us examine some fifteenth-century trends. The circumstances of peasants, some free and others still serfs or becoming so, and artisans working for a daily wage, remain absolutely central to our understanding of the medieval society and economy.

Contemporary appeals for liberty raise questions about serfdom in the fifteenth century – was it waxing or waning? In Eastern Europe, Poland, Bohemia, and Russia, there are signs of a new serfdom as landlords tried to impose rules and obligations on formerly free rural tenants, as is especially clear in Poland from the 1420s. In Hungary, lords created a serfdom out of nothing in their own culture – even though they may have known that across Europe their counterparts in England may have been hastening the end of serfdom by too blatantly oppressing the peasants. The extent to which landlords succeeded or failed in these endeavors matches the abilities of the peasants by whatever means to resist these encroachments. For the poorly documented areas of Eastern Europe, the answer seems to be that the potential profits in cereal cultivation, the timber business, and other rural resources motivated landlords to keep their peasants from leaving and get them to work as a personal obligation. It makes little sense to call this development a "second serfdom" in a region that had not witnessed a first. Yet the phenomenon, sometimes accompanied by force, seems to be a legitimate example of lordly unrest in the face of unrealized profits. The peasants as yet had few collective means to resist these trends.

In other parts of Europe, centuries of tradition and a bewilderingly complex terminology make generalizations even more perilous. The land tax, *taille*, death duties, and lordly control of justice remained the main issues on the estates of the abbey of Luxeuil in the fifteenth century. Across the Rhine in Franconia, German peasants valued freedom of movement and were also concerned about the free transfer of goods from one generation to the next. Lordly jurisdiction in the German lands in some places still enforced a personal serfdom usually defined by labor obligations. But the circumstances of land tenure and rent also defined some people as still subject to lordly jurisdiction, particularly if they were not free to leave. These various levels of unfreedom are another way of seeing the fundamental importance of personal liberty to the German peasants.

On the estates of the bishop of Laon and the villages he controlled, serfdom might have evolved in subtle stages as one obligation or another seemed to take the place of older ones. The *chevage*, or head tax, became a way to capture old income from death duties or marriage fines that had been formally abolished. In fifteenth-century Normandy, serfdom persisted and varied long after its official end in 1302. In the fifteenth century, marriage and death fines were still being collected by the new French lords, and the *corvée*, labor service, meant more in an era of higher wages. In Baden, new words surfaced for obligations the peasants thought had been abolished. Peasants were allowed freedom of movement, which seemed to matter so much to them, but owed servile fees to their original lord. In the Rhineland Palatinate, it was the policy of the rulers to intensify lordship and serfdom as a favor to the landlords and help them collect fines and find their subjects. Even where national myth says serfdom never existed, as in the German-speaking Swiss cantons, it can be found on monastic lands around Zurich. In Denmark there was no serfdom until the late fifteenth century, when landlords obtained rights of privatized justice to fine and physically punish their tenants, now tied to the land. From 1330 to 1400, the price of lease land had declined by 50 percent, a sign that labor shortages were driving the big landlords to find new ways to subject the peasantry. By 1500, ownership of Danish lands roughly amounted to the Crown 10 percent, the Church 40 percent, the nobility 35 percent, and freeholders 15 percent. This continuous process of peasants losing land accelerated after the Big Death.

In some places, peasants resisted these trends. In southwestern Germany and around the Black Forest, tenants on monastic lands opposed perceived new impositions. Peasants on the abbey of Kempten lands in the Allgau rebelled in 1423 (no one helped them) again in 1460–1462, and in 1491 joined a big league of Swabian peasants. The actual level of violence in these efforts is difficult to gauge, but this history of endemic troubles shows that the great rebellion in the next century had deep roots. The more historians look for social unrest in the centuries after the plague, the more they find. In the fifteenth century, Bruges, Ghent, Utrecht, Leiden, and other cities periodically revolted against the centralizing regimes of the dukes of Burgundy. Here a desire for traditional liberties and home rule faced a new-style fiscal-military state.

Catalonia experienced a terrible civil war from 1462 to 1472. The crown and peasants supported the Busca faction of disgruntled rentiers and merchants who faced the Biga traders who were dominant in Barcelona. This struggle eventually involved France and Castile as well. This civil war, reasonably viewed by Juan II of Aragon as a revolt, devastated the richest part of his kingdom. Catalonia, a prosperous region appearing on the verge of leading Iberian development, instead entered a long period of decline. In England factional strife led to a long civil struggle, the Wars of the Roses (1455–1485), eventually resulting in two changes of dynasty. Where rebellion did not occur, it is safer to assume effective coercion and spying than contentment.

War and social unrest certainly seem more frequent in the decades following the first onslaught of the Big Death. Yet, violence had been endemic in medieval culture, whose moral leaders extolled the virtues of crusades and extirpating heretics by any means necessary. Savage and terroristic reprisals were a fixture of warfare, private violence, and even the systems of justice. No part of Europe seems particularly peaceful, though its richest areas could afford more violence and attracted the best available mercenaries. It may be that the survivors of the Big Death thought they would live in a better world. If so, many were disappointed. Yet, the complex fifteenth century showed both new and old features shaping the Europe that was on the verge of opening its horizons to encompass the entire world.

SELECT BIBLIOGRAPHY

Daron Acemoglu and James Robinson, *Economic Origins of Dictatorship and Democracy*. Cambridge, 2006.

John Brewer, *Sinews of Power: War, Money, and the English State, 1688–1783*. New York, 1989.

William Caferro, *John Hawkwood: An English Mercenary in Fourteenth-Century Italy*. Baltimore, 2006.

———. "Warfare and the Economy in Renaissance Italy, 1350–1450," *Journal of Interdisciplinary History* 39 (2008):167–209.

Samuel K. Cohn, Jr., *Lust for Liberty: The Politics of Social Revolt in Medieval Europe, 1200–1425*. Cambridge, MA, 2006.

Paul Freedman and Monique Bourin, *Forms of Servitude in Northern and Central Europe: Decline, Resistance, and Expansion*. Turnhout, 2005.

R. H. Hilton and T. H. Aston, editors. *The English Rising of 1381*. Cambridge, 1984.

Norman Housley, "Costing the Crusade: Budgeting for Crusading Activity in the Fourteenth Century," in *The Experience of Crusading 1*, Marcus Bull and Norman Housley, eds. Cambridge, 2003, pp. 45–59.

Charles Johnson, translator. *The De Moneta of Nicholas Oresme and English Mint Documents*. London, 1956.

Gino Luzzatto, *Il debito pubblico della repubblica di Venezia*. Milan, 1963.

K. B. McFarlane, "War, the Economy, and Social Change," *Past and Present* 22 (1962): 3–18.

Edward Miller, "War, Taxation and the English Economy in the Late Thirteenth and Early Fourteenth Centuries," in J. *War and Economic Development*. M. Winter, ed. Cambridge, 1975, pp. 11–31.

Michel Mollat and Philippe Wolff, *Ongles blues Jacques et Ciompi: Les revolutions populaires en Europe aux XIVe et XVe siècles*. Paris, 1970.

Reinhold C. Mueller, *The Venetian Money Market: Banks, Panics, and the Public Debt*, 1200–1500. Baltimore, 1997.

Alexander Murray, *Suicide in the Middle Ages*. Oxford, 1998, 2000.

Michael. M. Postan, "The Costs of the Hundred Years War," *Past and Present* 27 (1964): 34–53.

Alan Ryder, *Wreck of Catalonia: Civil War in the Fifteenth Century*. Oxford, 2007.

9

FIFTEENTH-CENTURY PORTRAITS

HIS ECONOMIC AND SOCIAL HISTORY OF LATER MEDIEVAL Europe concludes in the fifteenth century because a modern economy was already emerging that eventually superseded older ways of organizing production and social relations. Inevitably some parts of Europe experienced these changes before others, which remained deeply tied to traditional social and economic norms. The surviving original sources from this century are also increasingly complex and abundant, which makes it possible to take a closer look at what in previous chapters was difficult or impossible to see. At the same time the wealth of evidence makes it harder to generalize about Europe, and this may be a good thing. Many regions and countries now have enough evidence to sustain their own social and economic histories, and many such fine studies point to the beginnings of the early modern global system. For us, the fifteenth century is the moment to summarize existing trends and to analyze the developments making some parts of Europe more durably prosperous than others. Rich sources also make it possible to examine some individual prominent lives that illuminate important social and economic changes. The collective and individual portraits that comprise the substance of this chapter have been selected from a nearly infinite list of possible images. Each portrait has a narrow and broad point to make about the social and economic history of later medieval Europe. Together they provide a prospect of this period, still enduring the stresses of epidemic disease and other calamities, but showing some new paths not taken in previous centuries.

THE FLORENTINE CATASTO OF 1427

The first portrait is a collective one, the remarkable snapshot of Florence's society and economy as revealed in a marvelous source, the amazingly complete records associated with a new system of taxation the commune imposed upon itself on May 24, 1427. The mass of details provided in these documents eventually baffled the Florentines who had to abandon the system as too cumbersome to maintain. But modern statistical methods and above all the computer have made it possible for us to ask and answer questions about Florence, which fifteenth-century contemporaries might have wondered about (or not) but were unable to answer with the precision now available.

The context of the new tax system is a brief resume and lesson in the problems of fifteenth-century political economy. Florence's commune traditionally relied upon these sources of revenue: a direct tax on rural real estate, the *estimo*; indirect taxes, the gabelles, falling on commodities like wine and salt; a modest tariff; the funded public debt of the Monte; forced loans, *prestanze*, levied only in Florence and not its countryside or subject towns like Pisa, Prato, and Pistoia. Each of these taxes had its problems. The *estimo* missed liquid capital and urban real estate, and by the 1420s was simply not yielding much revenue. High levels of gabelles were regressive and angered working people. Tariffs had the potential to distort trade, the lifeblood of Florence. Nonetheless, these sources of income sufficed in peacetime. In the 1420s, Florence faced new threats from its neighbors and the huge accumulated debt and interest payments from hiring mercenaries over the previous decades. Assessments for forced loans were intensely political decisions that in the end deeply offended some people who saw them as unfair. Yet in wartime, only the rich could speedily come up with the thousands of florins needed to pay mercenaries.

By 1427 the crisis required Florentine elites, the big employers and merchants in the major guilds, to devise a new system of taxation. Rounds of discussion produced a set of principles shaping the new policy. The Florentines decided that all forms of property should in theory be taxed, subject to certain agreed upon exemptions in turn reflecting social and economic goals. Every household was required to produce an inventory of those assets that yielded a return on capital. So they exempted the family house and its furnishings, which were not productive and really a form of saving (conspicuously in lavish family palaces), and all tools – a boon to those investing in expensive technologies needed to make a living. The assessments on farm and pack animals were reduced to safeguard the food supply and transportation. In Florence, there was also a 200 florin per capita exemption which fell to fifty florins in Pisa. (In practice, this astonishing high per capita exemption meant that most households would end up with little or no taxable wealth and they were expected to negotiate a kind of token payment.) Each household was to have a tax return. Servants were not to be included for tax purposes and the clergy and foreigners remained in a tax limbo. The decision not to tax servants or their employers shows how vital domestic labor, mostly female, seemed to Florentines. Servants were not capital.

A supervising committee and a large team of clerks rigorously checked the household returns, which were frequently updated because of changes in family or economic status. These changes provide precious historical information on social and economic trends in Florentine households. The difference between assets and exemptions and liabilities constituted one's working capital, in Florentine eyes taxable wealth. Experienced Florentine businessmen assumed that capital yielded a 7 percent profit per year, more than the Monte shares paid, less than safe returns from the wool business or a lot less than profitable, but risky ventures, such as banking and insurance. The level of taxation on this hypothetical profit was 0.5 percent in Florence, 0.25 percent in Pisa, and 0.19 percent in the countryside, figures revealing the principal of a graduated tax mainly falling on the center of wealth, Florence. For fiscal and ideological reasons worth pondering, a head tax also fell on every able-bodied Florentine male, defined as between the ages of eighteen and sixty. The household returns took years to compile and were not ready until 1430.

These returns, which all survive, are plainly more accurate on some matters rather than others. For example, the count of households in Florence, 9, 946, is clear enough, but the multiplier is somewhat speculative at about 3.75. This number yields the surprisingly low population estimate of 37,245. Even if we boost that total to compensate for some beggars, monks and nuns, babies in poor households where the head might have no incentive to dash off to the tax office to record the birth, we would still be left with a Florence of perhaps 40,000, again about a third of its preplague height. The distribution of wealth (Table 9.1) reveals that the city controlled most wealth, especially in real property, movables, and above all the public debt. Even after the hefty deductions, Florentines, comprising 14 percent of the population of their state in Tuscany, possessed nearly two-thirds of taxable wealth, making the city an island of riches. In Florence, this wealth was not equally distributed; 14 percent of households had no assets period, a figure rising to 31 percent after deductions.

Table 9.1. *Distribution of Wealth in Tuscany in 1427 (data from table in David Herlihy, "Family and Property in Renaissance Florence," in* The Medieval City. *Edited by Harry A. Miskimin, David Herlihy, and A. L. Udovitch. New Haven, 1977, Table 1.1, p. 6).*

	Florence	Six cities	Fifteen towns	Contado	Total
Households	9,946	6,724	5,994	37,226	59,890
Persons	37,245	26,315	24,809	175,840	264,210
Percentage	14.10	9.96	9.39	66.55	100.00
Real Property					
Value	4,128,024	1,137,466	614,446	2,178,253	8,058,189
Percentage	51.23	14.12	7.63	27.03	100.00
Movables					
Value	3,467,707	585,357	170,245	223,792	4,447,101
Percentage	77.98	13.16	3.83	5.03	100.00
Public Debt					
Value	2,573,378	3,438	1,888	1,337	2,580,041
Percentage	99.74	0.13	0.07	0.05	100.00
Total Wealth					
Value	10,169,109	1,726,261	786,579	2,403,382	15,085,331
Percentage	67.41	11.44	5.21	15.93	100.00
Deductions					
Value	2,504,041	332,763	135,341	321,205	3,293,350
Percentage	76.03	10.10	4.11	9.75	100.00
Taxable Wealth					
Value	7,665,068	1,393,498	651,238	2,082,177	11,791,981
Percentage	65.00	11.82	5.52	17.66	100.00

All sums in florins
Six cities: Pisa, Pistoia, Arezzo, Prato, Volterra, Cortona
Source: The Medieval City, p. 6.

The top 1 percent in the city controlled one-quarter of all assets (and a much larger portion of the Monte), more than the bottom 87 percent of their fellow inhabitants of Florence. The shares in the public debt, for all purposes, a monopoly of the capital city, represented a great transfer of wealth, in the form of interest payments, from rural areas and small towns to the glittering center. Gini coefficients (aptly named for a later Florentine statistician) calculate the concentration of wealth and yield numbers ranging from zero – a perfectly equal distribution of wealth, to one – in which one person owned everything. Hence, the higher the coefficient is, the greater the concentration of wealth in society. For Florence the Gini numbers are 0.70 for working capital, 0.79 for total wealth, 0.80 for movables, and 0.90 for shares in the Monte. Even if we allow for the fact that the records are naturally more accurate concerning the richest levels of society, these numbers reflect a high concentration of riches in Florence where a few hundred households owned most wealth. Prominent families, such as the Medici, the Strozzi, Pitti, and others invested in palaces and artistic works for which Florence was famous. The large numbers of people with little to spend suggested to David Herlihy that a city like this was not well poised to provide a mass market that might fuel even greater prosperity and economic development.

The household returns provide a wealth of social data. For example, they show a puzzling sex ratio of about 105 males to every 100 females at birth rising to 110:100 at all ages in Tuscany – raising the question – what happened to the missing women? Patriarchal values may have led to devaluing and under-counting baby girls. Other sources from the famous orphanage of Florence, the Hospice of the Innocents, reveal that about 70 percent of the foundlings there were girls – a sign that this society abandoned some female infants to this or maybe even worse fates. The Tuscans declared their ages and we have these patterns: age thirty-nine (259), age forty, (11,200), age forty-one (253). Plainly people averaged or guessed their ages at five or zero, and eighty-nine claimed to be over a century, an implausibly high number. Ages seem more accurate in the city than the countryside, for men rather than women, and for rich rather than poor – all suggesting a correlation between numeracy and literacy. The mean age was twenty-nine, and it decreased with wealth, revealing a skewed demographic snapshot of Tuscany with a dearth of adolescents and adults, and plenty of little children and the elderly. These facts probably reflect the long-term consequences of terrible bouts of plague – the last severe one around 1400 for Florence, when perhaps one-quarter of the population perished.

Corrections in the household tax returns are informative about ages at first marriage. In the cities, at first marriage the mean age for women was 18.86 and for men was 27.85. The comparable figures for the countryside were 19.28 and 23.80. The most common urban age for marriage represents a typical marriage between a sixteen-year-old young woman and a man of twenty-five. In fact, about one-quarter of Florentine women were already married before the age of sixteen, and the girls with higher dowries were more likely to marry later. An amazing 97 percent of all marriageable women over the age of twenty-five were either married or widowed. A full half of all women over the age of sixty in Florence were widows. A significant number of adult men, 4.5 percent, were permanent bachelors. Many demographic consequences flowed from these ages and the important gap between them, often greater than the standard nine years in the city. These family cycles produced the stereotype of the increasingly elderly husband and the younger wife. With children she became the mediator between generations. Childless, she became a topic for humor or the large numbers of younger unmarried men looking for trouble.

The many unmarried adult males in Florence have been held responsible for a number of social trends ranging from high levels of urban violence to general erotic tensions producing a large number of prostitutes as well as same-sex relationships for which Florence acquired a reputation across Europe. Women found it nearly impossible to marry without dowries because men demanded them. This marriage market led to an increase in dowries in the fifteenth century. All sorts of trends, ranging from epidemics to the spiraling levels of dowries, pushed down the age at first marriage for girls. Young women were unlikely to find husbands if they were still single at the age of twenty. These facts help account for the astonishingly high numbers of nuns in the city – not all Florentines by birth – but still there were about nine hundred of them. As a way to raise money and foster marriage, the commune had established, in 1425, its famous Monte for dowries, a kind of savings club that enabled fathers to save and plan for dowries for infants. The commune used the money in the meantime for its vast expenses, and paid interest on the principal for the lucky survivors to their first marriages.

The high numbers of children were most notable in the countryside, which was probably a healthier environment and hence responsible for keeping Florence from being even smaller. Yet, the city was not far behind in its numbers of children. Not so surprising given the nature of the tax records, households with more money tended to have more children, taking off at 400 florins household wealth up to a threshold of about 700 florins. These children were also more likely to survive. Poor and middling women were having fewer babies (as far as the tax office knew) and various social practices may account for this. The large number of abandoned children came from these households, where mothers also nursed the babies of wealthier women. These richer women were hence no longer lactating and more likely to become pregnant again than were the wet nurses. Economic necessity prompted some of these trends and may have encouraged birth control methods that preachers, such as San Bernardino of Siena, railed against. Estimates of birth and death rates depend on a variety of sources and remain rough, but for these years the death rate seems about 36.4 per 1,000, and births perhaps at about 40, but children were becoming the special victims in the plague years. The overall population levels remained stagnant at best until at least 1450.

These and many other findings make the population of Tuscany the best known and studied of any in premodern Europe. The obvious question remains: how typical is Tuscany in the broader context of the rest of Europe? Florence was an advanced commercial center in one of the most urbanized and rich parts of Europe. Its sophisticated public debt, high dowries, and capitalized agriculture with many sharecroppers in the fertile contado were local phenomenon that might cast light on similar issues in Venice and Genoa but not in Barcelona or Bruges. Other features, such as the age distribution of the population and even the ages at first marriage, may or may not reflect common problems and solutions across a plague-stricken Europe. The Florentine records illuminate the southern European marriage and family model, leaving historians of other regions to ponder whether these patterns hold elsewhere.

FRANCESCO DI MARCO DATINI (c. 1335–1410)

This famous merchant from Prato, near Florence, made a last will that resulted in a treasure trove of material for studying his career and the broader patterns of social and economic history. At his death, Datini had a huge fortune of over 70,000 florins. He left his house and the bulk of his estate to the poor of his home town, to be administered by a remarkable secular foundation that exists down to the present day. He wanted his papers to be gathered up and preserved in his house, a real tribute to his amazing personal archive. What survives today amounts to a collection of more than 150,000 business and personal letters (many very short), 500 ledgers and account books, and other documents and contracts – notably for insurance. (See Figure 9.1 for an example of a bank transfer order, in effect a check.) Datini's long career makes him easily the best documented person before 1500. Yet, once again the issue is to what degree was he a typical person – how may we generalize from his experiences to the rest of the business world in his times?

From a modest background, Datini was sent off in 1350 to the papal city of Avignon to make his fortune. His parents and two siblings had died in the plague, and his youth and self-reliance are typical of the postplague world. Beginning with a few inherited assets, he laid the foundations for his fortune

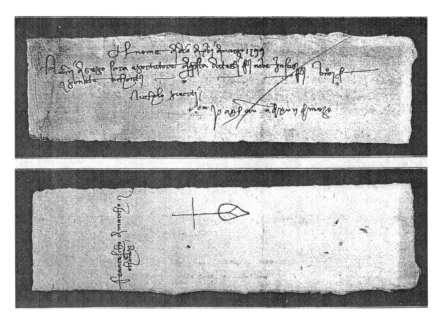

Figure 9.1. Datini Check (from Enrico Bensa, *Francesco di Marco da Prato*. Milan, 1928, p. 353).

in the cloth and armor business. People always needed clothing and warfare was constant. He had shops where armor was both assembled from pieces from Milan and elsewhere and made from raw materials imported from Germany and Genoa. The violence of his times made armaments a growth industry and mercenaries were reliable customers. By the 1390s, he was sending armor to Barcelona and would typically look for a 15 percent profit. He relocated to Prato in 1382 and moved his main business to Florence in 1386, where he was able to join the big merchants' guild of the Por Santa Maria. Prato was a wool cloth town, and Datini was able to continue his routine, safe business of importing wool from England and Spain, and organizing the weaving business at home – all this annually yielding a safe, respectable 8–9 percent profit.

Because his wealth made him welcome in Florence, Datini benefited from guild membership and business ties. He also became part of the pool that had to take up forced loans, and he was bitter about what he had to pay. Datini was a generic merchant who bought and sold whatever the market opportunities and his own astute sense of trends suggested. His firm, with home offices in Prato and Florence, eventually had branches in Avignon, Pisa, Genoa, Barcelona,

Valencia, Majorca, and Ibiza. He staffed these offices with employees, factors, and hence represents a new style of business where the firm was more important than temporary partnerships and traveling merchants. Datini stopped traveling, and one of the reasons we have so many letters is that he relied on the post and agents to conduct his astonishing array of trades. Datini remained active in wool and armor but extended his reach to spices and other luxuries, art, slaves, salt, religious vestments, and many other items like copper, which he exported to Africa. Datini was also active as an insurance broker buying and selling small contracts to reduce his risks and make money. He opened a bank in 1399 to facilitate his profitable use of bills of exchange that in turn funded his wool imports via partners from distant England. Like many successful merchants Datini put part of his profits into local farms, which he let out according to the standard *mezzadria* sharecropping terms in which he supplied the capital and received one-half the profits, a way to share risks and allow a landless peasant access to good farm land.

Datini wanted, from his agents, constant news about commerce and above all prices, and his records comprise a comprehensive source on fluctuating markets across the Mediterranean and beyond. He had a great friend in the notary Lapo Mazzei and their letters show how a strong sense of piety and a desire to make money formed the core principals of Datini's life. His letters to his much younger and childless wife Margherita reveal the ups and downs of an unhappy marriage that settled into a companionate truce. Because his wife stayed in the fine house in Prato and he preferred to live elsewhere in Florence, their many letters are yet another window onto family life and much more. Datini had an illegitimate daughter named Ginevra, whose mother was a twenty-year-old slave named Lucia. He married off the slave and raised the daughter as his own – in effect it fell to Margherita. Ginevra was honorably married with a substantial dowry of 1,000 florins, and like so many of her father's network, she learned to read.

Datini sexually and commercially exploited his slaves. Fifteenth-century Genoese data provides evidence on the ethnic origins of female slaves there. Figures 9.2 and 9.3 supply the numbers, divided at 1453, during the Ottoman conquest of Byzantine Constantinople, the great event affecting sources of slaves. These young women were the most expensive slaves. They worked as domestic servants and frequently became pregnant by someone, usually their owners. In the first half of the century, slaves from the Black Sea, Tartars, Abkhazians, and Circassians, predominated. Later, the Ottomans too preferred

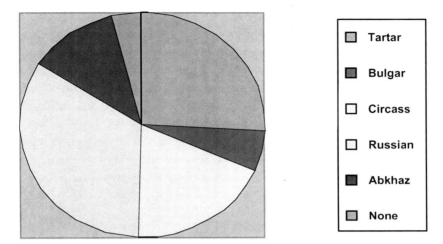

Figure 9.2. Genoa Women Slaves 1400–1453 (adapted from Steven A. Epstein. *Speaking of Slavery*. Ithaca, 2001, p. 190).

these women, and the Italians shifted to Moors and white women from the Balkans. Slaves became increasingly expensive and hard to obtain as the century progressed. Italian slavery was astonishingly gendered. Tax records from Genoa in 1458 show 2,059 slaves in the city: 2,005 women and only 54 men.

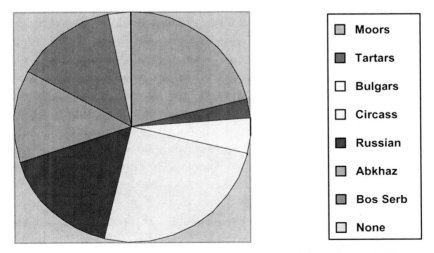

Figure 9.3. Genoa Women Slaves 1453–1500 (adapted from Steven A. Epstein. *Speaking of Slavery*. Ithaca, 2001, p. 190).

Datini had a wonderful mind for business and refused to specialize in anything except making profits. His letters reveal constant anxiety and a mania for detail. He found solace in listening to sermons, participating in the great religious revival/pilgrimage of the Bianchi in 1399, in the arms of his slaves, in reading Dante, and writing letters constantly. His letters reveal a cautious and vigilant businessman who was not likely to be cheated or to make his way to China. He was a perfect example of the postplague prudence and aversion to long-term risk that characterized the mercantile life in the difficult postplague years. Perhaps his most prized possession was a Spanish mule for which he paid the huge sum of more than 122 florins, more than enough to purchase two first-rate, young female slaves.

JACQUES COEUR (c. 1395–1456)

This great French merchant from Bourges in Berry was reputed for a time to be the richest man in Europe. His career makes a revealing contrast to that of Francesco Datini. This is not to suggest that the business of making money has become the sole focus of this social and economic history. Rather, these exemplary lives portray a very wide range of the types of experiences open to the intrepid, however defined. Coeur's career ended in disgrace, flight, and death on the island of Chios in the eastern Mediterranean. His failure meant that his archive did not survive in the great house he built in Bourges, one that, like Datini's, still stands (see Figure 9.4). Records of his accomplishments are scattered amid hostile notices and royal efforts to seize his wealth.

Coeur began his climb to great riches as part of a group that farmed the royal mint in Bourges. This concession guaranteed the Dauphin Charles, fighting for his kingdom against the English, certain revenue, and the "farmers" the chance to profit from minting money. Coeur first appears in the historical record in 1429, when he was charged with minting gold ecus at less than the eighteen carat standard – one of the many ruses for literally making money. These activities placed Coeur at the center of war finance, a subject he learned well and a useful skill in a century where war remained a significant consumer of national income everywhere.

In 1432, Coeur made a great journey to Egypt and Damascus that changed his life. His reasons for going remain unclear but he must have seen the opportunity for fabulous profits in the Mediterranean. He left the familiar surroundings of Bourges, which always remained the center of his northern interests, for

Figure 9.4. Palace of Jacques Coeur, Bourges (Art Resource ART 148386).

Montpellier and later Marseilles. What he learned in the Levant or already understood was that silver was overvalued in Egypt, where it formed the basis of the currency. Europe's silver famine, even in the age of stable currency in France from 1436 forward, may owe something to traders like Coeur. His genius was to understand that there was a fortune to be made by exporting silver, not cloth to Egypt, in exchange for spices. He entered the spice trade in a major way, eventually obtaining a monopoly from Charles VII, for supplying the large market in southern France. Importing Chinese porcelain, rugs, coral, and sugar diversified his mercantile activities, which threatened the profits of the Catalan, Genoese, and Venetian merchants who had dominated this trade. Coeur eventually purchased his own galleys, usually having four or five, and benefited from papal permission to trade with the Mamluk, sultans in Egypt, with whom he remained on good terms. This aspect of Coeur's career shows the French entering the Mediterranean trade networks in a major way. His competitors in a city, such as Barcelona, were also taking advantage of Aragon's royal connections to foster trading links, in their case to Naples, Mamluk Egypt, and Syria. Coeur, however, was not an itinerant merchant of the old style. Like Datini, he operated through a large network of trusted agents. And he did move around in southern France to supervise their activities. But he never returned to Egypt.

During the 1430s, Coeur also became a main financial advisor to the king. In 1436–1437, he took over the farm of the mint in Paris. In 1439, he obtained the court post of *argentier*, as Reyerson describes the post a bursar in charge of supplying luxuries to the court. His connections in the Levant trade and his northern office in Bruges, all operated from his headquarters in Bourges, made him the ideal person to run a kind of royal bazaar. Coeur supplied jewelry, silks, furs, spices, arms, horses, and whatever else the king and his people needed. This business gave Coeur ample means to profiting by supplying, from his own efforts, as many of these luxuries as possible, and also by extending credit to those who could not pay cash. So Coeur became a banker and eventually extended his activities into the very lucrative salt gabelle in Languedoc. He was also selling weapons to the king, and possibly in Egypt as well, and from 1444 was also profiting from his own silver and copper mines. The 1440s was his golden decade of prosperity as an archetype of a merchant who specialized in no particular commodity or line of business but who was quick to seize opportunities where he found them. Accumulating fiefs and estates in his home region, Coeur was ennobled in 1441, a tangible sign of the king's trust. He is one of the first in a subsequently long line of commoners across Europe who rose to wealth and power by providing monarchs with sound economic policy advice, and, as in his own case, even the luxuries they craved. Inevitably he became a model for the over mighty subject ready for a fall.

At some point Charles VII, who was quick enough to abandon Jeanne D'Arc when he needed to, must have begun to wonder how much of Coeur's fortune was really his own. In 1449–1450, Coeur was able to advance the king 200,000 gold ecus for the campaign in Normandy – where did such wealth come from? His great palace in Bourges, begun in 1442, also excited comment and envy. The king's advisor had profited from some royal subsidies for the galleys and favorable tax advantages that made his spices cheaper than anyone else's. Vast profits from the mint, salt taxes, and all of those baubles he supplied to the court were all quite obvious. In July of 1451, Coeur lost his king's favor and he was accused of a bewildering array of offenses, ranging from treason and corruption to the disgraceful trading of armor, guns, crossbows, and money to the Muslims. False rumors circulated that he had for some inexplicable reason poisoned the king's mistress Agnes Sorel back in 1449. More credibly, it was charged that he had in 1446 returned a runaway slave to Egypt, even though the slave had claimed to be a Christian. Coeur was arrested, imprisoned, tortured, and condemned on May 29, 1453, to pay a fine of 300,000 ecus, and he also had to repay the king another 100,000 ecus before he went into permanent exile. Presumably, Coeur had even more wealth, for he managed a remarkable escape in 1455 and ended up in Rome, where he retained papal favor. He sailed east in charge of a big fleet of sixteen galleys in 1456 as part of an effort to mount a crusade against the Ottoman Turks. He died on the Genoese island of Chios in the Aegean on November 25 and was buried in the Franciscan church there.

Coeur's perplexing portrait shows a merchant entrepreneur demonstrating amazing skills in everything he touched. He was also a faithful servant to the crown, one of those able men who helped Charles VII become the most powerful monarch in Europe. Reyerson views him as a transitional figure between the great merchant princes, such as Benedetto Zaccaria of previous centuries, and later financial geniuses, such as Nicolas Fouquet. The great German banking families, such as the Stromer of Nuremburg and the Welsers and Fuggers of Augsburg, later in the century, expanded the scale and scope of their businesses beyond anything even Coeur accomplished. Certainly he was a person blurring distinctions and boundaries between the public and private spheres of his activities. He retained a sense of open horizons and could, like Datini, contemplate business prospects in northern Europe via Bruges and in the south by putting French interests via Montpellier and Aigues Mortes back into the Mediterranean in a major way. The Mamluks in Egypt helped make him rich and in a sense the Ottomans killed him by causing the circumstances that brought him to Chios.

THE PASTONS AND THEIR EAST ANGLIA

About a thousand letters and other documents illuminate the rise and activities of the Paston family, originally from a village near the Norfolk coast. This family archive survived because members kept drafts of their own correspondence, some letters received, and most importantly wrote to one another so frequently. Their collective portrait is the story of how they mobilized sources of power and wealth, the law, and the land.

Behind every story of a successful social climb in the fifteenth century stands a shadowy figure like Clement Paston (d. 1419) No papers survive from this prosperous farmer, who controlled more than 100 acres, land held partly freely and also as a bondsman, a social rank still carrying the legacy of serfdom. He married a bondswoman, and the couple placed their hopes in a typical second generation riser, William Paston (1378–1444). His father's main accomplishment (in the eyes of his descendants) was to work hard enough on his lands to get the money needed for William's education. The law was the obvious choice, and William ended up at the Inns of Court in London. By a series of judicial appointments, he climbed up all the way to being a judge on the Common Bench. William married the formidable, literate, and well-dowered Agnes (c. 1405–1479) – an apparently large gap in ages. Agnes would enjoy a long and influential widowhood in the family, active in the affairs of her grandchildren. It is never entirely clear how lawyers grew wealthy in the king's service, because they had decent salaries, but only that, and were barred from collecting fees from clients. Nevertheless, money flowed William's way and the Justice, as he was known, entered the ranks of the gentry by buying manors, entire estates that came with income. William died rich, with £1460 in gold on deposit in London and another £958 in Norwich.

His son John I (1421–1466) is known from forty-four letters and documents, and his justly famous wife Margaret (c. 1420–1484), the mother of at least five sons and two daughters, from 107 letters and documents. John was an exemplary third-generation type – educated at Trinity Hall Cambridge and the Inns of Court, he became an important person in Norfolk and represented it in Parliament. He had to fight against other climbers to hold on to what he had and became the great friend of one of the leading men in the kingdom, Sir John Fastolf. When this patron and friend died in 1459, John inherited vast wealth in Norfolk and Suffolk, and spent the rest of his life fighting for the bequest. He managed to keep the prestigious Caister Castle but the scramble for the rest was a real sorrow and burden and was mostly lost. He depended on his canny wife to help defend their scattered wealth and manage the family affairs during his occasional imprisonments. Margaret was up to the challenge.

Their son John (1442–1479) never married but was not the end of the Paston story, yet here we can note some aspects of a fourth-generation success story. King Edward IV knighted this John in 1463, and he was a MP (Member of Parliament) several times and a person of substance at court, in the king's retinue at home and abroad. This great-grandson of a serf also fought on horseback. Across Europe, families like the Pastons were finding ways to climb the social and economic ladder in the fifteenth century. Sometimes theses letters enable us to look beneath the surface and see the real basis of their power. The family's correspondence with Richard Calle, who became their head bailiff, opens a window on exactly how they prospered. Calle first worked for the Pastons around 1455 when he must have been at least twenty, and he was still living in 1503. The Pastons kept some letters that they had received from Calle – their instructions to him, which must have been frequently oral, do not survive. Also, in 1469 Calle married Margery Paston, John's sister, and Margaret Paston in particular felt that her heart had been pierced by this marriage she never approved of or accepted. In fact, the Pastons tried to get the bishop of Norwich to break up the marriage because it was clandestine, secret, but in this age all that mattered was the consent of the parties. The one letter from Richard Calle to Margery suggests that this was a love match. At any rate, the Pastons put Margery out of their minds but still employed Calle, probably because he had proved his worth many times.

Calle's main job as bailiff was to be an estate agent for the Pastons and this involved him in two main activities. He was vigilant in the sheriff and county courts as the many Paston lawsuits worked their way through the system. These law cases invariably concerned who controlled manors, and Calle's other main responsibility was to lease the lands of these estates. The Pastons could not live everywhere on the estates that came their way through marriage, inheritance, and purchase. The benefit from owning these lands was principally the rent rolls, the price, usually per acre, that the tenants paid to put the land to work to generate an income. The manors also had courts, and these were lucrative assets Calle understood well. Calle needed technical knowledge of agriculture and soils in Norfolk and, even more important, who was a good farmer. Calle was supposed to balance the perpetual needs of the Pastons for as much money as possible against the competition in Norfolk for good tenants at the right price. So he also was responsible for striking the right decisions about whether the rents should be in cash or in-kind, and who was liable for what repairs and everything else that was required to keep the lands productive. Each manor had a steward, beneath the notice of the Pastons who were not farmers any more, and that is why the needed a local man like Calle. He also understood prices and markets. The Paston estates brewed beer for market and Calle knew the malt business and had a good sense of the market for it in London and Flanders. He bought herring by the barrel and kept the main Paston residences stocked with supplies and news. The profitable cutting and selling of the Pastons' timber depended on Calle's market timing. He spent a lot of time on horseback and dealt with his social superiors and dependants across East Anglia and the counties around London.

Calle risked much in serving the Pastons because sometimes he was caught up in their legal battles, and he was also engaged in defending all of his masters' rights, like securing the Fastolf inheritance by violence or whatever means necessary. Calle's hard work, as well as the watchful gaze of astute members of the family like Margaret, kept the patrimony together and exercised power through the courts and their rent rolls. The Pastons thrived though royal favor and other lucky aspects of patronage. They mattered to the king and their friends because they controlled wide productive lands leased to other families, some, like the Pastons, who were scheming to enter the rentier class themselves. The entire Paston correspondence has served social historians well for its rich evidence on family feelings, literacy, reading habits, diet, and many other aspects of domestic life. The economic historian asks about who paid their bills. Beneath the letters were hundreds of not completely free men and women paying rents and fines in the manorial courts. Men like Calle squeezed hard so that Sir John had a horse and armor to follow the king to France or to conduct his daughter to Bruges for a wedding. London mattered to this family as it was a big market and safe haven for capital, but in their Norfolk home, hard-working agricultural labor done by other people paid the bills.

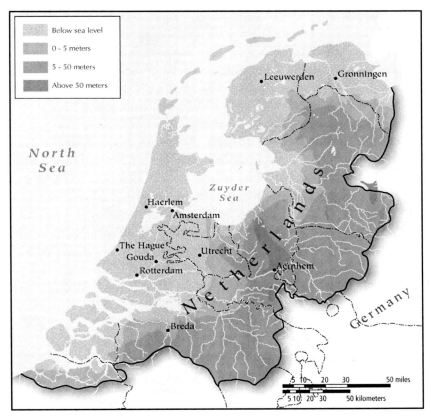

Figure 9.5. Netherlands around 1500 (map by Keith A. French and Darin Grauberger, University of Kansas Cartographic Services).

PRELUDE TO THE FIRST MODERN ECONOMY

The home of the modern Dutch, the Netherlands, around 1500 was a region of maritime and alluvial zones roughly defined by the estuaries of the Maas, Scheldt, and Rhine rivers (see Figure 9.5, not the modern coastline). These seven provinces, centered on Holland, experienced amazing growth and prosperity during the long sixteenth century. It is useful to look back before 1500, when this region, containing less than a million people scattered in 100 urban areas and about 1,500 villages, provided only a few hints of its future dynamism. Yet, the late medieval economy and society laid the foundations on this promising soil. Land and the sea were the only natural resources worth noting. There were no forests, quarries, mines, or other natural resources that fostered growth in other areas. The Dutch, however, enjoyed some advantages. Their territory was isolated and not easy to conquer. The great city of their region, Antwerp, was the focus of the older cloth towns and more intensely farmed southern part of the Low Countries. In the north, the later Middle Ages witnessed a patient effort to gain lands and create inland water routes connecting the river estuaries. Easy access to the North Sea had made this region a potential entrepot for trade since the heyday of the Frisians in the early Middle Ages. A pattern of decentralized enclaves and small cities gradually expanded. People on the local level used a system of dikes and mounds to create *polders* – areas of land below sea level that could be drained and then farmed or used for livestock. Local cooperation in Zeeland and the boggy areas of central Holland made some lords, such as the bishops of Utrecht and the counts of Holland, wealthy. These old and new lands were never really suitable for a feudal agrarian regime, and in the Frisian lands in the north, manors made no sense and they were uncommon throughout the provinces. Hence, serfdom was also rare and the late medieval Dutch enjoyed a high degree of personal freedom even as a typically large percentage of land belonged to nobles, the Church, or wealthy townspeople.

As we have seen, in the fifteenth century, the Dutch began using rotating windmills to harness wind power, one of their main resources, to raise water out of the polders. A community approach to maintaining the dikes assigned individual farmers the responsibility for their bordering drainages. Work was constant because the land was always sinking. This common problem may have helped the Dutch develop a strong communitarian ethos, although in the fifteenth century the first signs appeared of a switch to professional maintenance paid for by the taxes raised for the common good. In addition to the wind, peat supplied the main fuel needs for the Dutch, but this resource was a mixed blessing. Waterways made moving peat from where it was dug up to where people burned it relatively cheap. Dutch cities as well as Antwerp provided good markets for peat. Digging peat ate away at the land and made the struggle against the sea even harder. Great storms, such as the flood of 1421, washed away generations of work and in this case flooded thirty-four villages and inundated some lands under water to the present day. What the sea yielded it occasionally took back.

The demographic patterns in the fifteenth century are hard to establish in the poor sources. A rural crisis for landowners caused by generally lower food prices and high wages was pushing people to the small cities, where there were some good opportunities to make money. The Dutch experienced high death rates and birthrates, but this region, sustained by rural migration, was one of the most urbanized in Europe. Sometime in the fifteenth century, a modest growth in population began, but the region was still below its preplague height even in 1500. Amsterdam merchants were beginning to import cheap Baltic grain in this century, which lowered food prices for the city workers and fishermen (and affected the Polish agrarian regime). Most political and economic power remained in the southern provinces. The core of the Burgundian state centered on Brussels. Antwerp and Bruges were major centers of international banking and exchange, and a natural place for Mediterranean merchants and ships to find customers and connect to the trading routes of the North and Baltic Seas. It would be a big mistake to read history backward and find reasons for optimism about the future of the Dutch in 1500.

Yet, even in this context, the Dutch enjoyed some advantages. Their geography and land resources had created a nonfeudal and noncommunal environment. The lack of open fields and labor services in the countryside fostered a high degree of personal freedom, flexible occupations, and open relations between the towns and rural areas, mainly linked by seafaring and fishing. In the cities, guilds were nonexistent or weak social clubs, which were strong on symbolism and good agents for urban elites who dominated city politics. In this sense, the Dutch cities resembled Venice, where merchants ruled as well. But the Dutch seem protomodern in the sense that their urban societies were market-oriented, individualistic, and, above all, mobile. Wealth was concentrated, but not to the degree elsewhere, as far as we can tell. What little evidence that survives suggests that even the Dutch household structure was "modern" based on the nuclear family without the siblings or parents of the husband and wife present. Family members worked hard and acquired habits of industriousness that served their ambitions to have better lives. In short, Dutch society benefited from a high degree of urbanization and abundant water transport systems, a well-monetarized economy, the legacy of Burgundian and Hanseatic influences, and, above all, access to ocean resources.

The Dutch were in an ideal place to fish the rivers and seas. In the fifteenth century, the Baltic fisheries were becoming less productive just as the Dutch developed the perfect tools for making money and jobs from herring. The problem the Dutch faced was that the best fishing grounds for herring were just a bit too far away for ships to return to port with fresh fish. The problem was to preserve the catch while at sea. The method was obvious: the Dutch enjoyed abundant supplies of salt as a result of the salt pans dotting the coasts. The solution in the fifteenth century was the invention of the herring buss, a factory ship that integrated the tasks of fishing and quickly cleaning the fish and salting the catch at sea, preserved in barrels until the buss returned to port. These busses started out as very small ships in the range of 30–40 tons. Innovators tinkered with these ships, making them larger and more efficient in their use of mariners' labor. Dutch burghers formed partnerships to finance the new vessels. Soon hundreds of them were at sea, and their salaried crews attracted people tired of the rural crisis and its low returns to agriculture. The trade in preserved herring – on land they were also pickled and smoked – was even more lucrative as the Dutch became great suppliers to a wider region. By 1500, the Dutch had created a virtual herring monopoly, an integrated and sensible business that took advantage of the latest technologies in ship construction. It is too simplistic to see herring as the sole explanation for the future of Dutch prosperity. But it would be wrong to ignore how this resource galvanized other activities. The Dutch needed a great deal of salt, and here too the windmill made draining pans easier. The capital-intensive sailing buss required timber imports, mainly from the Baltic, to sustain the small shipyards scattered throughout the waterways, using hemp, canvas, and other raw materials. These yards used modern techniques, building the ship up along the frame with edge to edge planking that made them lighter and faster. By 1500, the Dutch were also skilled at turning out a three-masted caravel, more suited to their shallow northern waters than the great Portuguese and Italian ships they saw making the journey north from distant Lisbon and Venice. Smaller Dutch ships were more efficient and spread the risk against losses to bad weather and pirates.

Some Dutch cities like Amsterdam and Leiden were active in cloth production, wool, and their own linens; people always needed to be clothed. Because all wine was imported and expensive, brewing beer was a major urban activity, always at odds with cloth production because one trade needed good water and the other dirtied it. In the end, the Dutch opted for brewing. Over the course of the fourteenth century, the Dutch shifted to using hops, a better preservative and a crop that could be raised on their soils, especially around Gouda. Brewing in cities became an industrial activity with big ovens and copper kettles. Beer was an ideal commodity to produce around Holland because its many waterways made for cheaper transporting this heavy commodity, which was 90 percent water. Cities levied excise taxes on producers and consumers, a growing source of income for most of them in the generally increasing brewing activity in the fifteenth century. Dutch beer proved to be an ideal export commodity and gave their traders an edge on German producers.

Herring, salt, and English cloth were also main exports, and the Dutch were aggressively entering the Baltic trade in the fifteenth century against stiff Hanseatic competition centered on Lübeck and Hamburg for beer. The Hanse would not sell ships to the Dutch, so they made their own. Imported wood also stimulated another transformative industry as the Dutch learned to make good barrels for their beer and herring. The Dutch became good customers in places like Danzig for wheat, timber, and rye and found potential allies among the Danes and Swedes tired of German domination and prices.

The real payoffs to all of these trends are a post-1500 story. Yet, the Dutch were located in just the right area to connect the Baltic and North Seas to the Mediterranean and Atlantic trade routes so recently pioneered by the Portuguese. Merchants from Portugal, including some crypto-Jews, would very soon be supplying pepper and other spices to canny Dutch traders who would resell them across the north. Outside of the mainstream of certain medieval legacies like manorialism and a communal movement at odds with rural society, the Dutch, so few in numbers (almost the same as Portugal) were finding a distinctive path out of the fifteenth-century crisis. The lesson here is that one of the least medieval societies was well positioned to become one of the first modern ones, even though by 1500 there was no university in any of its provinces. Dutch neighbors in England and northern Germany had to respond to these challenges; in the sixteenth century, peoples across the globe would soon meet the Dutch and their ways.

ACCOUNTING

Luca Pacioli (Figure 9.6) (c. 1445–soon after 1514) was born in Borgo San Sepolcro in the Apennines and his great book, or *summa*, on arithmetic, geometry, proportions, and proportionality was published in Venice in 1494. This practical work on numbers contained a small section on accounting but was suffused with the practical needs of an active life, from a deeply humanistic and religious perspective. In short, Pacioli, a great mathematician, saw the world from the point of view of numbers. Living in an age of printed books, he wrote one of the first contemporary and widely circulated books on best business practices at the end of our period of study. His work is a useful summary of

Figure 9.6. Luca Pacioli (Art Resource ART 57019).

several important features of the late medieval society and economy, as well as a manual for merchants and others who kept books. His portrait shows a calm, even bland Franciscan monk with his book and the tools of a geometer.

Pacioli pointed out that any business needed three things – cash, someone who understood math and accounting, and good records of debts and credits. Wealth came first, and Pacioli could cite a Latin tag from Aristotle that wealth was the necessary prerequisite. Yet, he complicated matters because he knew that good faith and reputation could obtain credit and establish one in business, just as bad records could cause confusion and ruin everything. So in effect worldly success boiled down to good character and math skills! He assumed that a merchant could read and write, and was thus able to compile a proper inventory of one's property. His book jumps from one proverb to another as a way to drive home points – he clearly believed in the value of experiences within the fund of common knowledge. For example, Pacioli was convinced that it took more skills and effort to learn how to be a good merchant than it took to be a doctor of laws. He was not disparaging the law, which he saw as necessary for cities to function. A passage from Dante explained well what Pacioli had in mind. He recalled it inexactly but Virgil's advice from *Inf* 24:46–51 remained vivid and had become over the last century and more a part of the common fund of received wisdom. What merchants needed to do was remain awake, cast off sloth, and spend one's life in such a way as to leave something behind, to win fame. An unknown poet in Latin supplied another piece of proverbial advice – "no one gained victory who rested" – very close to Pliny the Elder's simple truth that life consisted of being awake. Pacioli reminded the lazy about the virtues of the busy ants, and St. Paul's teaching that he who was worthy of the crown was he who fights for it. The accumulated weight of all of this advice validated the active life of buying and selling, not at all inconsistent with praying and seeking the kingdom of heaven.

An accountant could be proud – provided he had good records! Pacioli explains and codifies the best practices of double-entry bookkeeping and more – already more than a century old but here set out in a printed manual. First was the memorandum – a kind of household book composed of scrap notes of everything large or small in chronological order. These raw materials of daily economic activities should be posted in a journal, a neat copy of business that was still a personal, private record. Examples of this type of record survive in the Datini papers and elsewhere, and in some famous cases (especially in Florence) became the basis for diaries that noted family matters, personal concerns, and even dreams. As a kind of personal economic chronicle the journal served merchants well, but it was hard to consult unless one had a fine memory for what happened on a specific day. So Pacioli urged the transfer of journal information to the great notebook or ledger that contained separate pages for debts and credits running down the pages. Hence, at a glance a merchant was able to see both ends of the business and consult the literal bottom line at the end of the pages, the total of debits and assets (credits). Kept in a separate place, a document box, were all of the individual contracts, bills of exchange, and all other papers constituting the proof of what was in the journal and ledgers. Cash was always on the debit side of the books, because it was not out there as a credit working for its owner. Here is an entire philosophy of business.

Pacioli intended his book to be a help and not a curse to business people. He cited the old Roman maxim that the law did not concern itself with trifles as reason enough to assert that there was no need for separate written accounts for everything. Here is the origin of the petty cash fund. Pacioli also recommended ᴋs be closed every year – and where business records survive we find ᴊs practice of opening a new ledger at some agreed upon beginning of ᴗᴄ₁l year or partnership. Finally, in the real world, so much business was now conducted by letters to partners and agents that it was necessary to observe some rules about correspondence. We are just on the verge of the great age of business letters so we cannot expect too much practical advice from Pacioli. Nevertheless, he urged letter writers always to note the place (town) where the letter was written, so the recipient could be sure it did not come from the next world (!), and day, important to assume that the letter was not written in the dark, gloomy, and confusing time of night. Anyone who could read Italian could benefit from all of this good advice, which had not been for some time an Italian monopoly of best business practices anyway.

REASONS TO PAUSE IN THE 1490s

A few final strands of social and economic developments point to the 1490s as a time when old and new trends meshed into the first hints of modernity. First, if we examine the post-1348 market economy, its social context operated in a temporary exception to the old Malthusian limits. For at least a century after 1350, the traditional checks of limited food supplies and land were not constraining household size and consumption. Instead, the great age of inheritances and Europe's open horizons seemed to end the worse effects of scarcity and famine as relatively cheap Polish, Lithuanian, and Ukrainian grain helped to feed diminished populations in northern and southern Europe. Gregory Clark concluded that later medieval Europe was a wealthier place, not only because it was more efficient, but because there were fewer people. The Malthusian argument acknowledges a Golden Age of Labor in this depopulated world. Yet, Clark contends that Gini coefficients, which are lower even today than they were in the later Middle Ages, suggest that inheritances concentrated wealth more than labor and technology found greater rewards after the plague. This important point suggests that for average people there was no real progress in this period. Indeed Clark thinks this is true up to the Industrial Revolution. Even increases in real wages in this view would produce few comforts and instead would end up funding more children, who were an eventual drain on family incomes. Clark's argument is too pessimistic and misses the genuine improvements in the standard of living and technologies after the plagues.

A long-running debate considers the alleged "economic depression of the Renaissance," an idea growing out of a close scrutiny of the Italian economy after the plague. A wider perspective considers the place of Italy in the European economy especially as the Atlantic states entered the New World in the sixteenth century. For present purposes, we note two phenomena. After the Big Death and subsequent outbreaks, the Italian (and European) economy certainly contracted as the overall size of fleets, wheat harvests, and many other measurable outputs fell. Economic contraction of this magnitude has been in other eras described as a depression. And certainly after the Big Death social attitudes about risk and confidence changed. Nonetheless, if we focus on per capita production (more output per worker), wages, and new technologies, the fifteenth century abounds with signs of development and prosperity. Greater competition across Europe in items like wool and cotton cloth, furs, and weapons, made the gap between Italy and its neighbors smaller. Closer looks, for example, at the Russian, Dutch, and Danish economies in the fifteenth century, show no signs of depression. So, although diminished populations produced many fewer goods overall, their individual consumption in many cases increased, but not necessarily for everyone. The pursuit of personal comfort after the plague, and undeniable advances in technology, contributed to a world apparent in the Arnolfini wedding portrait. For elites the level of material comfort certainly expanded. After the fourteenth-century crises, signs of recovery by the late fifteenth century suggest that Europe had entered a kind of "Indian Summer." Rather than simply enduring the winding down of the old social and economic order, Europeans by the 1490s were ready to begin their great migrations across the globe.

The jury remains out on the lives of ordinary people, most of whom remained in the European countryside. For them, food, clothing, and shelter consumed (as today) most of their income. After the Big Death, as Christopher Dyer observed for England, common people ate more baked bread and meat and drank more ale and beer . Eating in the rural society remained seasonal, with bouts of feasting and dearth, punctuated in many places by war and pillaging. Plagues still occurred and a great famine in the north in 1437–1440 caused severe problems. Nevertheless, increased consumption fed investments in new techniques in brewing, cloth production, and other activities that made many people more comfortable in the basic needs that comprise the standard of living. Again, fewer people were alive to enjoy simple comforts, but they were more available.

Shortages of silver and gold, most notable from about 1395 to 1415 and in the mid-fifteenth century, kept many prices stable (or even falling) and encouraged, as we have seen, a new wave of silver mining in Bohemia, Austria, and elsewhere. John Day has stressed the value of the standard Fischer equation for understanding this economy, where $MV = PT$. Simply put, the money supply (M), basically the stocks of coins, times the velocity of money (V – how quickly it circulated) equaled the general price level (P) times the volume of transactions (T). Each factor has attracted research and advocates who view it as the fundamental part of the equation. Bullionists, monetarists, favor M and look at changes in the money supply, and stocks of silver and gold as the main limiting factors in the economy. Checks and bills of exchange seem to have the potential to increase M, especially if merchants were willing to accept a bill in lieu of cash. Some bills were assigned to others but most observers conclude that commercial paper made a minuscule addition to M before 1500. The focus remains on metals, and so – who is looking for gold and silver? We can explore the careers of Vasco Da Gama and Columbus from this perspective, and others.

$V, P,$ and T have attracted varying degrees of study. The velocity of money, its rate of turnover, how many times a coin changed hands in a year, remains impossible to study. We cannot follow a florin's life cycle or measure how worn all of the surviving examples are. Prices are relatively easy to find because late medieval people have left an increasing volume of actual records that reveal prices of staples, such as wheat, wine, beer, squirrel fur, and even common wages in the weaving and construction trades. The problem, as we have seen, is the standard of measure to use. Gold and silver were themselves commodities with fluctuating supplies and prices. Daily wages have increased in real terms but so too had some other commodities like wine, butter, and cloth, which in their ways were labor intensive. If we could agree on and construct a market basket of commodities and expenses, we would have a better sense of the changes in the standard of living. The problem remains that for the vast majority of the population the basics, food, clothing, and shelter, took up a very high percentage of income. We do not generally have good information on simple items like common urban rents for rooms and how often people renewed their clothing. Hence, although one can find the price of bread or renting land fairly easily, in practice it becomes very difficult to say anything useful about big issues before 1500. So we are stuck assuming that the velocity and volume of transactions must vary according to the population levels and degree of market penetration or activity. Where cities were relying on rural people to sustain their numbers, as for example in Flanders, Holland, and Tuscany, *V* was buoyant because people worked and used cash for many daily expenses. Up in the Swiss Alps or the highlands of Scotland, the opportunities to spend money were not nearly as common. And so we are drawn, like late medieval people, to take a closer look at *M*.

Consider the Portuguese efforts to explore the near Atlantic and their patient voyages in the fifteenth century to find the end of Africa in the south. The steps are well known: the conquest of Ceuta in Morocco in 1415; the discovery and settling of Madeira and the Azores (1420s and 1430s), reaching Gambia in 1446, the Gold Coast in 1471, Congo in 1483, and the voyage of Bartolomeu Dias, who rounded the Cape and found the path to the Indian Ocean in 1487–1488. The Portuguese crown and the merchants of Lisbon financed these ventures. The name Prince Henry the Navigator (1394–1460) has always been associated with the spirit that guided Portuguese mapmakers, explorers, slave traders, seekers of gold, and all the rest south. Clearly Henry was an important figure, but he sat mainly in Portugal while others risked their lives for his every increasing fortunes. He was not the only one who understood that Portugal's future was in the Atlantic.

Thousands of Africans from the 1440s were brought back to work in mainland Portugal and the nascent sugar islands, especially Madeira, over the course of the fifteenth century. Sugar had made its way from Syria in the east and island hopped from Cyprus to Sicily, and the few spots in southern Iberia with enough rainfall to sustain the crop. We know that sugar remains one of the great medieval European legacies to the world, be it Madeira or Barbados or Haiti. Labor shortages in Portugal, with its population barely reaching one million by 1500, naturally attracted an interest in African slaves. Portuguese merchants at first acquired slaves by expensive raiding that settled down to a mainly traded business, depending on cloth, iron, and whatever they could find that Africans needed. Slaves and sugar made money. The Gold Coast after all was the fabled source of the trans-Saharan gold trade, and Europe never could meet its demand for this item. Above all, Portugal was looking for gold not supplied by their North African Muslim enemies.

Finally, there was the point to going around Africa, to find spices and all of the treasures of the East not monopolized by Mamluk sultans or canny Venetians and their high prices. Our story here has only space to conclude with the name Vasco Da Gama (c. 1460–1524) and his most celebrated accomplishment, the journey from Lisbon (July 1497) to Calicut on the west coast of India (summer

1498) and back to Lisbon by early September 1499. The voyage demanded nautical skills and daring, and Da Gama lost most of his crew to scurvy and other problems. What ships he brought back were stuffed with as much pepper, spices, and other treasures as he could manage. The profits for his investors were fabulous, measured in excess of one thousand percent and beyond the avaricious dreams of the biggest optimists. The real lasting benefits to Portugal, and problems for Venetian merchants and other traditional middlemen remain subjects for early modern social and economic history. What we find is the synergies of late medieval accomplishments in mapmaking, shipbuilding, and a revived zest for risks and adventure mixed in with a search for cheap labor. The Portuguese and their followers in the slave trade would have no qualms about enslaving and subjecting peoples of a different color of skin. All of these activities increased M.

Yet in the months before Da Gama sailed, King Manuel's decrees resulted in the forced conversion of Portugal's ancient Jewish community and the expulsion of the smaller number of his remaining Muslim subjects. The end of religious minorities in Portugal was at least partly the result of the king's desire not to expel "his" Jews, perhaps 30,000 people, who would have been allowed to depart with their portable wealth. This vicious policy, as well as the crown's seizure of all Muslim and Jewish public properties, their cemeteries, mosques, and synagogues, maintained the money supply and probably spurred its velocity as much property changed hands.

As the Ottoman Turks extended their domains in southeastern Europe in the later fifteenth century after the symbolic conquest of their new European capital Constantinople in 1453, the Portuguese were not the only people to look west to the Atlantic for some way to balance Muslim wealth and power in the East. English and Dutch ships and fishing for herring and cod were already far into the resources of the North Atlantic. Even in distant Moscow by the late fifteenth century, western European and Ottoman traders found themselves competing for the luxury sable and marten and utilitarian squirrel that comprised the basics of the Russian fur trade with its great routes south to the Black Sea and west to the Baltic. The Russians expected to be paid in silver, or maybe a little gold, and this was one of the many demands on new sources of silver and gold. By 1500 Moscow was as populous as Florence. Think as broadly as this world, stretching from the fishing stations off Iceland to the Genoese and Venetian entrepots in the eastern Mediterranean, from the Russian fur markets to the steamy Portuguese stations in the gulf of Guinea on the islands of Sao

Tome and Principe. This is a big Europe, and we naturally, inevitably, conclude with one of its biggest and most successful dreamers, Christopher Columbus (c. 1450–1506).

Columbus remains, for better or worse, the best known late medieval European, as much as we might wish Leonardo Da Vinci could supplant him in popular awareness. Still, Leonardo had many brilliant ideas in a society not yet prepared to bring all of his technological dreams to the market. Columbus had one amazing insight – not that the world was round – most already believed this for many centuries, but that it was smaller than many hoped or feared. A trip west across the Atlantic would find China and Japan before the fresh water and food ran out. This was the idea he sold to Ferdinando of Aragon and Isabella of Castile, in that memorable year 1492 when they conquered the last independent Muslim stronghold, Grenada, in Iberia. After having taxed the Jews to pay for their war, the monarchs decided to expel the Jews from their lands. Here too we have the culmination of many medieval trends. The respite from expensive warfare made a chance on a small fleet of three modern if small ships seem worth risking. Columbus was a skilled storyteller who conjured up vast wealth and opportunities in a Castilian that all but concealed his Genoese roots. Columbus was a brilliant mariner and mapmaker and a great traveler – perhaps the only living person to have seen Chios, Iceland, and Madeira, and then Hispaniola. He well understood what the rise of the Ottoman Empire in the Eastern Mediterranean meant for Christian Europe. He took three small ships, the Niña (50 tons), the Pinta (60 tons), and the Santa Maria (slightly larger) to the Caribbean, but only the first two made it back to Spain.

Again, the story of the social, economic, and moral consequences of his activities belong to other textbooks. Let us simply look at him as the continuation of some old stories rather than a beginning of some new ones. First, Columbus is inconceivable without the context of trade, crusade, and mission with the Islamic world. The entire point to exploring the Atlantic, besides finding the back door to Jerusalem that so interested Isabella, was to realize the old Aragonese and Genoese dreams of acquiring the gold, spices, silks, and all of the rest of the East without enriching Muslim or Tartar intermediaries. Second, Columbus understood slavery and the slave trade very well as reasonable and profitable ways of escaping what we see as a Malthusian trap of stagnant population levels and labor shortages. Columbus simply valued people as profitable cargo to be acquired cheaply and sold dearly. In 1498, he wrote to his patrons and explained that Hispaniola, wherever it was, could export 4,000 slaves a year. Even if some died at first, the trade would settle down to useful numbers and profits. How did he learn these entrepreneurial skills? Finally, Columbus ended up Admiral of the Ocean Sea and viceroy of all the lands that he persisted in believing to his dying day were in Asia. In theory, if he and his descendants had been able to hang on to just a bit of what they had, Columbus would have been far richer than Jacques Coeur, Jakob Fugger, Cosimo de Medici, or even perhaps his masters the kings and queens of Spain.

Who really benefited from the world the Europeans had made by 1500? That is the story of the early modern world. Strong in guns, steel, and institutions, the Portuguese and Spanish led the other peoples of Europe into the wider horizons of the globe. The men and women leaving home included over the next five hundred years representatives of every national, ethnic, and religious group. These migrations were a struggle against poverty in the effort to live up to their diverse capabilities as human beings. Many later migrants were fleeing varieties of persecution that remained a durable fact of European society. By 1500, many Europeans, especially those lucky ones from prosperous regions, had markets and institutions embedded in ethical systems valuing cooperation. Their quest for security, food, clothing, and shelter was never ending. Rational maximizers of self-interest sometimes abandoned materialism for some purer, spiritual truth. Even these people chose to maximize one value over another. Most Europeans now saw that economic and social facts affected their values, and they understood that their behaviors had consequences in this world and in the next.

SELECT BIBLIOGRAPHY

H. S. Bennett, *The Pastons and Their England*. Cambridge, 1968.

Judith C. Brown, "Prosperity or Hard Times in Renaissance Italy?" *Renaissance Quarterly* 42 (1989): 761–80.

R. Gene Brown and Kenneth S. Johnston, *Pacioli on Accounting*. New York, 1963.

Gregory Clark, *A Farewell to Alms: A Brief Economic History of the World*. Princeton, 2007.

Alfred W. Crosby, *The Measure of Reality: Quantification and Western Society, 1250–1600*. Cambridge, 1997.

Norman Davis, editor. *Paston Letters and Papers of the Fifteenth Century*. Oxford, 2004.

John Day, *The Medieval Market Economy*. New York, 1987.

Jan de Vries and Ad Van DerWoude, *The First Modern Economy: Success, Failure, and Perseverance of the Dutch Economy, 1500–1815*. Cambridge, 1997.

Christopher Dyer, *An Age of Transition?* Oxford, 2005.

Steven A. Epstein, *Speaking of Slavery: Color, Ethnicity, and Human Bondage in Italy.* Ithaca, 2001.

Felipe Fernández-Armesto, *Columbus.* New York, 1992.

John Block Friedman and Kristen Mossler Figg, editors. *Trade, Travel, and Exploration in the Middle Ages.* New York, 2000.

David Herlihy and Christiane Klapisch-Zuber, *Les Toscans et leurs familles.* Paris, 1978.

Harry A. Miskimin, *The Economy of Early Renaissance Europe.* Englewood Cliffs, 1969.

Michel Mollat, *Jacques Coeur ou l'esprit d'entreprise.* Aubier, 1988.

Iris Origo, *The Merchant of Prato.* New York, 1957.

Kathryn L. Reyerson, *Jacques Coeur: Entrepreneur and King's Bursar.* New York, 2005.

François Soyer, *The Persecution of the Jews and Muslims of Portugal: King Manuel I and the End of Religious Tolerance* (1496–7). Leiden, 2007.

Richard W. Unger, *A History of Brewing in Holland 900–1900.* Leiden, 2001.

————, *The Ship in the Medieval Economy 600–1600.* London, 1980.

Diane Watt, *The Paston Women: Selected Letters.* Cambridge, 2004.

INDEX